T5-BQC-497

FLORIDA STATE
UNIVERSITY LIBRARIES

APR 15 1997

TALLAHASSEE, FLORIDA

THE FUTURE IS OURS

**Recent Titles in
Praeger Studies on the 21st Century**

Visions for the 21st Century
Sheila Moorcroft, editor

Creative Compartments: A Design for Future Organization
Gerard Fairtlough

Groupware in the 21st Century: Computer Supported Cooperative Working Toward the Millennium
Peter Lloyd, editor

The Future European Model: Economic Internationalization and Cultural Decentralization
J. Ørstrom Møller

Vitality and Renewal: A Manager's Guide for the 21st Century
Colin Hutchinson

The Foresight Principle: Cultural Recovery in the 21st Century
Richard A. Slaughter

The End of the Future: The Waning of the High-Tech World
Jean Gimpel

Small is Powerful: The Future as if People Really Mattered
John Papworth

Disintegrating Europe: The Twilight of the European Construction
Noriko Hama

THE FUTURE IS OURS

Foreseeing, Managing and Creating the Future

Graham H. May

Westport, Connecticut

Published in the United States and Canada by Praeger Publishers,
88 Post Road West, Westport, CT 06881.
An imprint of Greenwood Publishing Group, Inc.

Printed in the United States of America

The paper used in this book complies with the
Permanent Paper Standard issued by the National
Information Standards Organization (Z39.48–1984).

10 9 8 7 6 5 4 3 2 1

English language edition, except the United States and Canada,
published by Adamantine Press Limited, 3 Henrietta Street, Covent
Garden, London WC2E 8LU England.

First published in 1996

Library of Congress Cataloging-in-Publication Data

May, Graham H.
   The future is ours : foreseeing, managing and creating the future
/ Graham H. May.
      p.   cm.—(Praeger studies on the 21st century, ISSN
1070–1850)
   Includes bibliographical references and index.
   ISBN 0–275–95678–4 (cloth : alk. paper).—ISBN 0–275–95679–2
(pbk. : alk. paper)
   1. Forecasting. 2. Forecasting—Methodology. 3. Twenty-first
century—Forecasts. I. Title. II. Series.
CB158.M38 1996
303.49′09′04—dc20   96–15310

Library of Congress Catalog Card Number: 96–15310

ISBN: 0–275–95678–4   Cloth
          0–275–95679–2   Paperback

Copyright © 1996 by Adamantine Press Limited

All rights reserved. No part of this publication may be
reproduced, stored in a retrieval system or transmitted in any
form or by any means: electronic, electrostatic, magnetic tape,
mechanical, photocopying, recording or otherwise, without
permission in writing from the publishers.

*For Ian and Richard and their generation.
May they create a better future for themselves and those to follow.*

Contents

Figures ix
Tables x
Boxes xi
Prologue xiii

PART ONE: THE FUTURES DEBATE

1. The Future: Forgotten but Ever Present 3
   1.1. It depends what you mean by 'the future' 3
   1.2. The future: a forgotten dimension 5
   1.3. The future: always with us 21
   1.4. Conclusions 36

2. Some Problems of Futures-Thinking 37
   2.1. Different kinds of futures-thoughts 38
   2.2. Optimism and Pessimism 42
   2.3. Is there any point in futures-thinking? 45
   2.4. Can we usefully think ahead? 48
   2.5. Knowledge of the past, present and future 60
   2.6. Should we indulge in futures-thinking? 69
   2.7. Conclusions 74

3. If It Is So Difficult, Why Do It? 75
   3.1. History is made, not given 76
   3.2. Our responsibility to future generations 80
   3.3. The need for direction 86
   3.4. Controlling the agenda 91
   3.5. The shortcomings of reaction 94
   3.6. The future as a learning process 99
   3.7. The need for democratic futures-thinking 102

PART TWO: WAYS OF THINKING ABOUT THE FUTURE

Introduction   107

4. Foreseeing the Future   113
- 4.1. Prediction   113
- 4.2. Extrapolation   118
- 4.3. Analytical forecasting   139
- 4.4. Speculation   145
- 4.5. Judgemental forecasting   147
- 4.6. Conclusions   155

5. Managing, Planning and Creating the Future   157
- 5.1. Management   159
- 5.2. Policy-making   181
- 5.3. Creativity   186
- 5.4. Innovation   199
- 5.5. Conclusions   204

PART THREE: CHALLENGES AND OPPORTUNITIES FOR THE 21ST CENTURY

6. The Future as Paradox   207
- 6.1. Nine paradoxes of mature economies   213
- 6.2. Some further contemporary paradoxes   219

References   231
Index   243

Figures

1. Human perspectives — 7
2. The discounting effect in crisis perception — 12
3. The herringbone forecast — 40
4. The choice–determinism continuum — 47
5. The cone of the future — 48
6. Possible trends between two points — 120
7. Plot of live births in the UK 1951–1990 — 121
8. Linear regression by the method of least squares — 126
9. The S-curve — 131
10. Varied forecasts from an S-curve — 132
11. Availability of selected household goods — 133
12. The envelope curve — 135
13. Random or cyclical? — 136
14. The pattern of long waves — 137
15. The planning/policy-making process — 183

Tables

1. Annual economic growth rate: UK National Plan predictions and actuality — 51
2. Projected population of the USA — 52
3. Projected population of the UK — 54
4. Forecasts and recorded traffic at London's airports 1967–1980 — 55
5. Futures methods and techniques — 112
6. Live births in the UK 1951–1990 — 120
7. Three- and five-year moving averages for the UK birth data — 123
8. Exponential smoothing for the UK birth data — 125
9. A cross-impact matrix — 154

Boxes

1. Metaphors of the future — 6
2. A population model — 141
3. Developing a model — 143
4. Preparing scenarios — 165
5. Scenarios for Ilkley — 167
6. General procedure for impact-assessments — 174
7. Assessing alternative strategies — 201

Prologue

We seem to be convinced that thinking about the future is difficult, even impossible, but then spend much of our lives doing just that—thinking about and organising our future.

Our belief that the process is difficult probably stems from the fact that many of our past efforts to think about the future have been wrong. When the future that we had thought would happen did not happen, we may have registered any number of reactions, including surprise, annoyance, despair or relief, and we probably became more cynical about thinking about the future. If the forecast that proved inaccurate was someone else's, particularly an *authority*'s, we probably enjoyed a laugh at their expense and vowed not to believe them ever again. Then we went on thinking about the future and consulting forecasts just as before.

Thinking about the future is both easy and difficult at the same time. It is easy because our brain enables us to imagine situations that are different from anything we have known or experienced. The creativity of art, the genesis of a new product and the development of a plan or policy all rely on this creative ability to imagine the different, the new or the unknown. In most instances this involves an image of, or in, the future.

Thinking about the future is difficult because the image and the eventual reality are not always the same. When we conceive an image of the future or make a forecast, the situation imagined is some way ahead. Time must pass before the imagined, or forecast, future becomes the present. It is only then that we can compare our previously imagined situation with the present reality. If they do not match, we may easily conclude that the image was wrong and that thinking about the future is pointless. In fact, we probably notice the images and forecasts that turn out to be wrong rather more than those that prove accurate. Checking past forecasts against what actually happens is seldom done; it is too boring and possibly embarrassing, but it might be an illuminating experience. The purpose of this book is to examine some of the issues that arise when we think about the future.

- Why do we continue to think about, imagine and forecast the future when we believe we will probably be wrong?

- Why do we need to do so?
- What difficulties do we experience, and how can we think about the future in spite of those difficulties?
- What does 'The Future' mean and how do we relate to it?
- As we enter the twenty-first century, does the future require a different approach?
- Can we make a go of it, and how could more careful consideration of the future help?

PART ONE
THE FUTURES DEBATE

CHAPTER ONE
THE FUTURE: FORGOTTEN BUT EVER PRESENT

> In very general terms, the tendency to think, or at least to express thought about the future does not seem to be well developed. (Galtung 1976)

Galtung's conclusion is hardly surprising. If asked whether thinking about the future was an important part of their lives, most people would probably say that it was not, that they were more concerned about the present. At the start of a lecture I once asked a group of undergraduate students the same question. As expected, nobody answered Yes; most said No, and a few, perceptively, replied that their response depended on what was meant by 'the future'.

In Galtung's (1976) study the future in question was the year 2000. At the time of his research, in 1967–8, this implied a forward scope of some thirty years. In my own small exercise, a subsequent question revealed that there was considerable debate as to whether Christmas, then just over two weeks ahead, should be classified as in the future or not. It transpired that the definition was crucial, since the whole group, which did not think much about the future, were all keenly looking forward to the coming festivities! This small example serves as a useful indication of the paradox that is the concern of this chapter: although we quite naturally think, plan and act about and for the future, we seldom seem to acknowledge that this is the case.

1.1. IT DEPENDS WHAT YOU MEAN BY 'THE FUTURE'

Implicit in the belief that we do not think much about the future is the idea that the future is remote, a vague concept somewhere ahead in time. Like tomorrow it never comes, so we find it difficult to deal with. On the other hand, when it concerns something definite that can be easily imagined, like the impending celebration of a festival, a holiday or some other eagerly awaited event, it is clear that we think a great deal about the future. But is that really the future? It depends.

There are many different definitions of the future and frequently, implicitly, we use different ones in different circumstances. The *Complete Wordfinder* defines the noun as 'of time to come: an event yet to happen' and the adjective as 'going or expected to happen or be or become' (Tulloch 1993). It is quite possible to conclude from this definition that the future starts now, because whatever is to happen, even in the next few seconds, is still 'to come'. It is not yet, but 'going to be'. According to this approach, any thought we have about anything that is to come is thinking about the future.

This approach does have the effect, however, of making the future unattainable. It remains, like the will-o'-the-wisp, just out of our grasp, advancing ahead of us at precisely the same pace as we ourselves, in the present, are moving through time. The result can be a dismissal of the future as beyond the scope of our capabilities. It is never within reach. It remains dark and unknowable and not worth spending time on. It is better to live now, because we may not have to pay later after all. This is not a necessary reaction, but it is often an understandable one.

From this perspective the present becomes the interface between the past and the future, an infinitesimally small moment in time, a knife edge, between the two, which is always moving away from the past and towards the future. As we move with it, the present leaves behind the memories and experiences of the past, but what is ahead is unknown and unforeseeable. We can 'see' the past, since it has left evidence to be observed and studied; but of the future, not having been, there is nothing to see. This creates a powerful image of our approach to the future. We are moving from the light into the darkness while facing backwards. Like a skater hurtling backwards into the unknown.

Powerful as that image is, it is not the only image we have of the future. An alternative approach was suggested by Boulding (1978). It is the 'two hundred year present', defined as the period from the birth of those celebrating their one-hundredth birthday today, to the one-hundredth birthday of those born today. 'It is a continuously moving moment, always reaching out one hundred years in either direction from the day we are in. . . . It is our space, one that we can move around in directly in our lives, and indirectly by touching the lives of the linkage people, young and old, around us.' Slaughter (1989) made the concept more immediate by noting that 'we are connected to this span of time . . . through the lives of our families', by our links with our parents and grandparents in the past, and with our children and grandchildren in the future. Adopting this approach, he suggested, changes our attitude to the future. It becomes a mirror image of the past, in which our children and grandchildren take the place of our parents and grandparents. These personal and family commitments make the future important, immediate to our current concerns and worth considering carefully. It cannot be ignored if we wish to take our responsibilities seriously.

Box 1 suggests some other images, or metaphors, of our relationship to the future. Read through them and think about their relevance. Is one more appropriate than the others? Would you like to believe in one rather than the others? Do they all have an element of truth, perhaps in different circumstances?

I have not exhausted the differing definitions and approaches to the future, but have shown that there are alternatives. In different circumstances we automatically adopt differing definitions without being aware of it. Sometimes the knife-edge present confronting the unknown future is useful; on other occasions, such as when we use phrases like 'the present day', we imply a period of days, weeks or even years. The future depends on what you mean, and what you mean is affected by the circumstances.

1.2. THE FUTURE: A FORGOTTEN DIMENSION

The Club of Rome study *The Limits to Growth* (Meadows *et al.* 1972) suggested that different individuals have different perspectives on time and space, depending on culture, past experience and the nature of the problems faced. Galtung's (1976) research supported this view. The authors of *The Limits to Growth* suggested that the majority of people were concerned with immediate issues in time and space, and that although relatively few took a longer or wider view, some at least were concerned with the longer-term future (see Fig. 1).

Boniecki (1980) subsequently suggested that even this assessment of attitudes to the future overestimates the true position. In a study of the attitudes of 200 adults in Australia he found very little evidence to support the contention of *The Limits to Growth* and concluded that few concerned themselves with matters extending the length of their own lifetimes, let alone the lifetimes of their children. The large majority of individuals in his study had time horizons of ten years or less. Anything beyond the individual's time horizon was too distant and indistinct to invoke meaning. He suggested that it was the limited individual time horizon that renders futuristic studies like *The Limits to Growth* ineffective. People are unable to contemplate the issues raised, because they are unable to look fifty years into the future.

Box 1. Metaphors of the future

1. The future is a great roller coaster on a moonless night. It exists, twisting ahead of us in the dark. We can only see each part as we come to it. We can make estimates about where we are headed, and sometimes see around a bend to another section of track, but it doesn't do us any real good because the future is fixed and determined. We are locked in our seats, and nothing we may foresee or do will change the course that is laid out for us.

2. The future is a mighty river. The great force of history flows inexorably along, carrying us with it. Most of our attempts to change its course are mere pebbles thrown into the river: they cause a momentary splash and a few ripples, but they make no difference. The river's course can be changed, but only by natural disasters like earthquakes or landslides, or by massive, concerted human efforts on a similar scale. On the other hand, we are free as individuals to adapt to the course of history either well or poorly. Like white-water rafters, we can ride the rapids, avoiding the rocks, sandbars and whirlpools and pick a course by looking ahead, or we can just trust to luck.

3. The future is a great ocean. There are many possible destinations and many different routes to each destination. A good navigator takes advantage of the main currents of change, adapts their course to the capricious winds of chance, keeps a sharp lookout posted, and moves carefully in fog or uncharted waters. If we do these things, we will get safely to our chosen destination (barring a typhoon or other disaster that can be neither predicted nor avoided). At any point we can decide to change our destination in the light of the changing situation, and, having arrived somewhere, move on to the next stage of our journey.

4. The future is entirely random, a colossal dice game. Every second, millions of things happen that could have happened another way and produced a different future. A bullet is deflected by a twig and kills one man instead of another. A scientist checks a spoiled culture and throws it away, or looks more closely at it and discovers penicillin. A security guard looks carefully and discovers a bomb before it explodes, or takes a cursory glance and misses it. Since everything is chance, all we can do is play the game, pray to gods of fortune, and enjoy what good luck comes our way.

Source: adapted from Kaufman (1976).

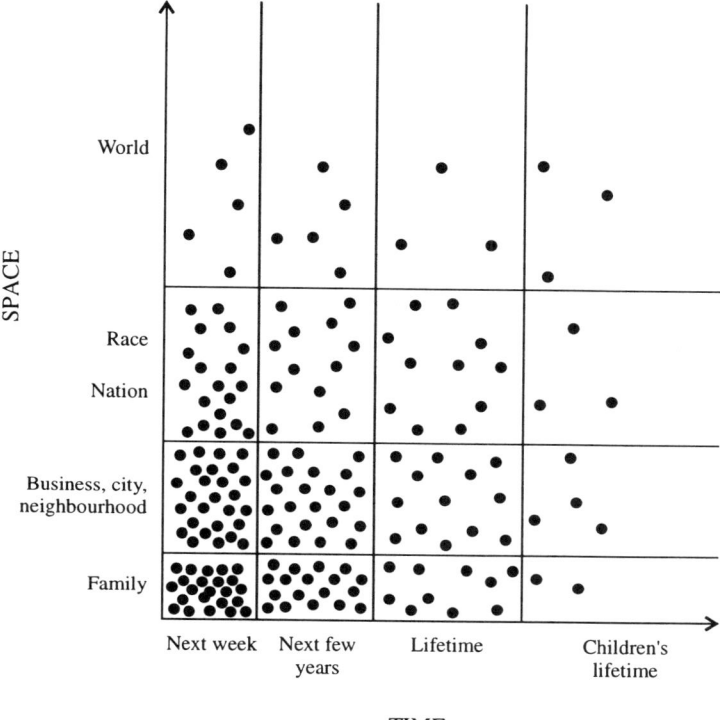

Fig. 1. Human perspectives

Although the perspectives of the world's people vary in space and in time, every human concern falls somewhere on the space–time graph. The majority of the world's people are concerned with matters that affect only family or friends over a short period of time. Others look farther ahead in time or over a larger area—a city or a nation. Only a very few people have a global perspective that extends far into the future.

Source: Meadows *et al.* (1972).

The main reasons given by the respondents in Boniecki's study for not thinking about the future were much as might be expected:

- coping with the present is enough; it leaves us no time for contemplating the future
- present issues are more important
- the perceived pace of change in modern society makes long-term thinking unrealistic
- by implication, there is an inability to cope, to imagine or contemplate even the personal long-term future, especially in a climate of rapid change.

1.2.1. Coping with the Present is Enough

The discussion of human perspectives in *The Limits to Growth* implies that individuals in advanced affluent societies might be expected to have wider, longer-term horizons than those living in subsistence conditions. Referring to the graph, reproduced here as Fig. 1, the authors suggested that

> most people's worries are concentrated in the lower left hand corner of the graph. Life for these people is difficult, and they must devote nearly all their efforts to providing for themselves and their families, day by day. Other people think about and act on problems further out on the space or time axes. The pressures they perceive involve not only themselves, but the community with which they identify. The actions they take extend not only days, but weeks or years into the future.

This follows the pattern of Maslow's (1952) hierarchy of human needs, which holds that once basic survival and security needs are satisfied it becomes possible for the individual to develop socially and personally. Thinking longer term is part of this. While this seems reasonable, Boniecki's (1980) work suggests that coping with the present still occupies all or much of an individual's time in a relatively affluent society. It appears to contradict the suggestion that thinking about the future is more developed in societies that do not need to concentrate on survival.

At first sight this may seem illogical. It is normally assumed that working hours are shorter in advanced societies than in subsistence societies, but this may not always be true, because subsistence may not necessitate working all hours to keep alive. It is possible to obtain enough to live on in a relatively short time, leaving the rest of the day free. There is no pressure to obtain more than is necessary for survival, because there is no means to exchange the surplus, nor anything to exchange it for. In Western society, on the other hand, there are many more (often costly) leisure-time pursuits to fill non-work time many times over, and social pressures to acquire consumer goods unheard of in subsistence society. In Western societies, therefore, we work much longer than is necessary for subsistence in order to obtain money to purchase some of the plethora of products available. The rest of our time can easily be spent making use of our purchases, whether in driving for pleasure, watching television, or indulging in sport or home-improvement. No wonder there is no time to think about the future: we are too busy coping with and, if we are lucky enough, enjoying the present.

An examination of the complexity of modern life shows that it is quite possible to suggest that individuals in modern society have no more, and quite possibly less, time to contemplate the state of the world and the possible future than their counterparts in a subsistence situation. It would be fair to point out, however, that the former have the opportunity to think about the future but, in conforming to the norms of society, prefer not to, whereas the latter may have no such choice, nor any reason to do so.

Galtung's (1976) international study offers further evidence to suggest that affluence does not necessarily create wider, longer-term perspectives: 'Future consciousness . . . is best developed among the non-European and the socialist nations [Eastern Europe at the time of the research], and least among the Western European nations.' Indeed, Galtung suggests that there may be something about the experience of development, particularly of science and technology, that tends to turn people away from thinking about the future rather than towards it. With the increasing dominance of the Western model since his research, future-consciousness may well have declined.

Two apparently contradictory explanations for this are suggested (Galtung 1976). First, the ease of affluence may tend to engender a sense of security, giving rise to the view that there is no need to think about the future because it is assured and can therefore be taken for granted. Things have been getting better, and there is no reason to think that they will not continue to do so. Second, and in almost total opposition, it is suggested that the future is seen as so uncertain or threatening that it is preferable to forget about it and make the most of the present. The future is just too frightening or depressing to contemplate. There are so many problems that seem insoluble and so many things that could go wrong, that it is better not to think about them but to enjoy the present while it lasts. A third explanation may be added—that increased affluence serves to increase the complexity of life, and thus space and time in which to contemplate the future do not, contrary to initial expectations, grow.

Simon (1974) suggested a further variation. Adopting the concept of the postindustrial society, he suggested that the West is beginning to move towards a 'temporary society containing temporary people'.

Post industrial man, we can expect, will be more rooted in a strong sense of the present. . . . The post industrial individual's sense of his own worth will derive more from what he or she is rather than what he or she might or must become. The essential value of what he or she is doing derives from the experiences intrinsic to the activity, rather than the instrumental value of that activity for the realisation of other ends projected into a uncertain future.

Twenty years later there is plenty of evidence to confirm this shift. As Yazaki (1994) noted, one of the difficulties we need to overcome in approaching the future is the prevalence of 'Nowism'. This does not mean, Simon argued, that postindustrial individuals will completely avoid thought or actions with a future-orientation, but that any such activity will be judged on its current value rather than on what it may offer in the more distant future.

This kind of development is perhaps seen in the apparently rapid decline in recent years of traditional middle-class attitudes. In the past it has been argued that the middle classes characteristically put off the satisfaction of wants, aims and desires by saving, indulging in long training programmes and adhering to strict moral codes, in the belief that as a direct consequence the end result would be enhanced satisfaction and success. With the development of hire-purchase, credit and renting facilities it is no longer necessary to save up in order to afford consumer goods; we can buy now and pay later. There is no better summary of the new attitude than an advertising slogan used a few years ago by Access, one of the main credit card companies in the UK:

'Access takes the waiting out of wanting'

Similar attitudes seem prevalent in society at large. It is enjoyment of the moment that is important, not putting it off in the expectation of greater benefit later. After all, since anything could happen to prevent us enjoying the benefit at a later date, it is better to have it now while we can.

Galtung's first explanation suggests that there is no need to think about the future where we assume a continuation of present circumstances, particularly if they are satisfactory, with little or no possibility of significant change. It will be like the present, so there is no incentive to contemplate any differences. Galtung's research was conducted in the 1960s, when Western societies tended to have a view of the future, not dissimilar to this, that equally discouraged serious thought about it. Since the end of the Second World War, and certainly from the 1950s on, the general trajectory of the economy, in particular, had been one of continuing expansion. Life seemed to be on an upward trend. There were slowdowns, but successive generations could normally expect an improvement over the living standards of their parents. The conflicts that had torn the world asunder twice in the century appeared to have been settled, and a peaceful future seemed reasonably assured by the large US military presence. It was Western European societies, according to Galtung, that expressed this attitude most strongly. They probably still do. Despite the conflicts affecting many parts of the world, despite the high unemployment in many countries, and despite the warnings of environmental collapse, the majority of the population in Western Europe are still living well and probably do not seriously contemplate any change for the worse, even if, at the back of their minds, some doubts exist.

Where those in Western Europe have moved away from such a complacent attitude to the future, Galtung's second explanation becomes relevant. Consideration of the future is discouraged—and concentration on the present is encouraged—by anticipated threats that are too unpleasant to contemplate. If there is a strong fear that tomorrow will either be much worse than today or even, at the extreme, nonexistent, it becomes logical to live for today. The two explanations are perhaps less contradictory and more the opposite sides of the same coin. The result, in terms of consideration of the future, is similar.

Present generations are continually reminded by the media of the depressing nature of the world around them. Wars, famine, natural and manmade disasters follow, apparently remorselessly on. The individual seems powerless in the face of the threats. Why bother? We are just as likely to be dead, unemployed or homeless tomorrow, so make the most of today. An interesting example of this attitude was provided in a letter sent to the *Guardian* newspaper in 1982 by a teacher from London. Quoting the attitudes of his ten-year-old pupils to the bomb, racial prejudice, the lack of jobs and housing, he concluded, 'Children today are painfully aware of the lack of a future facing them. Small wonder, therefore, that they see no point in working to get on.'

Other threats, for example those of future resource-depletion, may also be met with reactions totally opposed to the hoped-for response of the conservationists raising the issue. It is said that petrol will run out or become prohibitively expensive within a few years, unless we change our consumption habits. As an individual motorist it is possible to concede that, if all motorists changed their habits, supplies could be made to last longer; but unless I am convinced that everyone else will change their consumption patterns, all that will happen if I do not buy so much is that I will lose the benefits of using my car, while others continue to use theirs. That just means that I would inconvenience myself. On the other hand, if I believed everyone else would reduce consumption, I could carry on at my existing rate because it would not matter, since my consumption represents such a small part of the total. In either case, unless my demand is inhibited by rationing or prices I am unable to afford, the result is to encourage me to continue to gain the benefit of using my car while I can. Live for the moment and face tomorrow when it comes. Something might turn up anyway and the threats be shown to be unfounded.

1.2.2. Present Issues are More Important

It is customary in financial circles to consider currently available income more valuable than future income, and to apply discounting procedures to the latter to assess its value relative to money in hand. 'Given the opportunity to receive £100 today or £100 in a year's time, most people choose to receive £100 today. They do so because they have time preference for money. Money has time preference, or value, because its early possession opens opportunities for investment or early consumption' (Copeland, Dascher and Davidson 1980).

12 THE FUTURES DEBATE

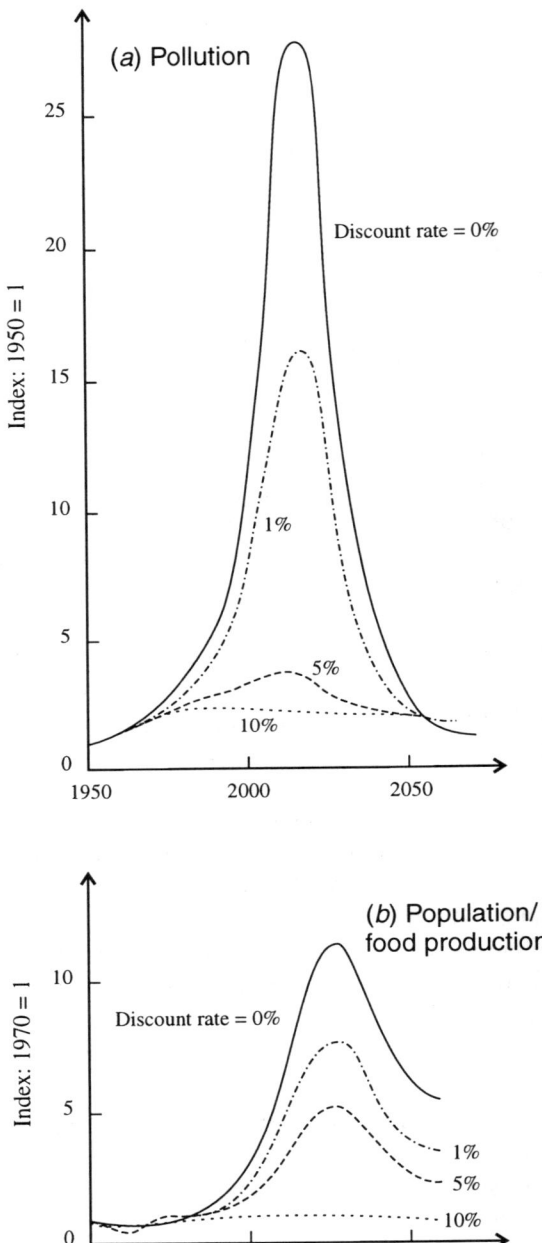

Fig. 2. The discounting effect in crisis perception
Source: Linstone (1973)

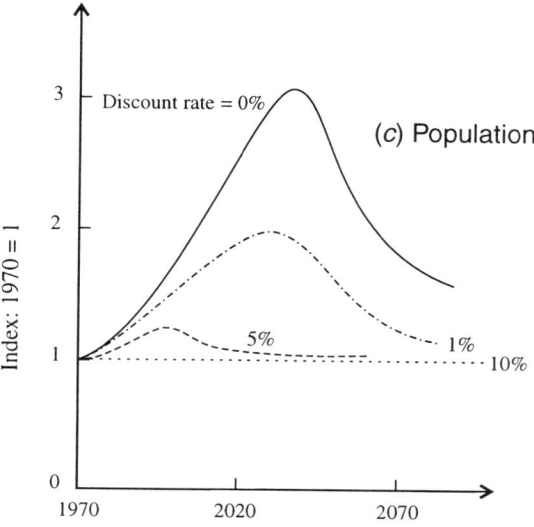

Fig. 2. (*cont.*)

With inflation, the advantage in receiving the money now, rather than in a year's time, is increased. In a year's time, £100 will be worth less than £100 in today's value. By receiving the money now we could invest it and receive interest (making the money more likely to retain its value) or purchase now more goods than we will be able to buy in a year's time. If we buy the goods we would have a year's benefit from them as well.

Linstone and Simmonds (1977) argued that the same process occurs when we think about events in the future: 'We apply a psychological discount rate to our perception of future problems and opportunities the same way a businessman applies a discount rate to future income.' Using examples of future crises predicted by *The Limits to Growth*, Linstone (1973) showed that if a similar discounting of the impact of these events is applied 'no dramatic worsening of the current situation is perceived by today's observer. . . . The forecaster points to remotely located threats and opportunities only to find a frustrating and maddening unresponsiveness.' Despite the apparently frightening prospects of the standard model run of *The Limits to Growth*, the application of discount rates rapidly reduces the perceived impact of the problems. 'An oil shortage thirty years from now is not perceived nearly as serious a crisis as the same shortage occurring in six months. We look at the future as if through the wrong end of a telescope' (Linstone and Simmonds 1977). Fig. 2 demonstrates the effect of applying a range of discount rates to some of the problems identified by *The Limits to Growth*. Their application significantly reduces the impact of the problems seen from our perspective in the present, or even, if the rates are high enough, makes them disappear.

Problems with which we are currently faced are real; they must be considered now and cannot be put off. Potential future problems, unless perceived as imminent, can be left, since they are unlikely to become much worse as the result of a small delay in consideration. Individual delays in consideration can, of course, always be argued to be marginal, even if, when taken together, they could become significant. Besides, there is no guarantee that a potential future problem will become a reality; it may never happen. In the face of the demands on resources made by coping with current problems, support for preparations to deal with problems that may or may not occur can be difficult to justify. The effect is to discount the importance of future problems in comparison with current concerns.

As individuals we are inclined to believe that whatever our current situation, we have enough to deal with without dreaming up other problems we might have to face, should they occur. We prefer, quite reasonably, to adopt an approach that says 'let's deal with that if and when it happens'. It takes great self-will even to give up habits, such as smoking or overeating, that we know are very probably harmful to us. Rather than change our habits in the interests of our own future, we persuade ourselves that it is not really necessary since we might escape the consequences. Anyway, we enjoy it and prefer the present satisfaction to possible future benefits. We can always rationalise our feelings by pointing to the continually changing opinions of the experts who argue at one time, for example, that low-fat margarine is healthier than butter because it contains no saturated fats, and in the next breath, in the light of further research, that other constituents of margarine are more harmful. You can't win, and if you cut out all the things you enjoy, 'you don't actually live longer. It just seems like it!'

On a societal level, when the scale of the currently perceived problems is appreciated, a similar attitude is adopted. With such crises as unemployment, poor industrial performance, inflation, rising crime rates, inner-city decay, famine in Africa, and civil war in numerous places already on the agenda, there is no room for other, less concrete potential dangers to be considered. Indeed, it may well be seen as an irresponsible waste of time and effort even to contemplate them. It would take scarce resources away from more critical issues.

In both business and government there is a tendency to look for the quick return, particularly, it is said, in Britain and the USA. The financial markets for exchange rates and shares respond to current events and perceptions rather than long-term prospects. Without the promise of good short-term returns, shareholders will sell their shares and move their investments into government stock or more promising securities. Governments and administrations are always accused of thinking no further ahead than the next election, when they could lose power. Their attention is concentrated upon the period leading up to that election and the creation, as far as possible, of a 'feel-good' factor among the electorate. That this may produce problems after the election is less important than remaining in power. In any event, there will usually then be time to work towards the election-after-next by getting unpopular measures out of the way before preparing the ground for it. Longer-term thinking beyond the normal electoral cycle could well be politically self-defeating.

1.2.3. The Perceived Pace of Change in Modern Society

It seems to have become an unwritten assumption of much 'Futures' literature, and an often accepted view of late-twentieth-century life, that we live in an era of almost unprecedented change. Possibly the most influential example of this idea is found in the striking concept of exponential growth. Several examples of this are quoted in *The Limits to Growth* and the more recent *Beyond the Limits* (Meadows *et al.* 1992), including a French children's riddle:

Suppose you own a pond on which a water lily is growing. The lily plant doubles in size each day. If the plant were allowed to grow unchecked, it would completely cover the pond in 30 days, choking all the other forms of life in the water. For a long time the lily plant seems small, so you decide not to worry about it until it covers half the pond. On what day will that be?
Day 29. (1972, 29)

This illustration assumes that the size of the plant doubles in the course of a day, a very rapid rate of growth.. But even at lower rates of growth, doubling time can be surprisingly quick. Quoting United Nations data, the Brundtland Report, *Our Common Future* (World Commission on Environment and Development 1987) showed that although world population had only grown at an annual rate of 1.9 per cent between 1950 and 1985, it had nevertheless nearly doubled, from 2.5 billion to 4.8 billion in 35 years. If it continued to grow at that rate, it would reach 10 billion around 2020. That is, even if the *rate* of growth remains unchanged, exponential growth means that the *amount* of growth becomes continually larger.

Small rates of growth, around 2 per cent, may seem insignificant, and for a time they are. It is only when they continue for some time that the amount of growth becomes larger. Two per cent of 100 is only 2, but 2 per cent of one million is 20,000, of 10 million, 200,000, and of 10 billion, 200 million. The rate of growth, when expressed as a percentage, is the same, but the amount becomes ever larger. At a growth rate of 2 per cent per annum it takes only 35 years to double the original amount, whatever that was. Higher rates double even more quickly.

The concept of exponential growth does not suggest that change is a new process, but that the further along the curve, the greater the amount, and consequently the greater the impact of growth. On an exponential curve, it is not necessary for the rate of change itself to accelerate for the scale of change to be very much larger than before. The acceleration of change in the twentieth century may strictly have been more apparent than real. What is less debatable, if exponential growth, or growth approaching exponential rates, is accepted, is its increasing scale and impact. The result has been the belief on the part of many observers that change in the latter part of the twentieth century is occurring faster than ever before.

While Toffler (1970) argued that 'the *rate* of change has implications quite apart from and sometimes more important than, the *directions* of change', later authors suggested that the type of change may also be of major significance. D. Bell (1976) and Marien (1977), among others, have argued that we are in the process of moving from industrial society to a very differently structured *postindustrial* society, while Harman (1976) writes of a transformation to *transindustrial* society, Ferguson (1980) of a *paradigm shift*, and Harvey (1989) of *postmodernism* and *post-Fordism*. Toffler (1980) suggested we are entering the *Third Wave*, a totally new style of civilisation that is markedly different from Second Wave or industrial society. He subsequently argued (Toffler 1990) that this will involve a *Powershift* with major implications for society. Less apocalyptically, the OECD Report *Interfutures* noted the emergence of 'A number of new problems . . . which have important implications . . . difficulties in maintaining growth and full employment, supply and demand imbalances in markets of important commodities, inflation, unprecedented balance of payments problems, concerns about the new patterns of trade, investment and monetary relations and the growing imbalance between the developed and the developing economies . . .' (OECD 1979). Few of these problems have gone away since 1979. Many seem to have become worse and others have joined them.

As a result of this change it has been argued that established methods and ideas are no longer adequate to deal with the new problems, or to provide us with an understanding of the events we are experiencing. Hence our feelings of an inability to cope.

W. E. Moore (quoted in W. Bell *et al.* 1971) suggested a further significant feature of change in the modern era, that 'most contemporary social change is either deliberate or is the secondary consequence of deliberate change'. According to W. Bell *et al.* (1971) this is a result of the rise of human mastery over the natural world, as a consequence of which humans in advanced societies find 'their chief struggle is with themselves and other men, not with nature or the lack of technology'. It is the growth of human numbers and the power of our technology that has brought this about (Suzuki 1992). It would be unwise to take this argument too far; but though nature still constrains us, in a society in which we are dependent on a vast array of unseen individuals, organisations and technologies for normal everyday life, human influence is increasingly significant.

Human life in earlier ages was subject to natural forces beyond our control. It still is, but today we find ourselves increasingly subject to forces that, while beyond our control, are the result of the actions of other human beings. These, as Isaiah Berlin points out, are different from limitations that result solely from natural forces. 'You lack political liberty or freedom only if you are prevented from attaining a goal by human beings' (Berlin 1969). Our inability to run 1500 metres in 2 minutes is accepted as a physical limitation arising from our physiology, but our inability to express our views freely because to do so would result in our imprisonment or death at the hands of those with power over us is a purely human-imposed limit. As such, in the West at least, it is usually considered unacceptable. When this kind of limitation by deliberate human action is believed to be a common reality of life, a certain resignation may well develop in the mind of the individual. If we are fighting against the elements, success or failure can be influenced to some extent by our own efforts in a heroic struggle. In any event, no one else can be blamed for our failure. On the other hand, if other human beings are responsible for preventing us from attaining what we want and they are beyond individual influence, like 'the Government', 'the Markets' or any identifiable powerful force, then we feel we can do nothing. There is no point in trying because our efforts are doomed to be ineffectual before we start: they will make sure we do not succeed.

Each of these three ideas—the speed and amount of change, the type of change, and our perceived inability to influence change resulting from deliberate human action—may be challenged as inaccurate interpretations of the current scene. For example, it has been pointed out that population increase in the UK and Western Europe was much more rapid in the nineteenth century than it is today, with a consequent impact on the development of Victorian cities (T. Williams 1981). The simultaneous transition from an agricultural to an industrial society was as traumatic, and as much the result of human actions beyond the control of most individuals, as are today's changes. The pressures exerted on the rest of the world by European colonists must have been equally traumatic for the local populations, many of whom were destroyed or disinherited as a result. Indeed, it is interesting to note that several writers, for example D. Bell (1976) and Toffler (1980), have pointed to the Industrial Revolution as a comparable transition to the one we are currently undergoing. We have experienced major changes in the past, but there remains one important distinction with earlier times: *information*.

Not forgetting, in the UK, such novelists as Dickens, campaigners like Chadwick and Booth, and the work of the great investigating committees of the nineteenth century, the level and speed of information then were much less than they are now. It took three weeks for information about the Crimean War between Russia and Britain to reach London; now instantaneous communication is possible and the Gulf War was seen practically live worldwide. The sheer weight of books, articles, newspaper reports and radio and television programmes examining, reporting and prescribing remedies for modern problems is far beyond that of earlier ages. Information and ideas are disseminated more rapidly, and given sufficient support, particular views of a situation can become widely accepted in a short time. Therefore, the features of change that are described, whether a true reflection of the situation or not, have become accepted as true. A generally agreed perception of change as being rapid and even accelerating, of major proportions, and beyond our control as individuals has developed, and it is this that influences our attitudes.

The replies in Boniecki's (1980) study suggest that the concept of rapid change has indeed become established in the minds of individuals in Western society. One consequence of this, and of the expectation that such rates of change will continue is the belief that the shape of the future becomes impossible to imagine:

'Change is inevitable and impossible to forecast.'
'Life changes too rapidly. Can't comprehend.'
'Given the rapid rate of change, I can't imagine what it (the future) will be like.'

These opinions appear to confirm the belief that, as Laswell (quoted in W. Bell *et al.* 1971) suggested, mankind is passing from the primacy of the past to the primacy of expectations of vast future changes. Our culture, which developed around a situation perceived as more stable, leaves us poorly prepared to cope with rapid change. As a result we become disoriented and unable to cope with the dynamic present or face the disturbing future.

Toffler (1970) coined the phrase *Future Shock* to describe this reaction to change. He defined it as 'the shattering stress and disorientation that we induce in individuals by subjecting them to too much change in too short a time'. His book of the same name is described on the dust jacket as a 'study of mass bewilderment in the face of accelerating change'. Quoting C. P. Snow, Toffler argued that 'Until this century social change was so slow that it would pass unnoticed in one person's lifetime. That is no longer so. The rate of change has increased so much that our imagination can't keep up.' Whether or not this is true, it is an opinion that many people seem to hold.

1.2.4. The Inability to Cope

The idea that limited human ability contributes to our difficulties in contemplating the future was also developed by Boniecki (1980). He suggested that the human cognitive–affective system, the means by which we perceive and react to our environment, depends on three capacities—intellectual, imaginative and emotional. Each, he suggested, is severely limited in its ability to enable us to think about the future. Limitations of intellectual capacity may result from lack of knowledge, insufficient understanding of complex processes or inability to comprehend the information available in a useful way. Whatever the reason, it can easily lead to feelings of inadequacy and effective paralysis. Bohler (1973) showed the importance of imagination in thinking about the future when he reminded us that, 'contrary to a widespread belief, future is not a concrete thing, but an abstraction loaded with affect. Future becomes a 'thing' only through the physical process of projecting our images into the other world.' The future is only real in our imagination; it does not exist anywhere else. In arguing that we are unable to cope with the pace of change, it appears that, with relatively few exceptions, we believe we are not able to imagine situations greatly removed from our past and present, things that are significantly different or other-worldly. This could have important implications: Boulding (1976), in describing the work of Polak (1973), suggested that a culture's image of the future constitutes an important, core capacity in its development. Polak argued that the Renaissance in Europe resulted from a dynamic image of the future based on optimism about humanity's ability to influence the course of events. He claimed that there has been a contrasting decline in imaging capacity in almost all aspects of Western culture in the twentieth century. Societies without this capacity, Polak argued, create few initiatives because they exhibit what he termed 'Essence pessimism combined with influence pessimism; the world is bad and there isn't a damn thing man can do about it' (Boulding 1976). Such a lack of positive images of the future leads, in Polak's view, to the decline and eventual death of a society.

An interesting light is cast on the argument of cultural inability to cope with the challenges of the future and the changing present by ideas about the functioning of the brain. The brain has two hemispheres and,

Although each hemisphere shares the potential for many functions, and both sides participate in most activities, in the normal person the two hemispheres tend to specialise. The left hemisphere (connected to the right side of the body) is predominantly involved with analytic, logical thinking, especially in verbal and mathematical functions. Its mode of operation is primarily linear. This hemisphere seems to process information sequentially. This mode of operation of necessity must underlie logical thought, since logic depends on sequence and order. Language and mathematics, both left-hemisphere activities, also depend predominantly on linear time.

If the left hemisphere is specialised for analysis, the right hemisphere (again, remember, connected to the left side of the body) seems specialised for holistic mentation. Its language ability is quite limited. This hemisphere is primarily responsible for our orientation in space, artistic endeavour, crafts, body image, recognition of faces. It processes information more diffusely than does the left hemisphere, and its responsibilities demand a ready integration of many inputs at once. If the left hemisphere can be termed predominantly analytic and sequential in its operation, then the right hemisphere is more holistic and relational, and more simultaneous in its mode of operation. (Ornstein 1972)

The distinction should not be taken too far for, as Rickards (1990) noted, there remain many uncertainties about the operation of the brain. The separate functions of the two halves of the brain should only be regarded as a working hypothesis, but using the hypothesis Loveridge (1977) argued that thinking about the future 'would seem to be associated largely with the right half of the brain, it requires imagination'. On the other hand there is a growing acceptance that, as Ferguson (1980) suggested, 'for both cultural and biological reasons, the left brain seems to dominate awareness in most of us', particularly in Western societies.

If this is true, it is possible to suggest that Western societies actually condition their members into inability to cope with the future. Westcott (1976), for example, found a cautious, pedestrian attitude among students on a course in Future Studies. He considered them patently vulnerable to Future Shock and attributed their attitudes to conditioning by an education system without a future-orientation, and the culture of the 'now generation'. Rickards (1990) suggested that our ability to recognise patterns, built up on the basis of past experience, may be part of the problem. We expect things to take familiar forms and to fit in with our established ideas. When they do not we may ignore them or reject them rather than accepting that things have changed. In a rapidly changing world this can be problematic. Ornstein and Ehrlich (1989) have even argued that our minds are fit only for the eighteenth century and that if we are to cope effectively with the twenty-first we need to develop a New Mind to cope with our New World.

This leaves open the suggestion that our disinclination to give serious thought to the future may be learned rather than inherent. Could it possibly be that we do in fact possess the potential to imagine the future, but in Western society have failed to develop it fully? Other cultures, as Galtung's (1976) study suggests, may be able to imagine the future rather more successfully. On the other hand, even in Western culture we do think about and imagine the future in many ways and situations even though we do not always realise that we are doing it.

1.3. THE FUTURE: ALWAYS WITH US

So far it has been argued that, in Western societies in particular, the prevailing opinion holds that thinking effectively about the future is so difficult as to be hardly worthwhile. It has been suggested that this pervades both personal attitudes and government and business, where short-term views are thought to dominate. On the other hand, it can be demonstrated that individuals, governments and businesses are inevitably concerned with the future in dealing with their current concerns, and therefore of necessity think ahead on many occasions and have gained considerable experience of doing so.

1.3.1. The Future in Everyday Life

The instinctive future

'What shall I have to eat tonight?' Anyone who asks themselves that question is concerned with the future. At the time the question is raised the meal remains a few minutes or hours ahead. This is quite obvious from our use of the future tense in asking the question. If we had already eaten we would have asked 'What did I eat tonight?' and if we were still eating, 'What am I having?' This may seem a trivial starting point but it usefully makes clear one important feature in our relationship with the future: we are unavoidably involved in dealing with, and thinking about, the future in living from day to day.

The example can be used to indicate certain other significant aspects of the future as well. Suppose that in answer to the question, I decide to have steak. If I wish to have steak for dinner and do not already have some at home it is obviously necessary to buy it; it will not make its own way to my house. This leads to the second important point about the future: we can, and do, quite naturally influence what will happen in the future. (There are many qualifications to be made to this statement because our actions are often limited by circumstances, but the basic truth remains.)

Of course it is always possible that when I arrive at the shop they will have sold out of steak and I will have to have something else instead. From this we can see two other features of our relationship with the future: the future is uncertain (we usually cannot be absolutely sure things will work out as we imagine or intend), and in thinking and making decisions about the future we take many things for granted; we assume, either explicitly or implicitly, that particular circumstances will occur.

What is taken for granted in this simple example?

- our continued existence (we will still be alive)
- we will want, and be able, to eat (we will be healthy and not ill)
- we will be eating at home and not change our plans, say, as the result of meeting a friend on the way home
- we will be able to buy what we want
- we will be able to prepare the food (the gas or electricity will be on so that we can cook)

The list could be extended.

If we were not able to assume (take for granted) these things, having a meal and most other aspects of everyday life as we know it would be virtually impossible. I do not mean to suggest that we should dwell on any of these matters each time we plan a meal: life would become unduly laborious if we did, and in ninety-nine cases out of a hundred there is no need to do so because everything works out as we expect. The important thing to establish is that dealing with the future, even if only in terms of minutes and hours, is a routine part of everyday life, something we do quite naturally without undue concern.

A few other examples of instinctive involvement with the future will help to show how normal an activity it is. A large proportion of the population undertake routine journeys to work, school or to similar destinations every day. Most walk, cycle, drive or go by public transport. From past experience we 'know' that if we leave home by such-and-such time we will arrive on schedule. If we use public transport, jokes about the reliability of the service apart, we 'know' because the timetable tells us that a particular bus or train will arrive and carry us to our destination at a particular time. A moment's reflection, however, indicates that we do not really know on any given morning that we will arrive in time, until we have. All forms of delay are possible. In reality, what we do is to assume, quite reasonably, on the basis of having done the same journey many times in the past, that today will be no exception. We expect certain things to happen rather than know that they will. This does not worry us and neither should it, but it is another example of how we continually deal with the future without consciously thinking about it.

Anticipation

'It is going to rain today. I had better take my raincoat.' To avoid getting wet we anticipate rain and act accordingly. Anticipation implies that we imagine, before the event, that something will happen. The event has, by definition, not yet happened and therefore we cannot be completely sure that it will, but nevertheless on the evidence available to us (the weather forecast, or the threatening clouds on the horizon) we conclude that rain is likely. We then adjust our actions to take account of our anticipation.

It is often suggested that anticipation in sport is the key to success. Great tennis-players often win points by being in the right place at the right time. In soccer goalkeepers are said to study the habits of penalty-takers in order to help them anticipate where a particular player will place the ball. They move in the anticipated direction in order to increase their chances of making a save, rather than waiting until they can clearly see which way the ball is going. If they wait there is usually not enough time to react before the ball has passed them. Though on occasions they look very foolish, diving away from the ball, the belief in the overall value of anticipation remains.

Any driver knows the importance of anticipation in the relationship between the position of their own vehicle and those of others a few moments hence. If another car pulls out of a side road in front of us, we brake or swerve in our attempt to avoid a collision, because we anticipate that continuing on our existing course will probably result in a crash. In doing so we do not wait to know that the crash is occurring before acting, but, in effect, imagine the likely future if we do not brake or swerve, and take action. If we wait to be certain we may literally be, as the phrase has it, 'dead certain'!

As these examples indicate, the problem with anticipation is that it is based on what we think the situation will be some time hence, and not on exact knowledge. In different circumstances this lack of certainty may discourage action in line with our anticipation because the changes or consequences of being wrong are considered too great. Unfortunately for those who require certainty, we are continually faced with situations that require the risk-taking that anticipation involves. On the brighter side, however, because we so often deal with such situations, we do have considerable experience to help us and in many situations do what is necessary without consciously thinking about it.

Appointments and other arrangements

'10.30 Wednesday—that's fine.' 'Same time, same place.' Making appointments, arranging dates or assignations, keeping an engagement diary or booking a holiday are second nature to many people. Every case is an example of thinking about the future. Arrangements of this kind are made hours, weeks, months or in some cases, years ahead of the expected event. It may be necessary to cancel the arrangement, or it may be impossible to get to the allotted place at the allotted time, but we still attempt to organise our time in this way. We do so for a variety of reasons.

If we wish to meet somebody it is necessary for us to arrange to be in the same place at the same time. Chance meetings do occur, but to be able to rely on meeting it is necessary to plan ahead. Advance booking is an established feature of much of the travel industry and holiday trade, and of such entertainment as concerts or theatres. By booking the customer aims to ensure they will obtain what they want at the time they want it; were they to leave buying a ticket until the performance or time of departure they might be disappointed. To judge from one area—the inclusive tour trade—there is an increasing tendency to look even further ahead. Brochures for summer holidays used to be available from the preceding January. More recently they have been published before Christmas and some are now available before the end of the holiday season the year before. To make reasonably sure of the holiday we want, at least in this section of the market, it therefore becomes necessary to increase the time-scale of our futures-thinking. We do it without a second thought, despite all the events that might intervene to prevent us taking the holiday in a year's time.

To organise our lives in work and leisure, whether to make them more manageable, easier or more enjoyable, we quite naturally indulge in thinking about and planning for the future. Life would be much more difficult if we did not.

Aims and ambitions

At some age every little girl, according to tradition, wanted to be a nurse and every little boy an engine-driver. Some firm up these ambitions and act in order to achieve them. Ambitions, be they for a future career or of the 'sail round the world' or 'climb Everest' variety are often long-term propositions. Considerable time and effort has to be expended in preparation for the desired future; few happen automatically.

Not everyone has ambitions on a grand scale but we all have aims, or things we would like to do. At the time of writing, my aim, or one of them—because there are others not directly relevant to this exercise—is to write a book about futures-thinking. Obviously this is going to involve a great deal of work in collecting material, writing and making arrangements for publication. There is no way of knowing at this moment whether the attempt will succeed. At some moments optimism reigns and everything seems to be going well, at others depression sets in and the task seems nearly impossible. Still the aim remains like light at the end of a tunnel, encouraging continued effort. If you are now reading the book, my ambition was fulfilled. Had I not imagined a future in which the book existed, you could not now be reading it. (I hope you are enjoying it.)

Without considering our actions at all unusual we all do things in the present that we hope will lead to benefit in the future. It may be for our own benefit, for our children, or for others, but it is a normal and unexceptional part of everyday life. Many things do not just happen immediately, but need considerable investment in advance if they are to be realised.

Commitments

In making appointments or arranging a holiday we are involved in fixing what we will be doing in advance. In other words, we are committing ourselves to being in a certain place at a certain time. Life is full of commitments, many of which commit us to particular responsibilities and actions for long periods in the future. Twenty-five years is a common period for a mortgage when buying a house in the UK. Because it is such a normal thing to do, there are over 9.5 million house-owners who are borrowing money on a mortgage. We tend not to think a great deal beyond the present when committing ourselves to pay up to a third of our monthly salary for about one-third of our expected life-span. Many mortgages, of course, are held for a shorter time before they are terminated for another, usually larger one, but that again commits the mortgagor to payments continuing into the dim and distant future.

Other commitments that we enter into in the normal course of events may be even longer or open-ended. Taking a job, apart from the knowledge that we will ultimately retire, may well move to another job or be made redundant, as and when certain circumstances occur, is usually an open-ended commitment. It may end at any time, subject to any conditions of notice, etc., but neither the employer nor the employee is likely to know when, or to spend long considering the length of time involved at the moment the job is taken.

Family commitments often last a lifetime—or in the words of the marriage service, 'until death do us part'. Here again, with a growing number of divorces, it is increasingly likely that a particular marriage or relationship will not last a lifetime, but it remains probable that most couples when getting married or deciding to live together do not see the arrangement as a fixed contract that will end in the short term. If asked how long they expected to remain together, they would probably answer 'forever', 'for life' or 'don't know', rather than 'for five years' or 'until next Thursday'. In entering such a commitment we are, then, fixing our future in certain respects for probably many years ahead, and possibly life. Having children is a similar open-ended commitment, one that could perhaps be said to extend beyond the term of our own life.

Precautions

Many jobs, particularly in the so-called white-collar sector, have linked pension schemes whereby arrangements are made for the employee to continue to receive income after retirement. For those without such schemes there are a variety of private pension plans on the market through which individuals can make similar arrangements for their old age. All such schemes are, at least when they are entered into, concerned with the future. To a twenty-year-old entering a job for the first time, a pension scheme that promises a continued income in, say, forty years time is probably a minor consideration, because it is so far in the future as to be virtually inconceivable. To someone nearing retirement, on the other hand, it may be much more relevant and the lack of such provision a considerable worry.

All car-owners are required by law to insure themselves against the occurrence of certain events while driving. Many in fact have insurance policies giving wider cover than the minimum required by law. Most householders (certainly those still paying a mortgage) have insurance policies on their house, and many others insure their possessions and themselves. Such policies are not normally taken out because the policyholder hopes to have a crash, have their house burned down, lose their possessions or die young, but as a precaution against these events. The whole of the insurance industry is based on our desire to protect ourselves, as far as possible, from the consequences of these events should they occur, and the premiums reflect the calculations of the insurance company of the anticipated future likelihood of such occurrences among their policyholders. Insurance does not prevent the occurrence of the event, but provides financial recompense should it occur. If we could be sure such things would not happen there would be no need for insurance. We cannot be sure, so we take precautions. Insurance is one of the ways in which we deal with the inherent uncertainty of the future.

Having a flutter

National lotteries, betting on the horses and gambling in casinos are all forms of futures-thinking. People place bets on a particular horse because they believe, or hope, the horse will win a particular race. If it does so, they—and this is probably the main reason for the popularity of betting—stand to win back more, sometimes much more, than their stake money. It is a matter of chance, of beliefs and hopes, rather than certainties. Many 'certain' winners fail to make the first three or even finish. The attraction of betting and the existence of a considerable gambling industry are based on the unpredictability of the future. If everyone knew which horse would win the Grand National in advance no bookmaker would take bets, and the odds would be so poor that there would be little point in placing a bet anyway. If you remain unconvinced just try placing a bet on the 3.30 *last* Saturday!

Capricorn: the Goat

'An unsettled atmosphere has been surrounding you recently, but various people will be making adjustments both to their own lives and to yours, with far-reaching and beneficial effects. Do not allow sentiment to colour business or home decisions. Be firm, but fair.' How many of us can truthfully say we have never read our horoscope? So many popular newspapers and magazines print them, it is hard to avoid them completely. Such frequent occurrence indicates, too, that many people must read them, or at least that newspaper and magazine editors believe that they do. The fascination of horoscopes lies in their claims to foresee the future. We may believe them or be totally sceptical about them, but they constitute a further and apparently growing example of the place of the future and its fascination for us in our everyday lives.

Science fiction

'Star Trek', '2001', 'The Terminator', 'Aliens', 'Jurassic Park'—just some examples of popular films and television series set in the future. Science fiction has experienced considerable popularity in written, and then also visual form since the beginnings of the current vogue early this century. As I. F. Clarke (1979) and others have pointed out, such writing about future worlds has a long history and is closely related to the tradition of utopian literature. That there exists a mass market for science fiction indicates that even if only as entertainment and an escape from the trials of our present world, the future has a popular attraction.

As individuals, therefore, we do spend a considerable amount of our time dealing with matters related to the future. As a result we have a wealth of experience in doing so. Thinking about and planning for the future is not so unusual or impossible after all. Rather the reverse: life would be much more difficult and haphazard if we did not.

1.3.2. The Future in Industry and Commerce

Business as usual

'Business activity, and therefore management activity, is entirely based on expectations. Management is about the uncertain future' (Milne 1975). Surely not; surely businessmen, more than anyone else, are too busy dealing with the present to bother about the future. Milne argued, however, that most, if not all, business activity is concerned with the future. Even current production schedules are geared, Bratt (1958) suggested, to *expected* rather than actual sales. The reason is obvious. Between the production and sale of most products there is an inevitable time lag, resulting from the necessity to produce goods and transport them from the place of production to the place of sale. With perishable products, especially food, this time lag must be brief, and it may be necessary to cope with demand variations by varying production only shortly before or immediately after changes in demand. If the production process is relatively short and simple, and there are few constraints imposed by raw material or labour difficulties, short-term flexibility can be maintained. Where, on the other hand, the production process is long and/or complex, and it is not possible to vary the level of output at short notice, the need to think and plan ahead will be greater.

Such planning is necessary to avoid the inability to meet demand, the loss of potential sales, the problems of overproduction, and the need to spend large sums on storage. The inaccuracies of forecasting are such, however, that it will probably be impossible to obtain an exact match between current production and future sales. Therefore, on the basis of past experience producers may prefer either to maintain relatively steady production schedules or base production on the pattern of demand in earlier years, with a reserve of stocks to cope with the variations in sales. Here again, however, it is important to note the relevance of Bratt's (1958) argument that this decision is no less based on expectation: the expectation that future sales will follow the same pattern as those achieved in the past. In today's competitive world, successful firms increasingly need to respond to changing markets to avoid producing unwanted goods or being unable to supply a growing demand. Speed of response and, even better, successful anticipation of changing market conditions give firms a competitive edge. In a recession, if firms expect a decline in sales to continue they need to reduce production through short-time working or suspending production completely. If they do not and are unable to sell their products, more drastic reductions will eventually occur, if by the different route of bankruptcy. Where sales are expected to increase, firms will look to boost production to meet the anticipated demand. If they do not they stand to lose market share to competitors who have been more successful in anticipating the expansion. It is sometimes argued that the shifts in world production are in part a result of the failure of companies in the West, and particularly in the UK and the USA, to adapt to changing conditions as rapidly as those in Southeast Asia have done and to assume too readily that the future will be like the past rather than anticipate or plan for change.

It is important to stress that this process of working to expectations occurs whether it is stated explicitly or not. Even the firm that continues to produce at a given level because it has always done so is assuming that the future will be like the past, and that its level of sales will remain much as before. In making that assumption it may well be quite justified, and there is no guarantee that the firm which indulges in careful, explicit sales forecasting will make more accurate estimates. The point to emphasise here is that both firms are unavoidably thinking about the future, though one may realise it and the other may not.

Pearce (1971) listed a number of problem areas, other than those mentioned above, in which he suggests thinking and planning ahead are necessary:

- inventory control—the need to ensure a sufficient supply of raw materials and components for the production process;
- manpower requirements—the need to maintain a sufficient and adequately trained labour force;
- distribution problems—the need to predict market distribution, or have the right goods (colour, style, type and so on) in the right place at the right time; and
- price and discount policies—the need to estimate the effect of an increase or decrease in price, or a special promotion on sales.

To these Chisholm and Whitaker (1971) added

- financial management—the need to plan cash and borrowing positions during the year ahead;

and Makridakis and Wheelwright (1989)

- the need for forecasting in research and development and top management and for views on likely changes in the economy and the environment.

Hard-headed businessmen, then, who would probably be among the first to argue that they were concerned with today and had little time for pipe dreams of tomorrow, nevertheless think about the future in the course of their everyday work. As Jones and Twiss (1978) pointed out, 'there is nothing new in all this. The terms "far sighted" and "forward thinking" have long been attached to successful managers.'

It may be argued that companies with modern, flexible production systems operating to the 'just-in-time' philosophy do not think, or need to think, about the future. That these systems do not require their operators to think so far ahead as the methods they have replaced may be true, but they require even better short-term flexibility in order to cope with any variations in demand. If they do not anticipate an upturn they may be 'just-too-late', and failure to anticipate a reduction in demand will leave them with 'just-too-much'. Such production methods are, in fact, a recognition of the need to deal with an uncertain future and of the problems that can arise if the response to rapid change is too slow. As such they are, ironically, examples of a more developed Futures approach, one that accepts future uncertainty and attempts to deal with it, rather than assuming that it will be like the past.

New products

If the future inevitably enters into the production process of existing products, it is more obviously important where new products, new production methods or new investment to increase production are concerned. Of necessity this is often a long-term process. Before making any large-scale commitment to the production of a new product, be it a new model or a completely new line, any company will wish to be reasonably certain that it will be able to obtain the necessary sales to make production profitable. Few firms embark on ventures they expect to be unprofitable unless they have non-financial reasons for doing so. This confidence may be based on hunch, detailed market-research surveys or test marketing—all forms of dealing with the future.

Having made the decision to go ahead, if that is the case, quite possibly several years before the first sales are anticipated, the firm will then need to make a host of arrangements to bring about eventual production. Product designs must be finalised, new plant designed and constructed, new equipment obtained, people trained, prototypes made and tested, a sales trial carried out, and advertising and other preparations for the launch of the product, and probably many other smaller items, considered and organised. All of these steps are undertaken with one aim in view: the success of the new product in the future. Much can go wrong, forecasts can be inaccurate, plans prove misguided, but the necessity to think ahead is unavoidable.

Galbraith (1969) argued that as technology has grown more complex, 'An increasing span of time separates the beginning from the completion of any task.' The future—the appearance of the product on the market—in effect becomes more remote. Accordingly, from the time and capital that must be committed, the inflexibility of this commitment, the needs of large organisations and the problems of market performance under conditions of advanced technology, comes the necessity for planning. Planning, as Chadwick (1971) defined it, is 'a process of human forethought and action based upon that thought'. It is and must be future-oriented.

At the same time, however, technological development has made planning more difficult. As improvements to existing products, more competitive products and completely new products are brought on to the market with increasing rapidity, it becomes more difficult to foresee what the market situation will be when a new product is eventually launched. The result may well be to create the opinion that in such an uncertain situation thinking ahead becomes so difficult and liable to such great error that it is not worthwhile. This is precisely the kind of argument that was discussed in the first part of this chapter. On the contrary, Hage (1981) argued that as product life decreases there is a need to plan further in advance in order to survive. It is necessary, in effect, to be one jump ahead of the competition. This is so because, as Trist (1972) pointed out, 'The greater the degree of change, the greater the need for planning, otherwise precedents of the past could guide the future.' An analogy can be seen in travelling in a car at increasing speeds. At slow speeds we need only look a short distance ahead because we can quickly change direction or stop. At faster speeds either action takes much longer, partly because we travel considerable distances before reacting and partly because our actions take longer to take effect. As a result we need to think that much further ahead both in distance and time in order to drive safely.

The value of such future-thinking and planning in industry is indicated by the example of the Japanese. Under the heading 'National strategy is boosting Japan into fifth generation', *Computer Weekly* described Japanese plans in the early 1980s for 'what they intend to produce in the next ten years' (Camill 1982). The success of Japanese industry in competing with other countries (Done 1982) is at least in part based on similar thinking and planning ahead. Ten years after these particular examples the success of Japanese plans was clearly apparent in the continued expansion of their industry. They then moved on to their next targets with equally carefully laid plans because planning for the future is a continuing process, not a once-and-for-all task. A fascinating insight into the Japanese approach to technological forecasting and its role in their industrial success was given by Bowonder and Miyake (1993). Outlining the activities of both companies and government they made it clear that Japan is planning to dominate the information technology, new materials and biotechnology industries in the twenty-first century. As Hamel and Prahalad (1994) emphasised, this kind of foresight 'gives a company potential to get to the future first and stake out a leadership position . . . to control the evolution of its industry and, thereby, its own destiny. The trick is to see the future before it arrives.'

1.3.3. The Future in Government

One of the oft-quoted sayings of British government, attributed rightly or wrongly to Harold Wilson, Prime Minister in the 1960s and 1970s, holds that 'A week is a long time in politics'. This clearly reflects another opinion about politicians—that they are only concerned with short-term political advantage and the next election. Be that as it may, it is clear after a moment's reflection that politics and government are nonetheless essentially concerned with the future.

Before an election each political party spends considerable time and effort setting out its policies in an attempt to persuade the electorate that a future in which they are in government will be better than one in which their rivals are in power. These policies are presented as the way to solve the main problems seen by the party—poor economic performance, inflation, unemployment, crime, the environment and so on. They outline how the party proposes to act should it be given the chance, and what improvements it expects from its actions. The policies are expected to take effect over the term of office that follows the election, though some will be couched in terms that indicate that the current mess cannot be cleared up that quickly and will need a longer period to yield the promised results.

The same is true for a party in government. As McMahon (OECD 1965) pointed out, governments are unavoidably dealing with the future because they are faced with three distinct time lags: the *information lag*, the *decision lag* and the *policy–effect lag*. The first, though not strictly in the future, creates similar effects and problems to the other two. Most information is to a degree out of date, because it takes time to collect and process into a usable form, and because even if it were physically or economically possible to obtain a continuous stream of updated information, it would usually not be possible to use it immediately. Therefore, the latest available information, which we commonly consider current, is in fact more usually historic, past. In relation to it, the present, which may be significantly different, is in the future. This is true, for example, of a census. Census information, which is collected in the UK every ten years, is used as a basis for many public sector decisions, particularly in urban planning. When the information from the census becomes available considerable attention is given to comparing it with the previous census ten years earlier. Conclusions are drawn about the changes that are seen to have occurred between the two dates, which are interpreted as representing the latest trends. Unfortunately the information from a census usually takes at least eighteen months to publish, by which time the comparison being made is between information eleven-and-a-half years old and information one-and-a-half years old. The trends identified occurred between these two historic dates. Whether they are still operating is open to question.

It is on the top of this information lag that the decision-making process takes place and the decision lag comes into play. Information is received, interpreted and evaluated. Opinions will be formed as to whether the situation requires any action or not. Unless it is seen as a crisis requiring immediate action, further time will be spent deliberating over the type and amount of action required. Once some form of policy proposal is established it may be further discussed with interested parties before the decision is announced. The changes may be planned to come into effect at some still later date. This may be a relatively rapid process, as when changes in the tax on petrol are announced during a Budget Speech as taking effect from six o'clock the same afternoon. If legislation is involved, it may be a much longer one. Consider for example the time taken over the reorganisation of local government in Britain.

Pressure from a number of quarters for the reform of local government had been building up during the post-war period, but it was not until 1965 that the then Minister of Housing and Local Government, Richard Crossman, stated that 'The whole structure is out of date ... our councils are archaic institutions ... increasingly ill-adapted to fulfilling the ... functions with which they are charged' (Richards 1970). The following year a Royal Commission was appointed 'to consider the structure of local government ... and to make recommendations'. Its report was published in 1969. In February 1970 the then Labour Government published a white paper outlining its proposals, but the election of June 1970 brought a new, Conservative administration to power. The new government published its own proposals in February 1971 and introduced a bill into Parliament in November. The Local Government Act became law on 26 October 1972 and the new local authorities brought into existence by it took over on 1 April 1974. Some nine years had elapsed from the time of Crossman's speech to the completion of the reorganisation. Subsequent changes, in particular the abolition of the Greater London Council and the Metropolitan Counties, were achieved in a shorter time, but it still took three years from the publication of the white paper 'Streamlining the Cities' outlining the policy to the abolition of these councils in April 1986—about the same time as that part of the process took a decade earlier. Further changes in progress at the time of writing are little quicker.

Decisions taken by governments also affect the future for varying lengths of time. Some will have only short-term effects, but others, like the decision by governments to embark on nuclear weapons programmes and nuclear power, have left humanity with radioactive products which have a half-life of 24,000 years: that is, after 24,000 years half of their radioactivity will have decayed. By comparison, humanity's recorded history goes back about 4,000 years. In developing such programmes governments are looking for short-term advantage and are not deterred, even if they give it a thought, by the longer-term significance of their actions. There are longer-term implications, nevertheless. There is some evidence that in the USA, at least, some thought is now being given to the long-term problems created by nuclear programmes, particularly the need to warn future generations not to interfere with our nuclear waste dumps (Kliever 1992).

Not all government policies influence the shape of the future for as long as this, but they often remain in effect for some time. In many cases, policies take time, following their introduction, to take full effect: even if petrol taxes are increased from six o'clock not all garages increase their prices at that time; some prefer to maintain the old price until they purchase new supplies at the revised rates. Where legislation attempts to introduce new modes of operation or new schemes, or—even more—attempts to change attitudes and habits, the policy–effect lag may be even longer. As a result of these lags, the formation of policy is obviously an exercise in thinking about the future. Whether that is acknowledged or not, it does not stop governments and opposition parties continuing to make promises and devise policies for the future.

Any government therefore needs to look ahead. For example, McMahon (OECD 1965) reports that the governments of Canada, France, The Netherlands, Sweden, the UK and the USA all forecast the following variables: public expenditure, consumer expenditure, private fixed investment, investment in stock, exports and house building. In addition *Social Trends 1982* (Central Statistical Office 1981) indicated that at that time the UK government prepared forecasts for population to the year 2001, households to 1991, school pupils to 1991, the labour force to 1986 and the number of social security benefits recipients to 1982. More recent editions do not include projections, but some forecasts are still published, notably *Population Projections 1987–2027* (OPCS 1989), Treasury economic forecasts and Department of Transport traffic forecasts.

The time needed to make provision for changes in the demand for services such as school and higher-education places, social services and traffic makes forecasting and planning necessary. It may be relatively easy, apart from the political opposition that will have to be faced, to cut back by closing schools and reducing the numbers of teachers, when fewer are needed, but it is more difficult to increase provision to meet expanding needs. Unless a reduction in standards, such as increased class sizes, higher teacher : pupil ratios, or less space per pupil, is accepted, there will be a need for new schools to be built or existing ones expanded, and for more teachers to be trained. None of these can be achieved in an instant.

A survey of long-term planning activities in Swedish government prepared by the Swedish Secretariat for Future Studies indicated the range of such thinking that was undertaken (Ingelstam 1974). The survey included:

- actions in intergovernmental bodies
- international development co-operation, especially development programmes
- defence
- international trade policy and industrial policy
- long-term economic policy
- manpower policy
- locational and residential policy
- national physical planning
- transport
- education
- welfare and the care of the sick.

By way of illustration, two of these areas may be selected for further consideration. First, the need for long-term thinking in defence is created by three salient lags in the system:

- the time it takes to develop matériel—for 'heavy' matériel the plan-to-plant period may range anywhere from five to ten years
- the service life of matériel—this varies greatly, but fifteen to twenty years encompasses the normal range
- the training of personnel

In deciding to develop new types of military equipment any government is, therefore, quite clearly thinking far ahead, up to thirty years in Ingelstam's estimation.

The second example is the area of urban planning. 'It is safe to say that nowhere in the society are people's futures mortgaged so far ahead as when the municipalities plan housing projects, earmark uses of land and build highways' (Ingelstam 1974). Buildings, judging by past experience, may be expected to last on average for between sixty and a hundred years, in some cases much longer. Many towns in Asia and Europe were founded centuries ago and their basic street patterns and building plots can often be traced back almost as far, and some of their buildings hundreds of years. Though current efforts may not, for whatever reason, last as long, they are likely to be around for many years to come. It is obvious that forward planning that attempts to lay down policies or detailed proposals for the use of land is concerned with the future. Less clear, but nonetheless significant, is the importance of day-to-day development decisions by landowners, developers and planners. The decision to build housing on a particular tract of land certainly commits the future of that land for the life of the houses concerned, and quite probably for longer. It may therefore be a decision with very long-term consequences.

1.4. CONCLUSIONS

This chapter has attempted to show that in many aspects of life, individuals, businesses and governments think about the future. It is unavoidable. It has also attempted to show that we frequently overlook the amount of time and effort spent in thinking about and planning for the future, and hence underestimate the experience we have of doing so. Though it would be wrong to pay insufficient regard to the difficulties of futures-thinking, it can be argued that we do ourselves an injustice when we perceive our future as totally unknown and completely beyond our control, as we often tend to do. The influence of our current ideas and activities on the shape of the future is profound, whether by intention or default.

Of course, forecasters, futures-thinkers and planners occasionally make predictions and prepare for futures that do not actually come about. But if thinking about the future is unavoidable, is it not preferable to do it consciously, rather than turn our backs on the attempt because it appears, at first sight, to be too difficult?

CHAPTER TWO
SOME PROBLEMS OF FUTURES-THINKING

Thinking about the future, whether minutes, days, months or years ahead, is a normal aspect of human life. It is easily done. The problem is not that such thinking is itself difficult, but that what we think about the future is often at variance with what actually happens. Quite obviously we can think about the future; the critical question is whether beyond the intellectual stimulation and enjoyment such exercises may provide, it is really worthwhile.

There are two obvious answers to this question, yes and no. In the next chapter we will examine why, in the late twentieth century, thinking about the future is both worthwhile and important. Here the concern is with the problems of such activity; in effect, the reasons for answering no to the question.

An important qualification to the discussion should be made at the outset. The literature of and about Futures is divided between the enthusiasts and the critics. Both sides bring forward powerful arguments for their point of view. Both can be very convincing. At the end of the day, however, the suspicion remains that the result is to confirm the views already held by those presenting the arguments. Views may be qualified by the attacks of the opposition, new defences may be developed to counter particular points, but the principle remains intact. Baldly stated, 'You either believe in futures-thinking or you do not.' Futures-thinking is in no respect unique in this. It is no doubt apparent that I do believe in futures-thinking, but I am aware of the criticisms that can be raised to the theory and, particularly, the practice as they have so far developed. Careful consideration of these criticisms is useful in the refinement of the activity, particularly in the check it provides to unbridled enthusiasm.

2.1. DIFFERENT KINDS OF FUTURES-THOUGHTS

The problem comes not in thinking about the future but in attempting to 'foresee' what is going to happen in advance of the event, with more than a chance possibility of being right. One of the difficulties we encounter arises because we can have more than one kind of thought about the future. Jones and Twiss (1978) suggested that in considering the future it is important to draw 'a clear distinction between what *could* happen, what *should* happen and what *will* happen'. It may also be useful to add, what we *hope* will happen and what we *fear* will happen.

What we think *could* happen covers the wide range of all we believe might possibly occur in the future. It can range from future situations we believe would be favourable to those we think would be unfavourable. There is no guarantee, of course, that the eventual future will fall within the range we thought could happen. We are often surprised by events, remarking that 'I didn't expect that' or 'I didn't think that could happen'. This suggests that the range of our thought about what could happen is sometimes not broad enough. Perhaps our thoughts are limited to relatively unsurprising projections from the present, rather than incorporating major change or surprise. Without really thinking about it, we may limit the futures we imagine to those we consider probable (likely) rather than possible.

It has been suggested by Inayatullah (1990), for example, that 'Information about the future given to an administrator will only affect decision making if it conforms to the administrator's pre-understanding. If it is significantly different from that, the report will probably find itself filed far away from the real world of decision making.' Future images that are too different from our past and present experience are often rejected as unbelievable and therefore impossible. They could not happen. Unfortunately, sometimes they do.

Strictly speaking, what *could* happen includes all *possible futures* that could develop from the present state. It implies a very large number of potential events. Not surprisingly we reduce the number by, implicitly or explicitly, evaluating what we *think could* happen. We use terms like *impossible, improbable, possible, probable* and *certain* to reduce the range to manageable proportions. Impossible (in our opinion) futures either do not enter our consciousness or are rejected as not worthy of serious consideration. Improbable ones, though given some thought and considered possible, are felt unlikely to occur; to have a low probability. We give serious consideration usually only to those futures we reckon likely, or to have a reasonably high probability of occurring. Amara (1981) called these *probable futures*.

Our assessments of probability will be influenced by the evidence we have available in the form of information, opinions, beliefs and values. Different people, therefore, may well come to different conclusions about which futures are most probable. Closely influencing this process will be our hopes, fears and preferences. We will frequently *hope* that the future will be favourable to us, either personally, or by developing in ways that concur with our beliefs. Such hopes can be very powerful driving forces. The image of a future situation that we regard as better than the present is not simply passive; it encourages us to take action in an attempt to bring it about. Such images are one of the major forces for change in human history. They are translated into goals, aims, objectives and targets to be striven for. The Wright brothers did not just hope to fly, they actively pursued their dream until they succeeded. Governments introduce policies that they believe will influence events in a direction that will achieve their aims, be it lower inflation, faster economic growth or reduced unemployment. The fact that we are not always successful in achieving our aims or realising our hopes does not stop us having them. Rather, it may strengthen them and lead us to redouble our efforts to bring them about. Such future images exert a powerful, even on occasion an over-riding influence on our decisions and actions in the present. Without them we would have little or no reason to act.

Hopes can also affect our assessments of possible futures by leading us to believe that those futures we consider favourable will come about. Such hope value appears to influence the opinions of politicians. Take the British Chancellor of the Exchequer (the finance minister) who frequently stated during the recession of the early 1990s that the recession was at an end and the upturn just round the corner. Perhaps he believed it, but subsequent events proved that for a time at least these statements were more hopes than accurate forecasts. He may also have believed, not unlike the rest of us, that if he kept saying it he would be right some time!

Forecasters may fall into this same trap. When things are getting worse, particularly economically, they often forecast an upturn. If this does not occur and the trend continues downward, they may well continue to be hopeful, and despite continued evidence to the contrary still forecast the upturn. This can lead to a pattern of forecasts that when graphed looks like one side of a fish bone (Fig. 3).

The reverse of hopes are the futures we *fear* may happen. Some people may take great pleasure in worrying others with prophecies of doom and gloom, but most of us are not attracted by our fears. So much so that we may too quickly reject them from consideration among possible futures. They are too unpleasant to think about, so in the hope that something will turn up to prevent them from occurring, we conveniently ignore them. Sometimes it works, on

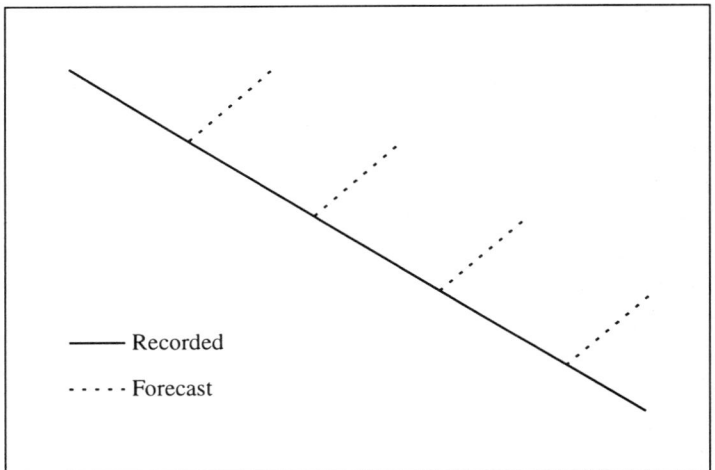

Fig. 3. The herringbone forecast

other occasions we are not so lucky. 'If only I'd thought about that I could have avoided it.'

Fear, like hope, can be an important stimulant to action. Like a rabbit caught in the headlights of a car, we may be transfixed and paralysed by the image of an event that would cause us harm or loss; but the image may also be an incentive to do something to avoid the event or lessen its consequences. It is fear of theft that causes us to take precautions like fitting an alarm to our house or carrying our money in a concealed belt. Such actions are intended to prevent, or reduce the risk of theft. Governments that fear attack by perceived enemies spend large sums on defence, and may even engage in a pre-emptive strike in order to reduce the enemies' ability to inflict damage in an anticipated attack. In both cases, fears, images of a future that we would find unpleasant, are instrumental in leading us to take actions aimed at influencing future events.

Closely related to our hopes, but not always the same, is our assessment of what *should* happen. Here we are applying our opinions about how things ought to turn out; what we want to occur. It would be good, right, just or better if a particular event occurred. These *preferred futures* will exert a strong influence over our actions as we attempt to shape events to bring them about.

Even this brief discussion serves to show that when we come to make conclusions about what will happen, it can be a complicated process. It is possible to reach conclusions without indulging in any evaluation of the alternatives or even believing that any exist. On the other hand, if we wish to take the future seriously and not just leave it to chance it can involve a great deal of thought. Even then the conclusion can only be what we *think will* happen, not what will happen. An element of uncertainty remains. What we think will happen—in formal circumstances, our forecast—is likely to result from some kind of assessment, either implicit or explicit, immediate or complex and time-consuming, of the possible, the probable, our hopes, fears and preferences. That we do not always—or even ever—go through such a process consciously does not mean that this discussion has no value. It indicates the process we go through even if we are not always aware of it.

Depending how certain we are about our conclusions, we may qualify them by reference to conditions that we feel will either bring the events about or prevent them. Or we may decide that we can only offer a range within which we are reasonably confident the future situation will lie. This process may be casual and rely on gut feeling or intuition, or it may involve long deliberation, perhaps including selected forecasting or planning methods. The results will still be what we *think will* happen. Whether or not what we think will happen does in fact happen, only time will tell. Such phrases as 'worse than I feared' and 'beyond my wildest dreams' indicate that actual events sometimes lie outside the range we considered. Predicting accurately what *will* happen is a complex task.

One other important concept to emerge from this discussion is that in our thoughts it is futures, plural, that emerge, rather than the future, singular. This can be disturbing. We are used to thinking about *the* past, *the* present and *the* future, all singular; one train of events leading through history. The suggestion that there might be more than one possible future is not immediately easy to accept. It appears to make the future different; not just a continuation of the past but a potential branching point where alternative directions become possible and different futures can emerge. We like to know, not be faced with the uncertainty of an indefinite future, as the existence of alternatives implies. On the other hand, we like to think that we have some influence over the course of events and not that our lives are controlled by outside forces, or that we are just living through a pre-ordained plan. If this is the case we need to be able to make effective choices about which direction to go in. For choices to be effective they must be between real alternatives, not just illusions. The consequences of choosing one alternative rather than another are likely to be different. If so, the very act of choosing will influence the future, one choice leading to one future and another leading to a different one. Depending upon the circumstances of the choice, the implications can be minor or of great significance. Deciding between steak or fish from a restaurant menu may have few implications, but a government weighing up the pros and cons of military action could open up vastly different futures.

The usual assumption that there is only one present and one past does seem logical, since we experience what appears to be one reality. But how do we know that the reality we experience is the same as someone else's, or that our reality remains the same while we are asleep? Consideration of the many debates and conflicts in the world suggests that the reality seen by different groups is not the same. To some environmentalists, for example, there is ample evidence that the planet is in a crisis created by our industrial lifestyles. In another camp, Bolch and Lyons (1993) argued that 'the world is not about to come to an end and that by nearly any measure the people who reside in the . . . West enjoy a cleaner and safer environment than ever experienced in modern history'. It is this different opinion about what *is* and the direction of *past* trends that critically influences the alternative images of the future. Which present are we in—the one as seen by Meadows *et al.* (1992) or the one apparent to Bolch and Lyons? Alternatives may, then, not be limited to the future; alternative images of the past and present can also exist.

2.2. OPTIMISM AND PESSIMISM

Our thoughts about what will happen in the future are influenced by a number of factors, including our hopes and fears for the future. A common observation further suggests that some people (optimists) tend in most situations to emphasise their hopes, while others (pessimists) are dominated by their fears. The *Concise Oxford Dictionary* gives the following definitions:

Optimism: doctrine that the actual world is the best possible; view that good must ultimately prevail over evil in the universe; sanguine disposition, inclination to take bright view.

Pessimism: tendency to look at the worst aspects of things: doctrine that this world is the worst possible, or that things tend to evil.

Modifying an analysis by Sicinski (1976), three significant facets of these definitions may be identified: the state of the world, the direction of change through time, and the general approach of the observer. Attitudes to the state of the world may be further examined in terms of (*i*) a general world-view concerning the nature of humanity and our place in it; for example, that it is the human lot to struggle in the face of adversity, or to master the universe; (*ii*) an opinion of the actual situation in relation to the theoretically possible; that things can get better, or will inevitably become worse; and (*iii*) an evaluation of particular events or states as better or worse than other happenings or situations. The first of these may be held irrespective of time. General world-views or opinions about the human situation may refer equally to past, present and future. They are likely to be timeless—that is, constant—whatever time-frame is under consideration. Comparative views, such as the second and third, can either be within one time period or applied to situations in different periods. The terms are often used with reference to opinions about imagined future situations in comparison to the present, but these may well be influenced by comparisons between the past and present. Those who view the past nostalgically as a long-gone Golden Age much preferable to today are likely to be pessimistic about the future, which they will regard as continuing the decline. Conversely, those who see the past as 'the Bad Old Days', when life was nasty, brutish and short, are more likely to be optimistic in relation to future events, as long as they can envisage continuing improvement.

Our approach to events may be general or specific to particular situations. Someone who exhibits a general tendency to see the worst of all situations is usually called a pessimist, but it is quite possible for an individual who does not normally express such views to see a specific situation in a pessimistic light, as indeed it is possible for a pessimist to be optimistic in particular cases. This approach leads to certain complications in the use of the terms pessimist and optimist. We may use the terms to refer to ourselves, our attitudes in general or to specific issues, but it is probably more usual for them to be applied to us, or our opinions, by others: 'Don't be such a pessimist', 'You're being a bit optimistic', and similar phrases. As evaluations made by others, they are external assessments and may differ from the feelings of those expressing the views. Pessimists, for example, frequently justify their attitudes as being realistic and optimists, as looking for the best in people.

One use of this external assessment is in the classification of opinions about the future. Gordon and Suzuki (1991), with their predictions of environmental doom if we continue on our present path, would usually be classified as pessimists, while Naisbitt and Aburdene (1990), who saw a very different future in which the environment was not a problem, would be seen as optimists. It is, however, quite possible to see the world envisaged by Naisbitt and Aburdene pessimistically. Those who consider high technology as undesirable, either of itself or because it is thought to have undesirable consequences, will view the coming of the superindustrial age pessimistically. On the other hand, it is also possible to take an optimistic view of the threats of environmental doom, as the most promising way to encourage people to change their attitudes and create a more desirable and sustainable lifestyle. The same events may be viewed pessimistically or optimistically, depending upon the values of the observer. What one hopes for in the future, the other fears.

This leads, then, to another, internal rather than external approach to the definition of optimist and pessimist. In this light an optimist is someone who expects their hopes to be fulfilled, or expects to succeed in their efforts, while a pessimist expects to fail or to see their fears become reality. It is quite possible for external and internal assessments to be opposite to one another. The threats of environmental disaster, which most tend to see as pessimistic, may be considered optimistic by those who see the simpler lifestyle envisaged as desirable.

Polak (1973) provides a further dimension to the examination of optimism and pessimism by differentiating between *essence* optimism/pessimism and *influence* optimism/pessimism. 'The essence categories refer to an unchangeable course of events; the influence categories refer to the supposed or rejected possibility of human intervention. The first point of view sees history as a book that has already been written; the second sees history as a process that man can or cannot manipulate.' Here the object of our concern is combined with our ability to influence events through time. Four resulting combinations can be envisaged:

- Essence optimism combined with influence pessimism: the world is inevitably moving towards a better future, but humanity plays, and can play no part in its development. We are carried along by events which, fortunately, are changing for the better. Thinking about the future is interesting because we may be able to foresee the improvements.
- Essence pessimism combined with influence pessimism: 'chaos overrules the cosmos from beginning to end, and man can do nothing except resign himself to the inevitable' (Polak 1973). Things are bad and getting worse and we have no control over them. Classic fatalism. There is no point in looking ahead and, because the future can only get worse, good reason not to do so.
- Essence pessimism combined with influence optimism: existing reality may be unpleasant and problematic but human beings can both imagine and effectively work for a better future. It is bad but we can make it better.
- Essence optimism combined with influence optimism: 'the world is good and man can make it even better' (Boulding 1976).

There is no way of proving the truth of any one of these combinations, but to adopt one as our approach to the human condition and our ability to influence it is critical to our attitude to the future. Futures-thinking generally assumes influence optimism. The examples of everyday thinking about the future in Chapter 1 mostly assumed influence optimism. We do those things because we assume that by doing them we can affect what happens to us in the future. To Popper (1988) it is this 'attraction, the lure of the future and its attractive possibilities that entice us: this is what keeps life—and indeed, the world—unfolding'.

2.3. IS THERE ANY POINT IN FUTURES-THINKING?

Influence optimism assumes that we can affect the course of events, that our decisions and actions are an important shaping force. This implicitly suggests that we reject the idea of determinism in favour of at least an element of free will and effective choice. R. Williams (1976) suggested that 'In its most widely used sense determinism assumes pre-existing and commonly "external" conditions which fix the course of some process or event.' The result, in its extreme form, is a situation in which human beings are totally unable to influence the processes or events in which they are involved—in Polak's terms complete influence pessimism. Determinists hold that the pattern of human history, from its origins onwards, has in some way been inevitable or pre-ordained. Pre-ordination implies a prior plan setting out the course of history; all that any generation does is to put its section of the plan into operation. Choices, decisions and deliberations are only a charade; the results, if we had but known it, were already established. A plan of this sort is often taken to imply a planner, a supernatural power external to the human race, who prepared and enforces the plan. The course of events is seen as the implementation of the will of the supernatural power. Other approaches are, however, possible. The inexorable march of history may not be the result of a plan but arise from the workings of the underlying processes of human society. It may be argued that processes necessarily change along particular lines that may be understood from a study of history but not influenced or diverted. Thus, in the Marxist view Feudalism was replaced by Capitalism, which was itself in turn to give way to Socialism and Communism. The trajectory is seen as inevitable though not preplanned. The idea of historical inevitability is reflected in phrases like 'It had to happen' and 'It was inevitable', which are often attached to events that, with hindsight, seem obvious. In the process, outcomes that beforehand we considered possible are dismissed.

Some people take the stance that, as individuals, we are determined by our biological inheritance, not only in respect of our physical characteristics but also in our relationships with other people, our personality and our responses to situations. Others argue that the social aspect of our existence is controlled by learned patterns of behaviour instilled by parents in our early years, or throughout life by the culture and society in which we live. Yet others take the view that the environment in which we live determines our actions, attitudes, economic circumstances and our life chances. Whether singly, through one overarching force, or through an accretion of many constraints from various directions, the result is the same. In any situation, either as individuals, societies or the human race, only one course of action is open to us; alternatives do not exist.

In such a situation any efforts to think about the future can only be couched in terms of attempts to foresee what is to come. Particularly if it is assumed that there is a plan already prepared for the whole of human history, the point of any effort can only be curiosity about what is going to happen, a kind of fortune-telling. Where inanimate processes are taken as the driving force a number of approaches are possible. It may be interesting for a Marxist to predict when the transition to Communism will occur, for a systems scientist to use models to examine how the system will evolve over time, or for a geneticist to predict that an individual is susceptible to certain diseases. All these fields are complex and far from totally determinist, but where such an approach is taken the failure of predictions may, of course, be attributed not to the invalidity of determinism, but to the current shortcomings in knowledge and understanding of the systems involved. If we knew enough, accurate predictions could be made, because the track is fixed.

An element of free will, on the other hand, introduces other complexities. Even in a situation in which it is acknowledged that only two realistic alternatives are available , and where the results of choosing one or the other will not be the same, thinking about the future takes on a totally different complexion. No longer is the exercise an attempt to predict what is going to happen anyway. Instead, we must consider the possibility of two different futures conditional upon the choice made. Prediction is obviously difficult where we have insufficient information and knowledge to be able to forecast accurately. If we can do nothing to avoid or enhance what is to come the exercise may lose its point. Choice, however, is infinitely more difficult, because rather than one strand of history, complex though it is, we have to envisage a range of possible futures diverging from the current situation. The future becomes conditional: if this, then that.

The extent of the range of futures we contemplate, and the value attributed to forecasting and futures-thinking will be influenced by where we position ourselves in the free will–determinism debate. At the extreme of total free will, the range of possible futures becomes infinite and forecasting of little value because the probability of accuracy is practically nil. If all individual members of society are attributed total unrestrained free will, forecasting becomes almost impossible because the effort of assessing the range of possible individual decisions and their interactions would be beyond our imaginative capacity. At the same time, the value of futures-thinking may be enhanced. Whereas from a determinist perspective its only use can be to predict what is going to happen anyway, in an environment of choice thinking carefully about the consequences of choices is important if they are to be informed rather than random. As the consequences must, logically, follow the choices, and follow from the choices, they are of the future at the time the choices are made. Full consideration of them therefore requires futures-thinking.

If we consider total determinism and total choice as opposite ends of a continuum, the human situation seems likely to be at some point in between (Fig. 4). The debate revolves around where. It seems probable that in the present we are individually, and as a society nearer the determinist end. Our present situation, deriving as it does from the past, constrains our alternatives but does leave room for some choices. As we consider the longer-term future we appear to have greater choice: a wider range of alternatives becomes available because some of the earlier determining factors are no longer so constraining. Humanity as a whole and societies may well be considered to have greater freedom the further into the future the thinking moves. Individuals, on the other hand, must face the ultimate determinism of death.

At the societal level, and individually in certain situations, it is possible to conceive of the future as a widening range of possibilities the further ahead we think. The future can be considered to be fan-shaped, the handle representing the present. A rather better metaphor is a cone, which, as a three-dimensional concept, gives a clearer image of the range of possibilities. It must not be forgotten that the present, represented by the vertex of the cone, moves forward with the passing of time. Humanity is, without time-travel, always living at the vertex, where there is relatively little room for manoeuvre. The room, if it exists, is in the future, in our ability to envisage what may be possible years ahead and to move towards it by making the necessary adjustments now. It is only by thinking about the future and acting in advance that it becomes possible to move beyond determinism or fatalism. Thinking only of the present, where our options are limited, effectively reduces our ability to influence our own destiny. From this perspective futures-thinking and planning become a vital part of our ability to influence events.

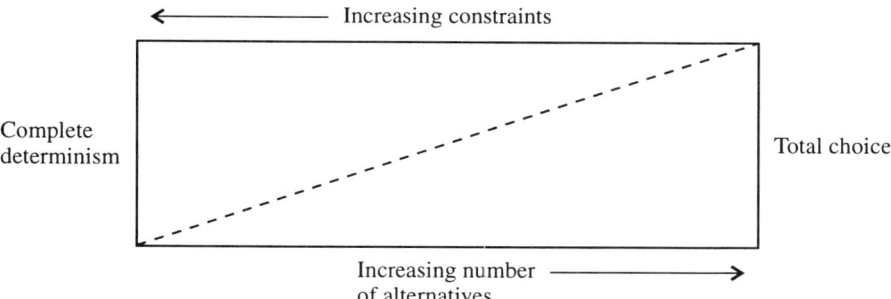

Fig. 4. The choice–determinism continuum

48 THE FUTURES DEBATE

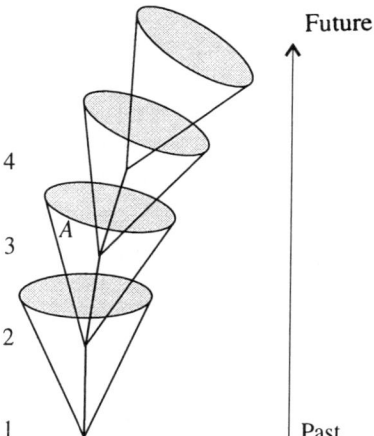

Fig. 5. The cone of the future

Fig. 5 shows possible alternative futures fanning out from the present at times 1–4. Point A remains a feasible alternative during periods 1 and 2, but by period 3 the chance of achieving it has gone. It is still in the future but it is no longer possible to reach it because the constraints of the, then, present situation do not provide sufficient flexibility. If we wish to reach point A we need to make the necessary decisions and take action well in advance; that is, we need to imagine it as a desirable future and plan ahead in order to achieve it. If we do take steps to achieve A the course of history will change and a different range of alternatives will be presented. Discussions about reducing the emissions of CFCs in order to preserve the Earth's ozone layer are a good example. Only by acting now can we halt the process of ozone-depletion some years hence, because past emissions will continue to destroy ozone for some time. It is difficult, if not impossible, to stop using them completely straightaway. They have to be phased out as alternatives are found. The process of phasing them out will affect the future and change its trajectory.

2.4. CAN WE USEFULLY THINK AHEAD?

There are different ways of thinking about the future and a wide range of methods of doing so. One of the most common is the making of forecasts. It is not the only method or the best, but it is generally known and attracts a good deal of criticism from those who doubt the value of futures-thinking. It attracts criticism because many forecasts become public and their results are exposed to examination. They can be checked for accuracy against observations made when the time for which the forecast was prepared becomes the present.

Shepherd Mead, the author of *How to Succeed in Business Without Really Trying*, wrote among other books *How to Get to the Future Before it Gets to You* (Mead 1974). At one point in the book he provided the following example of a forecast that was not actually made but might have been. It takes the form of a conversation between Mead and the MIT computer used to run the world model for *The Limits to Growth*, which had been published shortly before.

'Could you help me, please?'
'HAPPY TO, SIR.'
'I'm making a study of historical pollution in New York City, beginning in 1850. Are you writing this down?'
'OH, YES SIR. POLNY 1850. GOT IT.'
'The problem was chewing tobacco and horses.'
'YES, SIR, CHTO AND HO.'
'And the main problem was spit and horse manure.'
'YES, SIR. CHTOSP AND HOMAN.'
'I'd like to set up a dynamics system on this.'
'NO PROBLEM, SIR. JUST GIVE ME THE LEVELS AND THE FEEDBACK LOOPS, AND WE ARE OFF.'
'The spit level in the gutter was half an inch, and the manure level in the middle of the road averaged half an inch, too.'
'YES, SIR. CHTOSP LEVEL .5 IN., HOMAN LEVEL .5 IN. DO YOU HAVE THE FEEDBACK LEVELS, SIR?'
'They were feeding the horses oats and the men plug cut tobacco. By 1860 the rates on both of these doubled.'
'SUPERB, SIR. IT'S JUST LIKE WITH MR FORRESTER. YOU'VE GOT AN EXPONENTIAL SITUATION THERE, SIR.'
'You know how to deal with that?'
'OH, YES, SIR. POSITIVE FEEDBACK LOOPS AND LEVELS RISING EXPONENTIALLY, YOU'VE GOT A LEVEL THAT DOUBLES IN TEN YEARS.'
'Can you project that dynamically?'
'WON'T TAKE A NANOSECOND, SIR. WE'VE GOT A CHTOSP LEVEL OF 1.0 INCH IN 1860, 2.0 INCHES IN 1870, 4.0 INCHES IN 1880.'
'Just give me the readout for 1970.'
'YES, SIR.' (short buzz lasting 1 1/2 nanoseconds) 'I MAKE IT THAT BY 1970 WE HAVE 2,048 INCHES OF SPIT IN THE GUTTERS AND 2,048 INCHES OF HORSE MANURE IN THE STREETS. THAT COMES TO 170 FEET 8 INCHES OF EACH, PRECISELY.' (Equivalent to a fourteen storey tower block!) 'WILL THAT BE ALL, SIR?'
'Yes, thanks very much.'
'ANYTIME, SIR. WE'RE HERE TO HELP YOU.'

Had the conversation continued it would have suggested the equivalent of 28 storeys by 1980, 56 by 1990 and 112 by 2000.

No forecaster actually made that mistake, but there are plenty who, with the benefit of hindsight, have equally proved the difficulty of matching ideas about the future with events as they later transpired. Bertrand de Jouvenel (1967) quoted several historical examples of predictions that were not fulfilled, including a declining world population foreseen by Montesquieu in 1721, a future of fewer revolutions foreseen by Condorcet, five years before the French Revolution, and the following view of the future of war in 1791 by a Protestant pastor, J.-P. Rabaut.

Everything announces an age in which that madness of nations, war, will come to an end. The fury of the primitive hordes has already abated . . . wars are less wholehearted than among ignorant peoples; legions clash with one another with civility; heroes exchange greeting before slaying one another; soldiers from opposite camps visit one another before giving battle, just as men dine together before gaming. Neither nations nor even kings fight any longer, but armies and paid men. It is a game with limited stakes. War, once a frenzy, is now no more than a folly.

Unfortunately, we have continued to fight among ourselves for most of the intervening 200 years and, with every sign of continuing to do so, we now possess the capability to eliminate most if not all life on the planet.

Twentieth-century forecasters have on occasions been equally wide of the mark. The American astronomer Simon Newcomb argued, just before the Wright Brothers' historic flight, that flying in heavier-than-air machines was impossible. In 1945 Dr Vannevar Bush, the leading scientist in the American war effort, ridiculed the idea of nuclear intercontinental missiles (A. C. Clarke 1962). After quoting a number of similar examples from science, Clarke concluded that 'when a distinguished but elderly scientist states that something is possible, he is almost certainly right. When he states that something is impossible, he is very probably wrong.' Elsewhere, in a review of predictions, Ferkiss (1977) suggested that there has been a tendency, especially in the biological sciences, to be overoptimistic about the development of new techniques. Even acknowledged experts have a varied record of success with their forecasts.

In a study of 1,556 predictions made in eighteen technological fields between 1890 and 1940, Wise (1976) found that, by 1974, 40 per cent could be counted correct and 60 per cent incorrect. In more detail he found that 32 per cent had been fulfilled, 8 per cent were in process, 27 per cent were not proven, and 33 per cent had been refuted. He found also that technological events (such as innovations, inventions and resource crises) were predicted correctly more often than were the social, economic or political effects of those events—42 per cent against 25 per cent. This view that technological

Table 1. Annual economic growth rate: UK National Plan predictions and actuality (%)

	National Plan Prediction	Actual			
		1967	1968	1969	1970
GDP	3.8	1.8	3.1	2.8	2.5
Private consumption	3.2	1.6	0.0	2.5	3.0
Public expenditure	3.0	3.2	2.8	0.7	1.5
Investment	5.5	0.8	4.5	4.1	1.5
Productivity per capita	3.4	—	—	1.5	2.3

Source: Chapman (1976).

developments are easier to predict than social developments was supported by Clarke and by Ferkiss (1977).

Despite this opinion, and the conclusion that 'the record of long range predictions in science and technology, especially as regards its application to human affairs, is not one to inspire unbridled confidence' (Ferkiss 1977), considerable effort has been, and is, put into forecasting. Chapter 1 noted the efforts of the Japanese in technology forecasting; in addition, in 1993 the UK government proposed the creation of a Technology Foresight Programme to assist industry to develop promising technologies. The first results of the Programme were published in 1995.

Economic forecasting receives major attention from governments and other interested parties. Unfortunately, as G. Chapman (1976) demonstrated, forecasts and subsequent events have often varied widely. Overoptimism seems to have been a major feature. The UK National Plan prepared by the Department of Economic Affairs for the period 1965–70 provides a good example (Table 1), and more recent economic forecasts continue to have the same problems.

A similar tendency towards overoptimism was found by May and Green (1981) in a study of employment projections undertaken by British Local Authorities between 1974 and 1979. One of the most optimistic authorities was the County of Gwent, which in 1978 forecast that its unemployment rate, then 11.4 per cent, would fall to 2.5 per cent by 1991. In October 1991 it was 9.4 per cent, despite a number of changes in the way the rate was calculated that had the effect of reducing it. Both examples suggest that the hopes of the forecasters coloured their conclusions.

Perhaps the greatest effort in social forecasting has been put into demography, because estimates of future population are important in so many areas.

Table 2. Projected population of the USA (millions)

Projection		For year:								
		1920	1930	1940	1950	1960	1970	1980	1990	2000
Pearl (1925)		107	122	136	149	159	168	175	180	185
Whelpton (1928)		—	124	138	152	163	171	—	—	186
US National Resources Commission (1937)	High	—	—	133	147	160	174	187	—	—
	Low	—	—	132	137	138	135	128	—	—
US Bureau of the Census (1947)	High	—	—	—	148	162	177	—	—	—
	Medium	—	—	—	145	153	160	164	165	163
	Low	—	—	—	145	150	152	—	—	—
US Bureau of the Census (1958)	High	—	—	—	—	181	219	273	—	—
	Low	—	—	—	—	179	203	231	—	—
US Bureau of the Census (1967)	High	—	—	—	—	—	209	250	300	361
	Low	—	—	—	—	—	205	228	256	282
Observed		106	123	132	151	179	203	226	249	—

Sources: Duncan (1969), updated from *Statesman's Year Book* 1981 and *Whitaker's Almanac* 1993.

Duncan (1969) compared a number of forecasts for the population of the USA between 1920 and 2000 (Table 2). From these figures it is apparent that until the 1950s demographers in the USA tended to underestimate future population, but that, since then, they have overcorrected and tended to overestimate. Not surprisingly, it is also apparent that the shorter the time span between making of the forecast and the date for which it was made, the more accurate it tends to be. There is less room for significant change to occur.

Forecasts for the population of the UK in the years 2000 or 2001 (Table 3) show how forecasters, not unreasonably, respond to the latest information in adjusting their forecasts. In this case changes in the birth rate have been particularly important in affecting the forecasts. As a result the forecasts made between 1963 and 1989 have varied from 74.7 million to 57.5 million. The nearer to 2001, the smaller the variation in the forecasts, but they still change marginally. This suggests that once-and-for-all, long-range forecasts are unlikely to be accurate. Where long-range forecasts are needed it is better to continue to respond to new information as it arrives and rework the forecasts, but perhaps unwise to be swayed too much by short-term variations.

It would be quite possible to continue the catalogue of forecasting failures over many more pages. 'Make a forecaster look foolish' is a relatively easy game to play, and several attempts have already been made (see, for example, Ash 1991; G. Chapman 1976; A. C. Clarke 1962; Duncan 1969; Ferkiss 1977; I. Smith 1983; Wise 1976). Experience shows that forecasting, even when experts are involved, is a risky affair. Some commentators conclude from this experience that the effort is pointless. Discussing predictions for the 1950s made twenty years earlier, Nisbett (1971) argued that those predictions were wildly inaccurate. Further, he raised doubts about current forecasting efforts: 'The more important question is, can we at the present time go back to the population and economic data of the 1930s and working with all the techniques and instruments in our possession today, as well as with the priceless advantages of hindsight, see in those data anything that might remotely suggest what was actually to be the economic reality of the year 1951? I think not.' We could not even make accurate forecasts if we knew what the outcome was! Hoos (1978) went even further: 'To presume, then, that we have the techniques and tools to study the future is to delude ourselves—perhaps to the point of disaster if we depend on this methodology for accurate forecasts and for risk assessments of things to come.'

Clearly forecasters and futurists take their credibility in their own hands. Despite this, forecasters continue to try, and the demand for their efforts, particularly in business and planning, is as buoyant as ever. Is there anything to be learned from the unpromising record?

First, it must be noted that forecasts are not always wrong. The projections

Table 3. Projected population of the UK (millions)

Base date of projection	Projected population
1963	71.6
1964	74.7
1965	—
1966	—
1967	70.3
1968	68.2
1969	66.5
1970	66.5
1971	63.1
1972	62.4
1973	59.4
1974	59.9
1975	58.3
1976	57.5
1977	57.5
1978	58.1
1979	58.4
1981	58.0
1983	57.7
1985	59.0
1987	59.3
1988	59.2
1989	59.2
1991	59.7

Notes: projections from 1963 to 1968 estimate the population in 2000, those from 1969 onwards estimate the population in 2001. Projections were not made in 1980, 1982, 1984 and 1986; and that for 1991 is the latest available at the time of writing.

Source: *Annual Abstract of Statistics and Social Trends* (various years), Central Statistical Office.

for terminal passengers and air-transport movements for airports in the London area upto 1980 included in the white paper 'The Third London Airport' (1967) proved reasonably close (see Table 4). The observed levels remained close to the range of the forecasts throughout. The inaccuracy in this case resulted more from underestimating the passenger- and aircraft-handling capacity of the existing airports than from the traffic forecasts. This prompted the conclusion in the white paper that the latest date by which a third

Table 4. Forecasts and recorded traffic at London's airports 1967–1980 ('000s)

	Lower limit		Most likely		Upper limit		Traffic recorded	
	Terminal passengers	Air-transport movements	Terminal passengers	Air-transport movements	Terminal passengers	Air-transport movements	Terminal passengers	Air-transport movements
1967	14,300	244	14,600	246	15,100	251	15,477.7	293.5
1968	15,600	255	16,100	258	17,100	267	16,543.9	298.5
1969	17,000	266	17,700	271	19,400	284	19,186.6	328.0
1970	18,400	277	19,300	283	21,700	302	21,974.5	346.6
1971	19,900	288	21,000	296	24,300	320	24,449.6	368.0
1972	21,300	298	22,900	310	27,200	339	27,325.3	378.8
1973	22,800	308	24,900	324	30,400	359	29,791.1	391.6
1974	24,100	318	27,200	338	34,100	381	27,669.4	373.3
1975	25,600	327	29,600	353	37,800	402	28,946.2	360.8
1976	27,100	337	32,000	367	42,000	424	31,249.5	370.3
1977	28,500	345	34,600	382	46,600	447	32,466.5	366.9
1978	29,900	354	37,300	397	51,800	472	36,860.9	407.7
1979	31,400	363	40,300	413	57,400	498	39,408.6	430.8
1980	33,000	372	43,600	430	63,700	525	39,681.5	438.0

Notes: The forecasts progress smoothly and are intended to indicate trends; fluctuations about the trend from year to year must be expected. Forecasts refer to Heathrow, Gatwick and Stansted airports. Recorded figures also include Luton and Southend, which in 1980 accounted for 2,088,075 and 127,749 passengers and 26,306 and 10,642 air transport movements, respectively.

Source: 'The Third London Airport', HMSO Cmnd 3259, May 1967, and Civil Aviation Authority annual statistics.

London airport would be needed was 1976, which was not borne out by events. Subsequent developments, only partly due to the reduction in air traffic following the oil crisis in 1973–4 and during the recession of the early 1980s, led to a progressive extension of the timing of the need for the airport, until in 1978 it was estimated at 1990 or after. A third airport was eventually designated, at the existing airport of Stansted, and began operating officially as London's third airport in the late 1980s. Whether any loss of traffic, such as had been claimed would happen, actually occurred is not clear.

Successful forecasting by BAA, the operators of London's airports, has continued, according to Martin (1989). He quoted both seven- and thirteen-year forecasts that have been very close to recorded levels. A company like BAA clearly needs to think and plan ahead in order to provide the necessary capacity, because major expansion requires several years to realise.

Second, G. Chapman (1976), Ferkiss (1977) and Wise (1976) suggested that forecasts made by experts in particular fields often tend to be too narrow. Chapman argued that economic forecasts pay scant attention 'to the social and historical features which interrelate' with the economy, and, in particular, neglect 'non-quantifiable political phenomena which have had, and will continue to have, an all important bearing upon the outcome of events'. Ferkiss (1977) noted that 'it may be assumed that experts tend to be especially prone to ignore exogenous variables because of their specialised focus, yet the impact of outside forces often is determinative of developments in special areas'. Considering predictions of the effects of technology Wise (1976) concluded that 'the incorrect predictions ... were quite simplistic', and further, that 'it appears that social and economic conditions evolve in response to the entire complex of technology, rather than to a single innovation'. The tendency is, however, to predict the effects of particular technological development in relative isolation. This reflects limitations in our knowledge, our inability to cope with large amounts of information and our tendency to specialise in particular areas, as much as the shortcomings of forecasting itself.

In analysing the forecasting success of BAA, Martin (1989) identified three important features: a good data base, available in infinitesimal detail for 20 years to BAA as operators of the airports, but absent in many forecasting situations; the necessity to think creatively and not rely on trends, which are half over by the time they are identified; and the ability to convince the decision-makers of the credibility of the forecasts, which can have important implications. It can be shown that it is not always that forecasters make mistakes but that the users of the forecasts prefer not to believe them. A frequently quoted example is the M25 orbital motorway around London, which was built with three lanes although the forecasters had recommended four. Now, at much greater cost, it is being widened. The BAA case also indicates the importance of control. As owners of the airports they were able to take the necessary steps to provide for the forecast traffic and in fact make it possible. Had they not undertaken the necessary works it is unlikely that the forecast could have come about.

Third, the result of forecasting over a narrow spectrum is frequently either overoptimism (G. Chapman 1976) or, arising from familiarity with past and present developments, an expectation that the future will be like the past (Ferkiss 1977) and surprise-free. In a review of predictions in science and technology, A. C. Clarke (1962) suggested that experts in these fields often exhibit failure of nerve or failure of imagination and therefore underestimate the potential. More recently, the reaction against the observed or perceived potential effects of technology, particularly nuclear power, has tended to delay expected developments. Forecasts which do not take into account these wider issues obviously have a greater chance of being wrong.

Fourth, it is important to examine what is meant by a forecast being wrong. If I predict that a certain horse will win the Kentucky Derby and it does not, I am wrong; there can be little dispute about it. Not all forecasts are so simple. The Introduction to *The Limits to Growth* (Meadows *et al.* 1972) makes the following statements, which are repeated in the sequel, *Beyond the Limits* (Meadows *et al.* 1992):

(*i*) If the present growth trends . . . continue unchanged, the limits to growth on this planet will be reached some time within the next one hundred years. The most probable result will be a rather sudden and uncontrollable decline in both population and industrial capacity.
(*ii*) It is possible to alter these growth trends and to establish a condition of ecological and economic stability that is sustainable far into the future . . .

In other words, our industrial world will collapse if we continue on our current course. Should we, however, heed this warning and take the appropriate steps, this prediction will not come true.

Leaving aside the straightforwardly critical view that the prediction is wrong because things will not work out like that, it is clear that the authors of *The Limits to Growth*, and certainly the sponsors, the Club of Rome, did not publish their findings because they wished to present an accurate picture of the future. Their purpose was quite different, as the two statements quoted above indicate. They feared, as their model forecast, that unless the direction of current industrial society was radically changed, the future would be dire. Their hope was that, when they were presented with this vision of things to come, people would see the threat and act, in order to avoid the forecast becoming fact. Indeed, the last chapter, 'The State of Global Equilibrium', and the commentary which follows it set out several suggestions to help invalidate the forecast. That this was indeed the intention is confirmed by *Beyond the Limits*.

The intention of the prediction, therefore, was to encourage action in order that it be proved wrong. This is clearly in stark contrast with the view that inaccurate forecasting destroys the credibility of futures-thinking. Here, being wrong is the desired outcome and the proof of success. This is not an unusual occurrence: any time we take action to avoid the development of an undesirable situation we are doing the same thing. Pohl (1993) went further, arguing that 'The more complete and accurate a prediction, the less use it is.' If a forecast is accurate it is going to happen. There is nothing we can do but wait until it does. Such forecasts are not much use. The most useful forecasts are those which are not totally reliable and enable us 'to take actions in the present that will encourage the good futures and help avert the bad ones'.

As Encel, Marstrand and Page (1975) argued, 'any predicted future is subject to major modifications by deliberate action and decision-making within the time span for which the prediction is supposed to hold.' Some would conclude that it is this that necessarily invalidates the whole exercise, but others argue from the same evidence that therein lies the value of futures-thinking. If it were not possible to influence the course of events there would be little value in knowing what is going to happen, except perhaps to prepare for the inevitable. On the other hand, where we can guide the direction of the future by taking decisions and acting in the present, it is vital to forecast what the future is likely to be given different choices. Only then can we make effective decisions. Encel, Marstrand and Page argued that the purpose of forecasting should not be seen as prophecy, but as a contribution to the debate about the future we wish to create. Thinking about the future becomes a crucial part of our decision-making in the present. Without it we are almost inevitably going to be criticised for short-sightedness in a relatively short time. Thinking about the future does not guarantee success or the avoidance of approbation but it does increase our chances of influencing events in a direction we prefer.

Related to the idea of forecasting as a way of bringing about policy changes is the concept of the *self-altering prediction*. Henshel (1978) identified two distinct types of self-altering predictions, the *self-fulfilling* and the *self-defeating* or *suicidal*. The self-fulfilling prediction is defined as 'an initially false prophecy which becomes true because actions are performed as a result of public acceptance of the prophecy'. Examples would include a run on a bank following an initially incorrect rumour about its reliability, the devaluation or revaluation of a currency as a result of a similar incorrect assessment, and the individual who, believing he or she has no chance of being appointed to a particular post, fails to submit an application in time. The BAA forecasts quoted earlier had an element of self-fulfilment, the ability on the part of BAA to take action to bring them about.

Self-defeating predictions are, of course, the opposite, 'initially true prophecies which become false as a result of their acceptance'. Supporters of the front-runner in an election may conclude, as the result of opinion polls, that their candidate is so far ahead they need not bother to vote because the votes of others will see their candidate through. If too many supporters accept that prediction their actions may invalidate it and cause the favourite to lose. *The Limits of Growth* prophecy is of this type. Those who made it believe it is true but anticipate that actions will be taken to invalidate it. Henshel concluded that almost all predictions in social life are potentially self-altering because they 'become part of the interacting set of social conditions that result in future states' (Henshel 1978). It is not surprising that, in these circumstances, they are often 'inaccurate'.

Given this situation, in which forecasts become part of the information base on which we make decisions and can consequently affect the course of events, it becomes clear that forecasting should not be seen as a once-and-for-all process. This is reinforced by the population forecasts for the USA, which indicated greater accuracy in the short term, suggesting that it may be wise to continue to revise forecasts rather than rely on original estimates that appear increasingly inaccurate. We know forecasting is inexact and do not do ourselves a service by debunking all past efforts and giving up. Rather we might benefit by accepting the uncertainty and reworking our forecasts as new information comes to hand.

The Third London Airport forecasts suggest another reasonable approach. Initially the recorded levels ran slightly above the 'upper' limit, but after the oil-price shock of the early 1970s they fell back to nearer the 'most likely' level. Had just one forecast been prepared, the recorded levels would have been widely divergent for at least part of the period. The use of a range of forecasts, though not guaranteeing success, provides a more realistic way of dealing with the uncertainty we know exists when we attempt to predict the future. This might appear as a ploy to provide forecasting with more respectability than it deserves. Perhaps it is, but it is also a more realistic approach, which acknowledges the difficulties and attempts to provide a way of dealing with them. It is unsatisfying because we prefer to think that we know what pertains in a particular situation and want our image of the future to be the same, a single clear prediction, despite knowing from experience that such a prediction is seldom accurate and of limited use.

None of this makes forecasting any easier. It remains a minefield for the unwary. Examining these problems does, however, provide a more realistic platform on which to act. If we realise the problems we can at least act with them in mind and treat forecasts for what they are, a necessary part of the decision-making process, but one with inherent uncertainty.

2.5. KNOWLEDGE OF THE PAST, PRESENT AND FUTURE

The difficulties of forecasting are to a considerable degree based upon the belief that whereas we know, or can find out, about the past and present, we do not and cannot have such knowledge of the future. The past has happened and in the process left evidence which can be collected together to give a picture of situations and events long gone. It is the realm of facts. The population of Canada in 1993 was 28.8 million, 5,590 people were killed in road accidents in the UK in 1990, and Brazil won the World Cup in 1994. These no-nonsense recorded facts can be confirmed by reference to the appropriate sources at any time.

Similar attitudes govern our everyday approach to the present. Although it is possible to argue that, with the exception of live broadcasts, the media deal exclusively with past events, things that happened minutes, hours or perhaps days ago, it is normal to characterise the contents of news bulletins and papers as current affairs, that is, of the present. The speed of modern communications, by telephone, radio, satellite and television, means that this is more nearly the case than ever before. Indeed, it is now possible for people in all continents simultaneously to witness events occurring in one place, such as Olympic Games in Spain in the summer of 1992 or the World Cup in the USA in 1994. With only a small delay, events in space and on the Moon can be equally immediate, as the American Apollo landings indicated. The printed word or the evidence of our own eyes is, of course, readily accepted as fact, despite many arguments to the contrary.

As yet, in the absence of that dream of science fiction, the time machine, we cannot refer to facts about, or witness the future. We are therefore to some extent trapped in the envelope of our current knowledge. We have established ideas about the nature of the world in which we live, how it operates, what its problems are and how we might deal with them. On the other hand, the history of science suggests that ideas about the world, both physical and social, have a habit of changing. A good example is the observation that the continents look like jigsaw pieces that could be moved around to fit together. Wegener's theory of continental drift, which would account for this observation, was given little credence until a mechanism for movement was suggested. Once the concept of plate tectonics, the idea that the continents float on molten rock beneath the surface of the Earth, was accepted, the notion that the continents were once joined together became commonplace. But the difficulty remains. Though we can look back and see how ideas have changed in the past and how our current ideas evolved, it is a very different thing to attempt to imagine how our situation and our perceptions will change in the future. Some would, indeed, suggest that it is impossible and that any attempt is doomed to failure before it is begun. There is plenty of evidence in the past of the occurrence of the totally unexpected, through discovery or other means, to support this view; but it can also be argued that careful study of past changes may, if not help us predict accurately what will happen, at least prepare us for surprises to come and as a consequence make them, perhaps, less surprising. We can quite easily speculate about what might happen. Although in doing so we would envisage things that do not happen and fail to foresee things that do, we might avoid regarding as impossible today what becomes commonplace tomorrow. In effect, we need to accept the dynamic nature of our situation and our knowledge rather than be trapped into the false belief that the present represents a pinnacle that cannot be exceeded or a plateau that stretches unchanged into the future.

Jouvenel (1967) differentiated between information about the past and information about the future. Referring to the Latin roots of both French and English he distinguished between *facta*, which describe past events, things which have been 'done, accomplished, completed shaped', and *futura*, 'that which has yet to come about'. 'Strictly speaking', he suggested, only *facta* can be known. He went on to point out, however, with reference to someone wishing to fly to New York, that 'the only useful knowledge we have relates to the future', in the shape of the times of flights to New York tomorrow. It is all very interesting to know that any number of flights made the journey today—interesting, but no use if we wish to travel tomorrow. Strictly, of course, we cannot know that a particular flight, or indeed any of the flights scheduled to depart tomorrow will operate. The airport could be closed by fog, the airline we were intending to use go out of business, our plane be unserviceable or prevented from leaving by a strike. We might be unable to get to the airport or, for a host of other possible reasons, be unable to fulfil our intentions. In the absence of factual knowledge about the future we are forced to use other forms of information, *futura*. We think nothing of it and treat them as facts, though strictly they cannot be.

Basic to our approach is the *assumption*. We assume—that is we believe, or proceed on the supposition—that the timetable prepared by the airline represents what will happen. The timetable becomes a form of knowledge, because our past experience indicates this to be a reasonable conclusion. Of course, it is a substitute for exact knowledge, but one that, though it leaves room for uncertainty, is accepted in the absence of anything better. In making the assumption (that the timetable indicates what will happen), the future (in respect of flights to New York) changes from being completely unknown, to being reasonably precise (at least for the duration of the timetable). We 'know' how many flights there will be, when they will leave and when they will arrive in New York.

We make similar assumptions whenever we consider future situations and actions, and though we can all point to occasions in the past when our prior assumptions have not been substantiated, making them remains necessary. Many of the assumptions we make are implicit; they are not written down, put into words or even consciously made. For example, we assume our own continued existence and the continuation of the style of life to which we have become accustomed. Even at a time when there are nearly three million unemployed in the UK and many millions in Europe and elsewhere the tendency is for those in employment to assume that 'it won't happen to me'. Accordingly we continue to make arrangements for holidays, to move house or buy a new car, rather than saving for the occurrence of something we know could, but assume will not, happen. If our assumptions change and we are no longer so confident of continued employment, our actions will change in turn. Indeed, the downturn in the UK housing market and static levels of retail sales in the mid-1990s may indicate a shift in people's assumptions. Similar assumptions are made in government and business. Business assumptions are to some extent revealed by surveys of business confidence such as the one carried out by the Confederation of British Industry every three months. If businesses are confident they will invest; if not, they will cut back to avoid making losses.

Some assumptions contained in forecasts are explicit; they are consciously considered and articulated or even written down. In personal situations it is unusual for this to be done, but in the realms of research or forecasting it is much more common. In some instances it is a requirement of respectability. One particularly clear example was provided by an economic forecast prepared by the London Business School for the *Sunday Times* in 1982, which included the following assumptions: 'We *assume* the exchange rate is allowed to fall by about 10 per cent over the next two years' and 'We are *assuming* that the price of North Sea Oil is held at $31 a barrel for the rest of the year, and that it will rise back to $35 during 1983, as the world economy starts expanding.' In addition, there were assumptions about stockbuilding, investment, consumer saving and worldwide inflation. The importance of the assumptions was clear from the same article:

Oil prices, as much as the Budget [five days before the publication of the forecast] have outdated all the economic forecasts produced so far this spring [they had assumed higher oil prices than actually occurred in the spring of 1982]. . . . the fall in oil prices will significantly boost . . . world recovery, particularly in 1983—and so push up our exports. . . . The 10 per cent fall in the exchange rate over the next two years that we *assume* helps to restore Britain's competitiveness, which so badly eroded during sterling's rise in 1977–80. [*my emphasis*]

Many of the differences between the London Business School forecast and the Treasury's opinion, which were tabulated in the article, were also shown to be largely the result of different assumptions (Budd, Dicks and Robinson 1982).

Though similar to the assumption about flight timetables made earlier, in that they are made in order to make the future and thinking about it more manageable, the assumptions used in forecasting are often less reliable. According to G. Chapman (1976) errors in economic forecasting may often be traced back to the assumptions on which a forecast is based. The importance of assumptions and their necessity in forecasting is obvious, but it is often the assumptions rather than the forecast itself which are the cause of inaccuracy.

One significant difference between the assumption that flight timetables will be kept and assumptions about the economy derives from the scale of the subjects concerned and their susceptibility to control. Whereas the management of an airline has fairly direct control over activities within the organisation, a government possesses much less control over an economy. The airline organises its timetable and makes arrangements to fulfil it; a government draws up an economic policy or budget and then largely relies on industry, banks, individuals and many other actors in the economy to perform as expected in order to fulfil the forecast. The potential for control is much less.

In situations where an actor or group of actors has, and may reasonably be expected to continue to have, control over a situation, we can deduce that the chances of 'knowing' or predicting accurately what the future will be are considerably greater than where such control is lacking. Seldom, except where control is total and no outside influences can affect a situation, can anything approaching absolute certainty occur, but in many situations high probabilities of accuracy may be anticipated.

It may also be suggested that where control is low, the more specific an assumption, the more likely it is not to be substantiated. The assumption above that the exchange rate would fall by 10 per cent over the next two years was very specific. In times of floating exchange rates, the forecasters and, it may be argued, governments have no, or relatively little control over the price of currencies. The suspicion must be, therefore, that such assumptions have a high probability of proving inaccurate. Assumptions of this kind remain little more than informed guesses. They are useful in enabling us to build up a picture of what the future may be like if certain things occur, but it would be a bold or foolhardy person who would claim 'knowledge' of the future based on such premisses.

Associated with the idea of control over the future are the concepts of choice and decision. Consider for the moment that you are going to go out for a meal. You have a choice of Italian, French, Indian and American restaurants. At this stage the future remains 'unknown', though you do, of course, 'know' you will be eating out and not at home. It is accepted that a range of implicit assumptions have been made and are being acted upon. Having a liking for curry you decide to narrow the field of future possibilities by going to the Indian restaurant. Because it is a popular restaurant it is necessary to make such decisions a day or so in advance and to book a table. You 'know' therefore that on Saturday evening at 8.30 you will be going to the Indian restaurant. In much the same way you 'know', if you have booked it, what you will be doing for your next summer holiday.

In each of these examples, and in many similar situations, we assume that our decisions will become reality. Of course, they may not, but making choices and decisions is one of the main means we have of controlling what happens and increasing our 'knowledge' of the future. In so doing we may positively increase our 'knowledge', in the sense that given certain circumstances we 'know' we will be doing a particular thing at a particular time. Even then some uncertainty remains. At the same time we negatively increase our 'knowledge' by reducing the possibilities, by deciding not to go to the Italian restaurant or spend the summer painting the house.

Government and business decisions to adopt a particular policy may themselves increase 'knowledge' of the future in the same positive and negative ways. Such decisions are subject to reversal, following elections or other political and commercial pressures, but at least for the time during which they are operative they provide an indication of the likely future. In other words, they serve to increase 'knowledge' about the future by attempting to determine what the future will be.

In many instances we may also regard the future as 'known' because of the existence of established rules and procedures. We 'know' there will be a presidential election in the USA every four years, because the US Constitution says so. Similarly, in the UK there is an established pattern of local government elections and for a given area we can find out when elections will be held. We also 'know' with reasonable accuracy that they will be held on the first Thursday in May because that is traditional.

However, all of the examples and situations mentioned above, insofar as they refer to the future, do contain an element of uncertainty. The US Constitution could be amended, the pattern of local government elections changed, decisions altered, and assumptions proved wrong. But as Mack (1971) suggested, 'Uncertainty is the complement of knowledge. It is the gap between what is known and what needs to be known to make correct decisions. Dealing sensibly with uncertainty is not a byway on the road to responsible business and governmental decisions. It is central to it. The subject is complex, elusive and omnipresent.'

In making decisions, most of which in government and business are of significance in and to the future, knowledge is necessarily less than complete in many ways. Uncertainty, as Mack contended, is always present. Considerable efforts may be made to reduce uncertainty, through research, consultation, attempts to increase control and making assumptions, but an element of it is unavoidable.

Friend and Jessop (1969) provided a useful classification of uncertainty in decision-making situations that was derived from their analysis of planning in Coventry, a town in the English Midlands. Three broad classes were identified:

Class UE: Uncertainties in knowledge of the external planning environment including all uncertainties relating to the structure of the world external to the decision-making system—in the local government context this can be seen as including the entire physical, social, and economic environment of the local authority concerned—and also all uncertainties relating to expected patterns of future change in this environment, and to its expected responses to any possible future interventions by the decision-making system.

Class UR: Uncertainties as to future intentions in related fields of choice including all uncertainties relating to the choices which might in future be taken, within the decision-making system itself, in respect of other fields of discretion beyond the limited problem which is currently under consideration.

Class UV: Uncertainties as to appropriate value judgements including all uncertainties relating to the relative degrees of importance the decision-makers ought to attach to any expected consequences of their choice which cannot be related to each other through an unambiguous common scale—either because the consequences are of a fundamentally different nature, or because they affect different sections of the community, or because they concern different periods of future time.

The significance of uncertainty in relation to the future is clear from the use of the word 'future' five times in the classification. It is also apparent that, according to Friend and Jessop, there are uncertainties in knowledge of the external planning environment, which are distinct from the uncertainties deriving from 'future change in this environment'.

Uncertainty is not only a feature of the future, it is characteristic of the past and present as well. Pearce (1971) suggests that this is something we tend to overlook. 'While the idea of reaching a conclusion about some past event is generally acceptable, the concept of predicting some future event is often regarded with suspicion and mistrust. In one sense this mistrust is well founded, but in a more important sense it is illogical.' Using the example of trial by jury he argues that the process of establishing what happened in the past is often very similar to predicting future events. Evidence is collected and presented, a case argued, the jury then evaluate the information available to them and reach a decision about what they believe happened. There may well be disagreement and doubt about such past events, as the provision for majority verdicts indicates. There is also evidence that errors are made, and that on some occasions the guilty go free and the innocent suffer. Serious though that is, the jury system is not abandoned because uncertainty is present. The setting up of inquiries into accidents is also indicative of the difficulties of knowing what happened in the past. That there was an accident is known, but the inquiries are carried out in an attempt to establish the causes and assess who may have been responsible. Even at the end of the inquiry there may still be different opinions about the causes and who should be held responsible.

Uncertainty may also exist in a situation where all actors and observers concerned are quite certain about what happened. Take a soccer match between two teams as an example. The Reds are awarded a penalty from which they score to earn a draw. The referee decided that one of the Reds' forwards had been fouled in the penalty area. The Reds players and their fans are convinced the referee was correct; the Blues players and their fans are equally certain he was wrong. The event occurred, it is a fact, but the interpretation of the event is open to dispute. Was the award of a penalty just or unjust? It remains a matter of opinion about which there is unlikely to be agreement. Remarkably similar arguments are found in science and history. The conflict between the evolutionists and the creationists has continued on and off since Darwin. Recently it has entered a new phase of activity, with the creationists attempting to undermine the established acceptance of the evolutionary theory. Both sides are totally convinced that they are in the right, but for those not completely committed either way, uncertainty remains. Bronowski (1973) summarised the situation succinctly: 'There is no absolute knowledge. And those who claim it, whether they are scientists or dogmatists, open the door to tragedy. All information is imperfect. . . . That is the human condition.'

Why is this so? Philosophers have argued about the nature of knowledge for centuries and there is a whole area of academic enquiry, epistemology, devoted to the subject. The debate is long and complex, and extends far beyond the scope of the present discussion.

Though there are those who would challenge the approach, for the purpose of this discussion we shall assume that the real world exists and that we are part of it. It is quite obvious that as individuals our knowledge of the real world is less than total. There are parts of it that we have never visited, read about, seen films about, met people from etc., and know practically nothing about. Information does exist in the locality and in the minds of the people living there, but in all probability they know little or nothing about us. In our own locality we are surrounded by all manner of natural and manmade objects that we take for granted but know little about—our own bodies being, perhaps, the prime example. There are, of course, those who do know about such things, but even the experts do not know all the causes of cancer or have treatments for all its forms. Today's medical knowledge is greater than that fifty years ago, and we can now treat diseases and conditions that could not be treated then. Knowledge, then, is not static but changes over time. Today's knowledge is just as likely to be invalidated by tomorrow's discoveries as yesterday's was by today's (Kuhn 1970). We can conclude, therefore, that both individually and at the level of all humanity our information falls far short of the potential available in the real world. This shortfall may be absolute or relative. There are things yet unknown waiting to be discovered, and others of which we may know something but do not have complete knowledge because our processes of information-gathering are limited. The Office of Population Censuses and Surveys prepares annual estimates of the population of the UK, because for financial and social reasons a full census is taken only once every ten years. The estimates are carefully calculated and are, no doubt, as accurate as may be expected, but they usually differ from the probably more accurate census totals for the census years. The situation is complicated by the errors in the census itself. The US Bureau of the Census estimated that for various reasons, 'the 1970 census reflects a net undercount of 2.5 per cent, or about 5.3 million persons' (Hoos 1978). The UK census in 1991 was thought to be undercounted because a number of people avoided being enumerated, fearing they might be trapped into paying local taxes. Even in such apparently reliable areas, a considerable element of uncertainty exists. To have complete information on population would necessitate a continuous count which is both impossible and unacceptable. Uncertainty must always be present.

Having information is one thing, using it is another. The majority of researchers, opinion pollsters and surveyors of the social scene will in their experience have collected information they have been unable to use. Perhaps their time or their budget did not allow all the information collected to be analysed. One suspects this happens to much of the Census data, too; or at least that it is not used as much as it could be. In other situations information may be beyond the capacity of our understanding, either absolutely, or in relation to our existing ideas of what is or is not possible. In his novel *Timescape*, Benford (1982) provided an interesting fictional example of the dismissal of information because it was considered impossible, and Kuhn (1970) suggested this has in fact happened in the history of science.

Hoos (1978) argues that we must not forget that most information is not 'given but gotten'. Rather than information appearing ready to be used, it is collected, researched, sought out in answer to particular needs. If the government wishes to know the extent of derelict land in the country it will need to institute a survey to find out. Definitions of what to include and what to leave out must be drawn up, and depending on whether the purpose is to attract grants for reclamation or to establish which is the muckiest area of the country, a given local authority will probably try to maximise or minimise its own figures. Information, therefore, is seldom entirely neutral; it may be significantly different depending upon the means of collection, the purpose of collection and the use made of it.

The supporters of the Reds and the Blues in the example above received the same information but used it differently because they wanted their own team to win. Equally, in other situations we select consciously or unconsciously among the information available to us. The errors in the predictions of economists in the period 1961–75 were at least in part the result of their concentration on economic as opposed to social and political factors, which often appear to have been critical (G. Chapman 1976). This is not surprising; all disciplines are selective because they have particular areas of interest, and because in a world with ever more information available it has become necessary to specialise. Indeed, much of the extra information and knowledge has been brought about through specialisation and in particular specialist research. Renaissance Man could not have done it, and no one can cope with it all now. The situation does, however, create problems, because disciplines are only human constructs into which we have divided our knowledge of the real world to make it manageable. The result is a patchwork of knowledge with varying reliability as a representation of reality. One of the ways we make sense of or manage the plethora of information with which the real world presents us is through the construction of theories. Which comes first, theory or information, is a chicken-and-egg question, though within scientific circles there is an accepted approach, which demands a prototype theory as a means to differentiate between relevant and irrelevant information.

The typical scientific development begins with a hypothesis that such-and-such is the case. Experiments are conducted or evidence collected to prove or disprove the hypothesis. If it is confirmed, or at least not disproved, the hypothesis may then become the established view or theory of reality in that particular instance. It will be strengthened by further information that supports it, and weakened insofar as contradictory evidence becomes available. There is a tendency, however, for established theories to be defended by those whose reputations are associated with them and for those theories to be replaced only when the contrary evidence has become overwhelming or a new generation of scientists come to the fore (Kuhn 1970). Theories tend to be selective, either because information that does not fit into them is not sought out or known by those who hold them, or because it is consciously rejected as not relevant.

It is readily accepted that the social sciences are prone to the problem that 'you find what you look for'. It has been argued, for example, that 'Sociology is about opinion rather than truth, and that the sociological enterprise consists entirely in providing arguments which are accepted or rejected according to personal preference since no objective evidence can be brought to bear on their confirmation or falsification' (Saunders 1980). Kuhn (1970) and Bronowski (1973) suggested that 'seek and ye shall find' may also have truth for the natural sciences. Indeed, some recent scientific theories suggest that the observer cannot help but be part of the experiment and affect the result observed.

Not only is the future unknown, the present and past from which we try to predict are themselves far from certain. They may, as Jouvenel suggests, be the realm of *facta*, but not all the *facta* are available, and others we prefer not to notice. To some degree that makes thinking about the future even more difficult because we do it from uncertain ground, but it also suggests that the past, present and future are to an extent similar. They are all the realm of the unknown; the future has no monopoly over uncertainty.

2.6. SHOULD WE INDULGE IN FUTURES-THINKING?

Some years ago in a debate in the House of Commons, the UK Government proposed various measures to conserve energy supplies, particularly through increased prices for gas and electricity. It was thought that this would reduce demand and encourage conservation for the benefit of future generations. One Member of Parliament, Enoch Powell, challenged the policy, and specifically the underlying assumptions that present generations had a duty to worry about those yet to come and that future generations would be grateful for our concern.

A moment of reflection makes it quite obvious that we all live in the world created by our ancestors, and that our descendants will inherit the results of our actions. This will be considered further in the next chapter and is not the issue here. The debate revolves around different beliefs about how to obtain the most benefit for current and future generations. Those who take one view believe that present generations are the custodians of the future and that it is our responsibility to consider all the implications of our situation, including the effects our actions will have in the future. Those who reject the view argue that the best long-term result will only emerge if each generation makes those decisions it believes to be in its own best interests (that we should not penalise ourselves by paying more than necessary for our energy, for example, as this will not help and might well hinder the interests of those who follow). At first sight this appears callous, but how may it be argued?

It may be suggested that by attempting to consider the interests of those who follow, we place them and ourselves in a false situation. There are two sides to the issue. By conserving oil resources and extending their availability, for example, we may reduce our efforts to find replacement fuels because the urgency is lessened. This may well lead to false hopes now, and worsen the situation in the future if supplies do eventually run out. On the other hand, as Kahn (1978) argued, the 'advocates of the limits to growth positions . . . raise false, non-existent or misformulated issues . . . [and] pose as being basically insoluble real problems for which we believe rather straightforward and practical solutions can be found'. To those who are persuaded by the approach of *The Limits to Growth*, Kahn is himself guilty of raising false hopes in the form of future technological solutions that cannot, in their view, be relied upon. Meadows *et al.* (1992) argued that such solutions are only temporary in any event and do no more than postpone the inevitable. In thinking about the future from our current position, in which we are likely to have less information than will be available to future generations, we therefore run the risk of raising false hopes or spectres. It is better, some would argue, to avoid the risk.

If we go further and take action based on our present perceptions of what the future will be like, we may well reduce the range of options open to future generations. Any decisions have this effect to some degree, but the argument is often put forward that to maintain flexibility we should avoid making any decision that does not have to be made at the present moment. Advocating serious futures-thinking may be seen as a move in the opposite direction, because having perceived future situations it is perhaps logical to expect us to respond to our perceptions and act in the present. Indeed, this was the view of the value of forecasting held by Encel, Marstrand and Page (1975). Forecasts become part of the political debate and may indeed enlighten the discussions, but they may also be used as weapons of power to justify unpleasant, and what might well have been unnecessary courses of action. Stretton (1976) provided an instructive example of how this could happen via a coalition of environmental and dictatorial forces. Forecasts may, in other words, become powerful propaganda. Lal (1992) argued that environmentalism is exactly that and 'likely to harm rather than benefit humanity'.

The Club of Rome's *Limits to Growth* study was indeed propaganda. By presenting their forecast of the coming collapse of Western industrial civilisation, the Club hoped to bring about changes in policy and attitudes to avert the anticipated catastrophe. Their motives, it may be assumed, were of the best, and their intentions altruistic, but if Kahn (1976), Lal (1992) and Zey (1994) are correct, the results of the propaganda would be harmful if it were accepted.

The purpose here is not to offer an opinion in the debate but to indicate the potential power of forecasts in decision situations. Forecasts can be, and on many occasions in the past probably have been used to justify decisions of a doubtful nature. 'The energy gap of the 1950s which was held to justify the first nuclear power programme' in the UK, and 'the missile gap of the 1960s' are good examples (Miles 1978).

Forecasts of the growth of air traffic formed a significant part of the case presented in the 1960s for the development of Stansted Airport as London's third international terminal. The urgency of the need for new capacity to meet the demands of the predicted excess traffic at the existing airports of Heathrow and Gatwick seems to have concentrated attention on Stansted to the exclusion of other sites (McKie 1973). It had the potential to be in use much quicker than any other site because, as one Ministry of Aviation official explained, 'It has a runway . . . it is a very good runway, and we own it' (McKie 1973). The effect of this combined with the forecasts was to practically exclude any other alternatives during the early stages of the search. A similar argument was raised in support of the nuclear power programme in the early 1980s. Apart from the questions surrounding the credibility of the energy gap, based as it was on particular trends in energy consumption (Foley 1981), the assumption that there would be a shortage of energy in the 1990s led to an argument for urgent action. Only known, nuclear technology, it was argued, could deliver with any certainty the needed energy at the right time. The result was to dismiss alternative energy sources, particularly renewable sources like solar, wind and wave power, as incapable of sufficient development in the time available. Money was taken away from renewable energy research and the government pursued a vigorous pro-nuclear policy. The spectre of an energy gap was a powerful and persuasive propaganda weapon.

It is instructive to note who is in a position to make such forecasts and to question the motives of their current predictions. In the case of airports and energy the forecasts were all made by those in charge of the areas in question at the time of their preparation. This is not surprising; the authorities responsible for aviation may be expected to know more than most about air traffic, and the energy industries more about energy-consumption and supply. Unfortunately, experts have often been wrong in their estimates of future developments within their field of expertise. Estimates of the date at which the third London airport would be needed retreated by seventeen years over a fifteen-year period (Hall 1980), and energy forecasts have been wildly wrong (Foley 1981).

Not surprisingly, governments are often not prepared to present forecasts that suggest things will get worse. Politically such forecasts cast the government in a poor light. They suggest either that government policies are likely to fail or that the government is incapable of influencing events. For obvious reasons governments prefer to emphasise the positive and project an improvement. Such experiences caused P. F. Chapman (1978) to question the legitimacy of long-term forecasting. Part of his case rested on the problems associated with the techniques of forecasting—the need to choose what to forecast and select a method—and on the questions surrounding the reliability of the information used. The remaining issue he raised was values.

The cases quoted above—aviation and energy—are obviously areas in which those concerned with existing facilities understandably consider their functions important and wish to see them continue in the future. Few of us, whatever the evidence to the contrary, are prepared to accept that our existing roles are no longer valid. On the contrary, we often exert considerable effort to show how important our activities are and how necessary they will be in the future. This is exactly what the forecasters in air traffic, energy and the military set out to show. If they are successful, and their position and control over the relevant information gives them a good chance of being so, other policy options are unlikely to be given serious consideration. We are in danger of becoming locked into current ways of thinking that owe their dominance as much to the existing structure of responsibility and power as to the accuracy of their predictions. Options are not kept open in such circumstances; they are closed off until a crisis occurs to challenge the accepted view. Then we are inclined, with the advantage of hindsight, to argue that the problem should have been foreseen.

The danger is twofold. On the one hand, the present accepted wisdom may well prove inappropriate in the future, and on the other, the future may be constrained by today's evaluations ruling out what would have been quite feasible options. The first is the stuff from which crises are made, a one-dimensional vision of the future being held until circumstances force us to reconsider. The second may be even more serious in that possible ways to avert or alleviate crisis situations may not be considered.

Of course, decisions do have to be made, and decisions control commitments, and commitments to one approach necessarily rule out other possibilities. What is an unavoidable fact of life, however, may be made much worse by tunnel vision, which, in the words of the proverb, 'Puts all our eggs in one basket'. The danger is that visions of the future projected by those in control now effectively colonise the future for today's dominant attitudes and values. History should teach us that attitudes and values have changed and may be expected to change, over time. Much is currently made, for example, of the need to return to full employment, because employment is valued in present society for a number of reasons. But employment, in the form to which we are accustomed, is a development of the Industrial Revolution of the eighteenth and nineteenth centuries. It may well be that future generations, if they are allowed to, will have different values and consider our approach naively antiquated. The danger in our efforts to retain existing patterns of employment is that new developments may be stifled by our unwillingness to consider patterns based on different values. Robertson (1985) argued this cogently.

A criticism of futures-thinking along these lines is presented by Miles (1978). Although he does not conclude that all futures-thinking should be abandoned, he criticises much of the major effort so far, arguing that it has tended to be based on a variety of questionable assumptions that have had the effect of presenting only a narrow range of possible futures. Among the features he discussed are:

- *Historicism*: 'The attempt to predict the future on the basis of supposed laws of historical evolution, whose operation may be projected forward to provide a view of the future.' This is almost by definition one-dimensional.
- *Ethnocentrism*: seen in the projection of the continued dominance of Western industrial society and the development of the Third World on similar lines. Such projections are usually made in the West. Sardar (1993) argued that Futures Study is totally dominated by Western (mainly American) males. As such it ignores most of the wide range of alternative cultural perspectives, except where concepts are borrowed to enrich the Western model.
- *Scientism*: the attempt to apply techniques of the natural sciences, in particular quantification, to social issues and thereby obscure the assumptions and values built into the techniques.
- *Tech-fix and technological determinism*: the belief that technology will offer solutions to all problems and that technological development is the central mechanism of change in human society.
- *Mystification and elitism*: where arguments are so shrouded in technical wizardry as to be incomprehensible to non-experts and where powerful existing groups so control the flow of information as to ensure outcomes favourable to themselves.

Miles argued for a broad public involvement in the future debate to overcome the biases of establishment activity, but even this would leave the problem of potential divergence between the values expressed by today's public and those of future generations.

This, as Fowles (1978) argues, is the hub of the values problem. If we could be certain that the values of futurists would be the same as those of the future, designs initiated now could be guaranteed to fit in with the decades ahead. Unfortunately there is no such guarantee, but this of itself would not matter if current activities and decisions based on present values did not constrain the future. Housing projects, land-use planning and transport projects, for instance, determine people's futures far ahead (Ingelstam 1974).

We return therefore to the question with which this section began. Should we attempt to think about and make plans for the future? If we do, we have many difficulties and criticisms to overcome, but if we do not, we risk stumbling from crisis to crisis and condemnation for lack of foresight. We might well be excused for concluding it is a game we just cannot win. The problem is that it is also a game we are forced to play and in which we have to take sides. Resignation in the face of what may appear to be overwhelming odds only puts us on one side by default.

2.7. CONCLUSIONS

The difficulties of thinking about the future are considerable. They range from philosophical debates about humankind's ability to influence the course of history, to the more mundane issues of our poor forecasting record so far. There is sufficient evidence to develop a very good case against futures-thinking.

If we wish to continue in spite of the evident problems, we should do so with caution and in no doubt about the difficulties involved. As a result of the problems it faces, futures-thinking lacks respectability and credibility. It is easily dismissed as promising things it cannot deliver and as ineffective, if not dangerous. There is no established basis, it is claimed, in the academic or scientific sense, to justify the activity, but as we have already seen we continue to indulge in it because we need to.

CHAPTER THREE
IF IT IS SO DIFFICULT, WHY DO IT?

If thinking about the future in a meaningful way creates so many difficulties why should we bother? Some of the reasons should be clear from Chapter 1. Put simply, it would be almost impossible to live without thinking about the future. There are so many situations in which we instinctively think about and organise our future, both personally and collectively, that not doing so is practically impossible. This has always been the case, at least since the first humans planted seed to harvest the crop at a future date, but it has arguably become a more common need as society has become more complex. Thinking about the future, then, is a necessary evil, but why should we want to do so more than is absolutely unavoidable, when it is clear that it is so fraught with difficulties?

Our everyday speech gives us an initial clue. The English language, for example, clearly indicates the accepted value of thinking about the future. Words such as 'foresight', 'farsighted' and 'forward-thinking' have a positive image. In contrast, a lack of these attributes is described as 'blinkered', 'short-sighted', 'tunnel vision', 'narrow-minded'. All conjure up a negative image. Three common English proverbs also recommend careful consideration either in advance of action or at an early stage, before things develop too far: 'Look before you leap', 'Forewarned is forearmed', 'Prevention is better than cure'. The message is unmistakable. It will be much better if you think ahead, if you think about the future before it becomes the present. Problems can be avoided, preparations can be made to deal with situations before they arise, and problems tackled early are easier to solve than those that are left to become serious. Thinking about the future is common sense. We all know that but, in comparison to the amount of time we spend concerned about the past, we still do not take the future seriously. As Wells (1932) noted over sixty years ago, we have many historians but few professors of foresight.

3.1. HISTORY IS MADE, NOT GIVEN

Take a look around. Almost everything you can see was probably made or influenced by human beings. The chair you are sitting on, the desk, the building you are in, even the landscape, urban or rural, outside. They could be new or quite old. Writing this, I am sitting on a chair that is at least twenty years old, at a desk somewhat older, in a building constructed about thirty years ago. Nearby are other houses, some of them eighty to a hundred years old.

Think about where you live. If its anything like Ilkley, a town in the North of England, where I live, its appearance will owe a great deal to its history. Ilkley has grown in the last thirty years as people have moved into the area, but its history goes back much further. The centre is Victorian, dating from the second half of the nineteenth century. Some parts are older; there is the outline of a Roman fort, and on the hills around, the Moors, there are indications of prehistoric settlement. The countryside in the area is farmed, just as much the result of human action as the town. Although there are many places more remote from human settlement than northern England, relatively few, if any, have avoided the impact of human activity completely. Indeed, some scientists now believe that human activity past and present is affecting the whole planet.

The point of this excursion was simply to show that what we experience today is, to a large degree, the result of human actions in the past. Our surroundings and the ways we live our lives are a product of history. They have been influenced by the actions of people in the past, many of them perhaps long dead. Your life, too, has been influenced by past events. Where you were born, who your parents were, where they lived, their circumstances and your upbringing have all had an effect on you. Decisions that you have made and things that you have done have also had their impact upon your current situation. At some point you picked up this book, probably because in the past you have developed an interest in such topics. If you had not chosen the book you would not be reading this. The past and those who lived and influenced matters in the past have had a major effect on us. Some conclude from this that we are prisoners of our history and are effectively determined by it.

In their present (our past), past generations created our present (their future.) What would we say to them if we could talk to them? Would we thank them for all they did to make our lives comfortable? Would we remonstrate with them for all the mistakes they made? Probably a bit of both, in the same way that children regard their parents. Perhaps fortunately for us and past generations, such conversations are seldom possible.

If the influence of the past is so significant to us, it is most likely that, in the same way, we, in our present, are creating the future for the generations that will follow us. We know from the study of history that some events or decisions can have very long-term effects. The colonisation of large parts of the world by Europeans has had a major impact on the direction of history. Some of our decisions and actions are equally likely to have such effects, maybe over an even longer time span than in the past. As this chapter is being written, new plans that will affect the future of this area are being discussed. Some of the proposals, for a bypass and for the development of open land on the edge of the town could bring major changes that would have a long-term effect. Just as in previous generations, our decisions are creating the circumstances in which future generations will live.

With the assistance of hindsight it is relatively easy to distinguish those events that were of major historical importance from those that had little effect. Events that were thought, at the time, to be of little importance are usually unknown to us because they were not considered significant and thus were not recorded. Among those regarded as important, historians may disagree about the details but are more likely to agree on the principles. It is worth remembering that the study and interpretation of history is not without its different perspectives and even disputes. A tour of Boston, Massachusetts, including the Freedom Trail, which links sites important in the events leading up to the Declaration of Independence, is an interesting experience for an Englishman. The English version of history seldom portrays us as the enemy! The information used by or available to historians is likely to be selective, either by design or accident. It is often presented to make 'our' side look good. Historical ideas also change as the discovery of new information or new attitudes leads to a reinterpretation of the past, as the excavations on the site of the Jorvik Museum in York revised opinions about the Viking period of the city and changing attitudes influenced the interpretation of the European exploration of the American West.

It is much less easy to distinguish in advance those events that will become major influences in the future. The technological changes that occurred during the Industrial Revolution of the eighteenth and nineteenth centuries are generally agreed to have had a major impact on the course of history. It is less easy to determine the scale of the potential impacts of current new technologies on the future, though several authors, including Jones (1990), Sadler (1992) and Drexler, Peterson and Pergamit (1992), have suggested that information technology, biotechnology and nanotechnology will prove equally important in shaping the future.

Some measure of the future effect of today's decisions can be gained from the consideration of a few examples. Political leaders elected today are likely to remain in power, depending on the constitution of their particular country, for between four and seven years. Their decisions may have effect long after that, such as the decisions that led to the creation of the European Community in 1958. The British Department of Transport justifies the building of new roads by comparing the costs of construction with the benefits to be gained by road-users over the thirty-year 'life' of the road; the road itself is likely to be in existence for much longer. Building projects are typically financed over sixty years and may be let on 99- or even 999-year leases, and such is the scale of our cities that it has been calculated that, at current replacement rates, houses being built today will need to last for 800 years (Burns 1986). The clearance of virgin forest and the drainage of wetland may destroy unique environments and species, and extinction is for ever. None of this is new. Past generations also influenced our future and they do not seem to have concerned themselves unduly about us, so why should we bother about those who follow us?

There is some evidence that past generations took the future for granted. In the Middle Ages in Europe the pattern of life was established. Everyone had their place in society, ordained by God and enforced by the Church. The future for most people, as far as this life was concerned, would be a continuation of the present. There was no reason to think about it. The only future worth contemplating and working towards was in the next life, which, if the individual had deserved it, would be an improvement. It is sometimes argued that this emphasis on the next life inhibited thinking about the future in this one. It may also have had the effect of reinforcing the status quo.

In any event, changes in religious observance parallel the Renaissance and the Industrial Revolution, which were instrumental in the development of a new belief in human progress. The development of science and technology provided new opportunities and seemed to ensure the continued improvement of the human lot (I. F. Clarke 1979). People could look forward to a better future in this life and anticipate that their children would fare even better. This was a significant shift in attitudes, because the human future, for the first time, became something worth thinking about. The Victorian period in Britain is often seen as a time of great confidence. Britain was the dominant power, with an empire on which the sun never set. The future, as a continuation of the present, was assured and would be better than the present.

In the twentieth century this confidence seems to have been eroded. Della Vecchia (1986), for example, quotes several examples of research that indicate that the majority of American children in the 1980s had a pessimistic attitude to the future. 'Children no longer just focus on "what I will be when I grow up" but now ask "if I will be when I grow up".' There appears to be little worth looking forward to. Science and technology, it has been realised, offer no guarantee of progress or human improvement—in some respects just the opposite. More powerful technologies have enabled humans to continue their age-old squabbles but with much greater impact upon themselves and their surroundings. Among the most significant developments has been the discovery of nuclear power and its military and civilian uses. Great destructive power has been created and demonstrated, intentionally at Hiroshima and Nagasaki and accidentally at Chernobyl, to have life-threatening potential. Our technology, which has undoubtedly enhanced our lives, could also be the death of us. The growing reaction against science and technology can be seen as symptomatic of the loss of confidence in the future.

Doubts have also been raised about the ability of the planet to absorb the impacts of continually expanding technology (Meadows *et al.* 1972, 1992). Since the Industrial Revolution, and particularly during the twentieth century, the human population has grown rapidly, from about 750 million in 1750 to nearly 6 billion in the 1990s. If present growth continues it will have multiplied by ten times in less than 300 years. At the same time, technological development has increased the impact of a significant proportion of this larger population on the environment. 'The Greenhouse Effect'—the apparent warming of the Earth—is linked to the increasing use of fossil fuels over the last two hundred years. The depletion of the ozone layer in the upper atmosphere, and the consequent increase in damaging UVb radiation are linked to the use of particular gases; the worsening of floods in Bangladesh to the removal of tree cover in the Himalayas; increasing famine in Africa to overgrazing, and the worsening air quality in major cities to the internal-combustion engine in our cars. All are the result of human action undertaken for what appeared to be good reasons.

The use of coal and later oil were seen as great advances over the use of wood, wind and water for fuel and power. Since they gave more heat and were more flexible, they made possible many of the developments of technology and industry that have produced the comfortable lifestyle of the fortunate West. The invention of chlorofluorocarbons (CFCs) was hailed as an important advance, making a range of new products possible. The car, which is now estimated to create 17 per cent of the main greenhouse gas, CO_2, 85 per cent of carbon monoxide, 70 per cent of smog, and 50–85 per cent of lead pollution, remains a great liberator and the dream of those without one. The current figure of 500 million vehicles worldwide is expected to double by 2010 and treble by 2030 (Carley 1992). When only a few people had cars their impact was small; at the present level, the impact has become a matter of concern. Further growth can only increase it. It has been argued that 'We are the first generation that influences global climate, and the last generation to escape the consequences' (Orheim 1992). It appears that we are increasingly responsible for what happens to the planet. We are making the future.

Even if these events were to prove unlinked, the growing evidence that they may be should give us cause to think about what could happen. Quoting a poster he had seen in Sydney, Australia, Cleveland (1989) noted that 'If you act as though it matters and it doesn't matter, then it doesn't matter. But if you act as though it doesn't matter and it matters, then it matters.' For the first time in human history our generation is beginning to realise that what we do could have an important influence on the future of life on Earth. The fact may not be new, but the realisation is. This realisation has occurred as a result of advances in the technical capability that also caused the problems. We can now monitor and increase our understanding of our planet in ways not available to earlier generations. The hole in the ozone layer, for example, has been mapped with the aid of satellite images. We may not yet know for certain how the processes work, but the evidence is accumulating. When, as Pecci (1981) argued, 'The future will no longer be a mere continuation of the present, but a direct consequence of it,' and when the consequences, to a considerable extent, will be determined by what the human race does, can we risk not thinking about what we are doing and its affect on the future?

As the first generation to possess both this level of power to influence the Earth's future and the realisation that we are responsible for what is happening and will happen in the future, there are good reasons for us to take a different approach to the future from past generations. Surely we owe it to the generations that follow us to give very careful consideration to the future we are creating for them.

3.2. OUR RESPONSIBILITY TO FUTURE GENERATIONS

The growing realisation that what we do can have long-term or even permanent effects on the future and that we possess the ability to obliterate not only ourselves but also 'the fruit of four and a half billion years' (Schell 1982) dramatically illustrates the scale of our responsibility to and for the past. We are its custodians and, by our actions, can determine what happens to our inheritance. We can maintain, squander or destroy it. Schell pointed out that our ability to destroy now also stretches 'ahead from our present' to affect 'more billion years of life on earth' in the future. If we bring about the destruction that we are capable of, we could prejudice the future potential of humanity and many other lifeforms and possibly of the planet itself. Thus we are equally responsible for the future. Perhaps even more so, because although we can destroy the evidence of past civilisations, we cannot take away the fact of their existence or their achievements. By destroying the basic requirements for the existence of future generations, we could prevent their existence altogether or so reduce their life-chances as to severely limit their potential achievements.

In countries with a long history, like Britain, responsibility to the past is widely accepted. We are proud of our traditions and often unsympathetic to ideas of change. Some have argued that Britain pays too much attention to its traditions and loses out in consequence. Other nations without such conscious devotion to their history sometimes seem better suited to the rapidly changing world. Responsibility for the future is a more recent concept and one that attracts relatively little attention; but as Wenz (1988) points out, 'we are all in a position to be helpful (or harmful) to members of future generations, because we currently affect the earth on which they will depend for their survival.'

Many of the actions we take have long-term impacts or are irreversible. When we use a resource such as oil, or build on a piece of land, we incur what economists term an opportunity cost. In using the resource we lose the opportunity to retain it for future use or use it for some other purpose. Such costs are not one-off payments; they continue to be paid into the future, because the resource, once used, is not available again. Some resources—termed *renewable*—can be reused or regenerated. Wood, for example, is renewable, in that new trees can be planted where old ones have been cut for use. Others, such as oil, are not. The justification for consuming the resources is the benefit derived from their use. This too may be a once-and-only benefit, like using oil for fuel, or a continuing benefit, like that obtained from houses built on a previously undeveloped area of land. Whether or not we use the resource is determined by some implicit or explicit assessment of the advantages and disadvantages of doing so through techniques like cost–benefit analysis. Crucial in such analyses is what is included and how the effects are assessed. Conventionally, discounting procedures, which reduce the significance of longer-term effects, are used. These have the result of emphasising the interests of current generations at the expense of those to come. We saw the effect of such procedures in Chapter 1.

On the other hand, we can also create opportunities for future generations. Many of the everyday things that the Western world takes for granted were not available to past generations. They were discovered or invented by a wide range of people and gradually made available. We have the opportunity to fly around the world, for example, because in the past the Wright Brothers built the first aircraft, Whittle created the jet engine and a host of others constructed bigger, better and faster aircraft, set up airlines, built airports, provided navigation aids, and so on. This continuing process is still at work creating opportunities for future generations, perhaps to travel to the Moon, or 'visit' exotic locations without leaving home.

The problem is to get the balance of opportunities and costs as favourable as possible both for ourselves and future generations. There is much debate over our success to date. Some believe that we have made great progress and that our age is the best yet with the promise of an even better future. Others argue that our current position is untenable and that so-called progress has led us away from a more desirable and sustainable life. This debate has continued for more than a century, a period in which the generations of the industrial era have given little attention to the needs of the future, either thinking it assured, or more recently being more concerned for immediate benefit. Introducing a more considered approach to the future can only complicate the debate and the decision-making process, because thinking about the future has its own problems. There is also likely to be much argument about which future we should work towards, both in our own interests and in the interests of those to come, and how it may best be achieved.

It is often suggested that we have inherited the Earth from our ancestors. That appears to be true, but inheritance suggests ownership, and ownership suggests freedom to do as we please. As we have seen, our ancestors' actions have greatly affected our inheritance, and we have been presented with both the benefits and the problems of the world they created. Assuming that we are not the last generation, we are also creating the world that our successors will inherit. This puts a different perspective on our situation: rather than owning the world by inheritance, we may be seen as borrowing it from our children for the period of our lives. They will have to live with what we leave them. If we do not treat our home carefully, they will have to bear the consequences. Looked at in this way we do not own the world, but are tenants with a lease that was held by others before us and will pass to others after us. What sort of tenants are we, and how do we want to be regarded by our successors—careless, only interested in our own enjoyment with no thought for the consequences, or considerate, careful about the way we lived and what we would leave behind? If we wish to be the latter we will take the interests of future generations seriously and regard our tenancy as a 'full repairing lease' (Department of the Environment 1990) and ourselves as leaseholders with a responsibility to keep the property in good order and to ensure that we pass it on to succeeding tenants in good—or better—condition. Our freedom to do as we please is therefore constrained by the need to ensure the freedom of future generations from the effects of our inconsiderate action.

Discussing environmental hazards, Frankenfield (1993) suggested that we should guard against leaving future generations with (*i*) single hazards that on their own are likely to reduce the life chances of future generations, (*ii*) an aggregate stock of hazards that may interact to form complex toxic soups, (*iii*) hazards and mixes of hazards that are too complex for laypeople to comprehend or detect and as a result render them unable to control their own lives and force them to depend on experts, and (*iv*) hazards and soups that are too complex even for experts—and thus for society—to comprehend, detect, manage and/or foresee. We can appreciate the significance of this argument if we examine the environmental degradation left behind by earlier generations in their exploitation of mineral resources. Some are hazardous to life, while others impose high costs on current generations if we wish to reclaim our environment. Knowing this, we are hardly justified in doing the same to our successors.

There is a strong drive in most human societies to provide for children. Few like to think that the circumstances in which their children will live will be worse than their own. Most of us hope that our children will have a better life, and many parents make considerable sacrifices in an attempt to ensure that they will. Grandparents too are concerned about their grandchildren. If we lived that long we would also, no doubt, be concerned about our great-grandchildren and their children's children.

Assume for a moment that we each live for seventy-five years. Assume also that our children are born when we are twenty-five, and that this remains the case from generation to generation. From our birth to the death of our children would then extend for one hundred years, to the death of our grandchildren one hundred and twenty-five years and our great-grandchildren one hundred and fifty. Through them we have a direct and very personal link into the long-term future, just as we have a link to the past through our grandparents. Who would really want to be doing things that were going to make their own descendants' lives intolerable? Most of us would want to be helping them as far as we could.

This is a very personal indication of our responsibility to future generations. Perhaps we do not care so much for other people, particularly those in areas remote from us or those we consider unlike us, or our enemies, but our modern world brings them much closer than before. We can now witness events in any part of the world as they happen, thanks to satellites and television. We can see the misfortunes of others wherever they occur. That we do care and feel some responsibility is shown by the response to appeals like Band Aid and other charities and the agonising of the international community over intervention in local civil wars, the consequences of which are screened around the world. Children, in particular, attract sympathy. In our concern for their lives we reveal something of our interest in the wider future beyond the confines of our own lives and those of our immediate descendants.

Growing understanding of our responsibility for the future is indicated by the concept of sustainable development. There is a range of opinion about its meaning, but the definition give by the Brundtland Commission's has gained general acceptance: 'Development that meets the needs of the present without compromising the ability of future generations to meet their needs' (World Commission on Environment and Development 1987). It is a useful starting point, but it may not be easy to determine what the needs of future generations will be or to decide how we should go about satisfying our own needs without compromising theirs. Are the two compatible, or in order to achieve one is it necessary to compromise the other? If so which should take precedence? What is a need? When does it become only a want? Is a want less important than a need? Such questions have long been debated but the issue is further complicated by the difficulties associated with thinking about the future and the interests of future generations.

Tonn (1988) listed some of the difficulties in attempting to assess what the interests of future generations will be: they are not able to express their preferences and our assessment of them may well be incorrect; we do not know who will be alive to constitute the future generations; and the difficulties of predicting the future costs and benefits of potential policies are such as to be almost impossible. Ariansen (1994) pointed out that actions in the present may also determine, through the mating relationships they create, who future generations will be. Different relationships resulting from different combinations of circumstances would create a different set of people. Future generations are very much our responsibility because we determine who they are. Despite this very direct responsibility, Tonn (1988) noted that 'Future generations cannot hold their ancestors liable for irresponsible behaviour' or for their existence, nor can present generations receive effective rewards for sacrifices on behalf of their descendants. The only rewards that present generations can receive for sacrifices made in the interests of their descendants are psychic, a kind of feel-good factor. Such altruism does not appear to be a common commodity in present-day society, however desirable we may believe it to be. Indeed, how far are any of us really prepared to make real sacrifices for future generations remote both in time and kinship?

Particularly in the West, we seem quite prepared, beyond a certain commitment to charity, to continue our own privileged lifestyles in the face of clear knowledge of the deprivation experienced by many of our fellow human beings today. That the majority in Western countries are able to enjoy lifestyles beyond the wildest dreams of most of the world's population does not concern us unduly, and within Western societies we are prepared to tolerate gross inequalities of wealth and income, particularly if we are part of the 'comfortable society'. If we are not prepared to sacrifice our own current comfort for our contemporaries who are less well-off than we are, how can we expect to do it for generations still to come? 'Boy, do I love the Sunday *New York Times*. Apart from its many virtues as a newspaper, there is something wonderfully reassuring about its very bulk. . . . I read once that it takes 75,000 trees to produce one issue . . . and it's well worth every trembling leaf. So what if our grandchildren have no oxygen to breath? Fuck 'em' (Bryson 1989). Maybe this was intended to be irony, but it touches a nerve. When it comes down to it, are we really prepared to put the interests of future generations before our own comfort?

Despite any good intentions we may have, it is probably beyond us to establish with any certainty, except at a very general level, what the needs of future generations as yet unborn will be. It is difficult enough to be specific about our own future needs, without taking into account the probably different circumstances of future generations. Some help is offered by an approach suggested by Pearce, Markandaya and Barbier (1989). They contended that sustainable development may be obtained through intergenerational equity, whereby each generation is fair to the next by 'leaving them an inheritance of wealth no less than we inherited'. This has the advantage of linking closely with our acknowledged interest in our children's future. If we take good care of them and their generation, ensuring that they are at least as well provided for as we were, and they do the same, we do not need to attempt an impossible long-term assessment. Even that still requires very careful thought to implement, and it is based on an assumption that current levels of wealth are sustainable and not, as some would contend, already beyond the capacity of the planet to maintain.

It would still be possible to disregard our responsibility for the future. 'Eat, drink and be merry, for tomorrow we die' and 'Live now, pay later' are not unknown attitudes, but the more we understand our place in the continuing history of humanity the less tenable such selfish attitudes are. Tough (1992), for example, argued that the continued existence and flourishing of human civilisation is the most important issue of all. He further suggested (Tough 1993) that we should incorporate spokespersons for future generations into our decision-making to put forward their interests, because we can know what their interests will be and how we can best protect them. Their interests will, he asserted, be very similar to our own: peace, security, a healthy environment, the avoidance of catastrophe, improved systems of governance, increased knowledge, the well-being of children and continuing learning (Tough 1994). The details of how to achieve them may be debated, but the aims are clear. Tonn (1991) put forward a specific proposal for a House of Spokespersons for the Future in the US Congress, as a means of bringing the interests of future generations into current decision-making. Similar institutions could be envisaged elsewhere, such as a second chamber of the European Parliament or a new role for the House of Lords in the UK. As the members of the House of Lords tend to be older than the average of the population it would be an intriguing irony for them to have to use their experience for the specific benefit of future generations. Another suggestion is the requirement for a Future-Generations Impact-Assessment similar to environmental and technological assessments.

If we threaten the existence of future generations by our carelessness, despite being aware of the consequences, we deny a large part of our humanity and have to accept the heavy responsibility of endangering the human future. This might not be quite so daunting as it appears: W. Bell (1993) argued that the human future is, in part at least, our own future. Unless we assume our own imminent death, we have a continuing interest in the future. Would we consciously act in a way that we know is damaging to ourselves? Unfortunately, in particular circumstances, we do. We know that smoking is damaging to health, but we still smoke. We know that cars damage the environment and are responsible for many deaths and injuries each year, but we still drive. Perhaps we continue because although we know the dangers, we either find the risks exciting or believe that we will get away with it. Or is it another example of discounting the possible future costs in favour of immediate benefit? If we do not act in our own interests what chance is there that we will act in the interests of others, particularly others yet to be born?

If we do act in our own future interests, however, we also act in the interests of future generations, because our lives overlap. Generations are not watertight compartments but 'continuously intertwine with each other over the whole length of human history' (Laslett, quoted in W. Bell 1993). Could it be, then, that the problem really resides in our inability to understand our own true interests in the present rather than those of distant future generations? Bell reinforced this view by suggesting that in caring for future generations and making sacrifices for them we benefit as well. If we wish to leave behind something of ourselves, without which our life becomes meaningless when we die, we are automatically thinking about future generations in attempting to attain our own self-fulfilment. By acting in our own best interests we also act in the interests of the future.

3.3. THE NEED FOR DIRECTION

'If you do not know where you are going any road will take you there' (Enzer and Wurzburger 1982). The purpose of undertaking most journeys is to get somewhere, not just anywhere, but a desired destination. Only when we know where we want to go can we decide which route to follow. There may be different routes and we make our choice depending upon whether we want to get there as quickly as possible, take the scenic route or call at Aunt Mable's on the way . If we had no idea of where we wanted to go it would be difficult, if not impossible, to decide which way to turn. It would not matter anyway, because we would be equally happy or unhappy wherever we were. A fairly unlikely occurrence, except where we embark on a mystery tour just for the fun of it.

In any situation in which we need to make decisions we need some basis on which to make the decision—some thing we want, or want to achieve, that we do not currently have; a situation that we wish to retain but see threatened unless we take some action; a problem we want to solve. In each case we are comparing the present with an imagined, different future. What we decide to do is determined by the comparison. Without some idea of what we want we have no reason to decide one way rather than another. We might just as well save our time, energy, money and resources and do nothing—do nothing because we are prepared to accept whatever turns up, having no preference for one situation over another.

In many personal situations we will probably have aims we do not need to think about. We know what they are and our actions, almost instinctively, take us in that direction. At other times we may have competing aims and different ways of achieving them. The situation then becomes more complicated. You want, or maybe have, to finish this book, but you would also like to go out and have a good time. A tricky decision, which will be determined by the image of the future you find most attractive!

In more complex situations we may need to think more carefully about our aims and possible courses of action; to be more explicit about what we want and how best to attain it. We probably do that when we make more important decisions about moving house, going on a holiday, or selecting a course at a university or a career. We weigh up the alternatives and decide on the one we think will suit us the best. Effectively we imagine different futures and select the one we prefer. Not that success is guaranteed. Our actions may not have the result we anticipated or the end result might not be to our liking after all, which is a familiar problem of thinking about the future. But unless we take a completely fatalistic approach, we are unlikely to be happy not even trying to influence what happens to us.

Society, too, has aims. They may be clearly or poorly expressed, but they influence decisions. Economic growth is an aim often expressed by governments. Actions are taken which those in power believe are most likely to lead to growth in the economy. These actions will be influenced by opinions about which course of action is most likely to be successful. That it is not always achieved does not stop them continuing to try. Society's aims may also conflict and choices often have to be made. Should a new technology that promises considerable benefits but also has significant risks be developed? Nuclear power is a good example. Those in favour argue that it can provide abundant, cheap and relatively unpolluting electricity, while opponents point to uncertain health risks, the linked military uses of nuclear power and the dangers of major accidents like Chernobyl. Such choices are not easy to make and our attitudes to them are governed by what we think society's future should be and how we think it will most probably be attained. Without such future images, it would be difficult to offer an opinion. Such decisions about the future are difficult because we do not all share the same preferred images of the future and have different views of the possibility of particular events occurring. The supporters of nuclear power see an overriding need for energy that outweighs the low probability, as they see it, of accidents or other problems. Their future image is favourable. The opponents imagine other ways of supplying energy, or of reducing the need for it, and assign much higher probability to the dangers. Their image is of a future that would be better without nuclear power.

The difficulties we experience in making accurate assessments of the future consequences of our decisions, a form of forecasting, may lead us to conclude that we cannot make those decisions in a rational way. We might then be tempted to think that they could just as effectively be made by tossing a coin. But not thinking carefully about the consequences for the future of such decisions does not mean that those consequences go away. The consequences of earlier actions happen, whether those actions and their possible consequences were considered or not. By preferring not to decide or not to take responsibility for a decision, we do not avoid the consequences or the responsibility, just the opportunity to influence our destiny in a direction that we may prefer. The results may be different from those we imagined, and if they are less to our liking, we can only blame ourselves for not bothering to think about them in advance.

Modern Western societies, particularly the UK (Ignatieff 1993), are often criticised because they have no vision; no clear idea of where they want to go or what kind of society they want to become. As Polak (1973) has argued, societies without vision inevitably decline, because they lose momentum. Visions, dreams, images of a desirable future are the necessary driving forces that urge us to work for change in our current situation (Popper 1988). Unless we are satisfied with where we are, we need images of a different future to provide direction. There are so many problems in our modern world—hunger, disease, war, poverty, injustice, crime, pollution, etc.—that it is unlikely that we are satisfied with the current situation. To take action we need to have an image of the future, one in which the problems, at least, are reduced.

Problem-solving is an important impetus to thinking creatively about the future. The identification of a problem usually implies an intention to attempt to solve it. Since the process of problem-solving takes time, the development of solutions requires the creation of images in advance of their realisation. Depending upon the nature of the problem and the steps necessary to solve it this may be a short- or a quite long-term future image. Although it is a significant incentive to thinking about a future different from the present, the existence of a problem is not necessary for creative future-thinking. President Kennedy's commitment to put a man on the Moon by the end of the 1960s is a clear example of a goal that was not specifically problem-generated. It was an image of a future, distinct from the past or present, that was seen as a positive development to be achieved. Many problems had to be resolved en route to the goal, but the goal itself did not arise as the solution to a particular problem. Setting ourselves ambitions or targets does not start from a problem either; we see a particular future as desirable and set out to achieve it, no doubt encountering problems on the way but not being driven solely by the need to solve a problem.

Perhaps those who suggest that modern society lacks vision mean that they do not like the direction they see it going. Implicitly they imagine a continuation into the future of what they see as current trends for the worse and react against it, often looking back to a time when these problems were not so apparent. They prefer to attempt to re-establish the old rather than face change and create the new.

Even if they are not expressed verbally or as a vision of the future the society hopes to achieve, the values and aims of a society are made apparent through its actions and their results. The environment provides a good example. What a society considers to be important is reflected in the environment it creates. In medieval Europe religious buildings and castles dominated the landscape. In comparison to the living quarters of the majority of the population a medieval cathedral was a truly awe-inspiring edifice. It towered over the rest of the town and was visible for miles. Nothing else, apart from the temporal power of the state, reflected in the castles built to ensure the retention of that power, was anywhere near as impressive. Today neither churches nor castles stand out so clearly in Western cities. St Paul's Cathedral, which used to dominate the London skyline is now surrounded by the office blocks of the City. Modern British society does not strive for religious aims, but worships material success. In Leeds, a city in northern England, there are two buildings that particularly reflect this shift. One is built like a medieval castle. Apart from a well-guarded entrance it has no ground floor windows. It gives the impression of an impregnable fortress, even to the extent of having a portcullis that can be lowered to exclude unwanted visitors. It is the headquarters of a bank, a true 'Castle of Capitalism'. Some distance away is another building, which has a floor plan very like a medieval cathedral. The 'choir' is slightly offset from the true cruciform layout, but the similarity remains striking. At the east end, where the Lady Chapel honouring the mother of Christ would be found, is a shop. It is called 'Mothercare' and is devoted to the requirements of mothers and young children! This 'Cathedral of Commerce' attracts many more worshippers than the adjacent church, which is visually overwhelmed by the shopping centre.

Our values and aims emerge by default even if we have not directly considered them. They are exposed by the results of our actions, whether we like it or not. Without careful consideration they are likely to be even more muddled and inconsistent. If we do lack clear aims, or a vision of the future we want to achieve, it is difficult to establish priorities and take decisions that lead to their achievement. We are likely to end up judging each issue as it arises, on its own merits, with no criteria to compare it against and no particular reason to decide it one way rather than another. As one issue succeeds another we muddle through quite possibly taking mutually contradictory decisions, the results of which may work against each other. Of course, if we do not have any clear wish to proceed in one direction rather than another, this may not matter.

One of the difficulties of establishing an agreed set of aims in a society is that we do not all want the same things, or our wants may be incompatible: two groups of people claim the same territory, one group wanting to clear the forests for land to grow food or crops for sale, another wanting the forest retained to stabilise the climate or conserve wildlife. These conflicts become increasingly clear with our abilities to hear and see what is happening almost anywhere in the world, but it does not become any easier to solve them or decide who is right. Can we go on like this? When our decisions and our conflicts had only local significance, and our impact on the planet and its lifeforms was small it probably did not matter, but we may now be entering a phase in which if we do not think more carefully about where such disputes may lead us, we may not have a future, or at least a future any of us want. Perhaps we are moving into a phase in the development of humanity in which, if we are going to survive, we need to find new ways to resolve such conflicts and discover the desires for the future that we share (life, health, food, and somewhere to live) rather than concentrate on the experiences of the past which divide us. The future of the planet does not belong to any particular group or species but is shared by all residents, human and others. It seems to be becoming increasingly the case that we humans bear a responsibility for the future. Part of that responsibility must be to imagine what the alternatives might be, make a choice based on as clear an assessment of what we are striving for as possible and work towards it.

Working out a future in these circumstances will not be easy. There will be many disagreements, accusations of unfairness, mistrust and conflicts, but unless we dream of a future together we may be in danger of having no future apart. If that is a possibility, the importance of establishing directions and thinking very carefully about our future becomes even more important.

3.4. CONTROLLING THE AGENDA

New problems are always cropping up. Just when we think we have finished what we have been doing and are looking forward to a well-earned rest, someone finds us something else to do. They may not even wait that long but keep piling on new problems before we have finished. New problems arise because we live in a world of change. A significant portion of that change is caused by our fellow human beings, but change is also inherent in nature. Growth and decay are both natural processes. Both affect us as we grow up and grow older. At the same time, our social circumstances change as we meet new people and move into new situations. New situations and relationships pose new issues for us to think about. Our personal agenda, the issues that concern us from day to day, changes. Many of these changes happen to us either as the result of natural processes or the actions of others. In other circumstances we create change by making decisions and taking actions. Many of the examples discussed in Chapter 1 related to situations in which we are instrumental in bringing about change. Although we may feel that we are usually on the receiving end of change, there are circumstances in which we create it.

It is sometimes suggested that people do not like change. We are said to prefer familiar situations in which we know how to act, and feel comfortable and in control. In unfamiliar situations we are more likely to be unsettled and unsure what to do, and feel subject to forces beyond our control. Our reactions to new technology and other innovations are often like this. If we are told that new machinery is to be installed or new ways of working introduced, our normal reaction seems to be to oppose them, to look for all the negative results they will have and to disbelieve any positive claims. We are not in control, but feel forced to adapt. As a result we react against the change.

When we feel in control of change and new things, we are less likely to oppose them. We see the advantages more easily. As a result we go out and buy a video recorder or use the cash machine and willingly accept the changes they imply. Perhaps it is not so much change that we object to, but being changed, not being able to control or influence what is happening to us.

The same is true for societies, governments and organisations. The world in which they operate does not stay the same. Discoveries or inventions change our understanding of the world, new developments in technology or society raise new issues, or a new product from a competitor threatens existing markets. Their reactions are likely to be similar to those of individuals, unsettled by enforced changes but excited by the prospect of creating them or facing a challenge.

Changes can be gradual or sudden. We often do not realise that gradual changes are happening until they have been going on for a considerable time. Only when we compare situations after a considerable length of time do we notice what has happened. It is like looking at yourself in the mirror every day and not noticing how you are changing until you look at a photograph of what you looked like years ago.

In other circumstances we notice change but prefer to ignore it, perhaps hoping that it is just a blip and that normality will soon reassert itself. This usually means a return to an earlier situation which we found, or imagine with hindsight was, less troublesome, like the return to full employment beloved of politicians in the 1980s and 1990s. Policies to encourage this return are consistently called for, but few think to ask whether the economic changes affecting employment might suggest that employment was shifting away from being a central feature in society (Robertson 1985). That we have grown used to a particular situation or pattern of events is no reason to assume that it will always be present.

Sudden changes are more difficult to ignore because, by their very nature, they are more apparent and demand attention. They are likely to catch us by surprise, and in such circumstances we can only react to what has occurred. More gradual changes can be analysed and projected forward into 'what if' images of the future. We can anticipate the consequences should they continue and assess whether the situation they appear likely to produce is one we desire. If not, we often take action, in the present, to alter the direction of change to avoid or ameliorate the anticipated consequences. We do not have to wait until the situation becomes critical, but we often do.

Change does not just happen to us, forcing us to respond after the event; we also create it. Whenever we set out to achieve something, whether it is a grand scheme or a minor alteration to an existing situation, we create change. Many of the changes occurring in the world now are the result of human action; changes that we have made are themselves interacting with human and natural systems to create more change. A complex interrelationship of changes is developing in which our actions may be both reactive and proactive at the same time, responding to and causing change in the same action.

The desire for change is itself a powerful driving force. Without waiting for change to happen we set out to instigate it. Given a situation we regard as unfavourable we take steps to alter it into one we find more desirable. It is this which drives us on. If we did not believe we could change things we would not even try.

In many Western societies the population is ageing. Advances in medical science and better living conditions mean that people are living longer. As a consequence there are more older people than before and they form a growing part of the population. This presents new issues to society, particularly to governments, because the existing provisions of retirement, pensions and medical services were developed for a smaller number of older people. They are not able to cope effectively with the larger numbers. All the indications are that this situation is likely to continue, leading to an even larger number of older people in the future.

Should we wait for such changes to occur and the problems they will create to arise, or attempt to anticipate them? If we wait, we avoid the possibility of wasting time and resources examining problems that may not arise. By waiting we can know with some certainty that an issue is important because it has been presented to us as a problem needing immediate action, but we may well be faced with a problem that is much worse because it has had more time to develop and requires a greater input of resources to deal with than it would have done had it been tackled earlier. 'A stitch in time saves nine.'

Some issues, in areas like the environment in particular, may have severe consequences if we wait to be sure. Global warming is such an issue. There are those who remain to be convinced that warming is occurring or that human action has anything to do with it. They prefer to wait for proof before taking action. Unfortunately by the time we have proof, if such proof is possible or transpires, the situation may be so far advanced that solutions are not only very much more expensive and disruptive but even perhaps unachievable. At the very least we may have to live with the consequences for a very long time.

If we wait until we are forced to act we surrender control of the agenda, the issues we are dealing with, to natural forces or to other human beings. Either way we have given up any choice about which issues we tackle and quite probably reduced the options open to us. Actions may be forced on us by circumstances. We would have preferred to do things differently and to consider other matters, but we have no choice. Control of the agenda is an important part of influencing the outcome, as experienced committee people know. An important first step in getting the decision we want is to ensure that the issue is on the agenda, while ensuring that it does not appear is a valuable tactic in avoiding unfavourable conclusions. With control we can decide which issues are considered and which are not. Giving that up to chance means that we are much less able to influence our destiny.

3.5. THE SHORTCOMINGS OF REACTION

The development of techniques of impact- and risk-assessment acknowledges that it is worthwhile attempting to anticipate problems, weighing up the probability of their occurring and assessing their potential consequences before they occur. The techniques provide us with a measure of consideration and an ability to influence the outcomes before the event. Intended developments are scrutinised in an attempt to assess what their likely impacts will be. The assessments are forecasts, subject to all the difficulties of forecasting, but they provide an opportunity to weigh up the anticipated advantages and disadvantages before an irrevocable decision is taken. Decisions can then be made from a position of some knowledge, rather than blindly or in haste. There can be no guarantee of success, as the results may not be as forecast; but since the only way to prove what the effects of an action are is to undertake it and measure them, it is usually preferable to attempt to assess them in advance. If we wait and then decide that it would have been better not to have taken the action, we have all the problems of changing direction, and undoing what has been done, and we will have lived with the very impacts that led us to reject the action for as long as it has taken us to assess the impact and reach the conclusion that not doing it would have been better.

Nor is it possible to take two or more courses of action at the same time and compare the results before making our decision, because in the real world, unlike the laboratory, the very act of doing one thing rules out alternatives. Comparisons can only be made by imagining or modelling the results of alternative courses of action, and these can only give a measure of choice if they are carried out before the actions are taken—in other words, by indulging in thinking about the future. The kind of proof required by scientists is, as a result, usually unavailable in a policy-making situation. After the event it is a matter of 'if only' and recrimination for nor foreseeing what, with the aid of hindsight, is obvious. The techniques have become increasingly sophisticated, using a range of models based on research into previous similar situations, but in a particular case they must include that element of uncertainty associated with prediction. Even so, where we have an opportunity to anticipate the results of different actions before we take them, it seems better to try, even if it does not always work.

If we wait for proof we will always be behind the action, because problems can only be proved to exist by examining past data. By the time we have done that, the problem is likely to be well developed and probably more difficult to deal with than it would have been had we tackled it earlier. Unfortunately, as

Kettle (1993) argues, there are too many situations in which, with hindsight, we knew things were going wrong but failed to act. Had we been able to think ahead sufficiently clearly and acted upon our anticipations, we might have avoided the worst.

A good example of thinking ahead was the report produced in the UK 1993 by the Human Fertilisation and Embryology Authority. It was published to encourage public debate about potential new techniques of infertility treatment before they were available, rather than waiting until they had been used before trying to decide whether they should have been. The techniques raise many moral and ethical issues about which many people feel very strongly. The question that the Authority wished to address was whether these techniques should be used if they became available, as seemed probable. This was an exercise in attempting to choose the future rather than waiting for it to happen.

Life is full of 'If only's. 'If only I had thought about the saucepan on the stove I could have stopped it boiling over.' 'If only there had been more warning we could have prevented that accident.' 'If only we had had more information we could have stopped the attack.' Some are inevitable, but there are also plenty of examples where we do anticipate that things could happen and take steps either to prevent them or, at least, reduce their consequences. Some years ago the British Airports Authority (at that time still government-owned) published an advertisement that depicted a fire engine at London's Gatwick Airport under the headline '£224,000 of Public Money Doing Nothing'. It is to be hoped that the fire engine never has to be used, but not to have the capability to deal with an accident would be the height of irresponsibility. Is anyone really going to suggest that if it is never used it was a waste of money? Attempts to prevent aircraft accidents, although not always successful, have influenced the design of the aircraft themselves. Back-up systems working on the principle of fail-safe are built in so that if the main control systems fail there are others which can be used to fly the plane. Most of the time they are redundant but in an emergency they become vital in preventing disaster. The cost of preventing aircraft accidents through improved safety measures is considered worthwhile, but if the worst happens we need to be ready to reduce the loss as much as possible. Emergency services carry out exercises just to be ready in case a real disaster occurs. If they are never required to act in a real emergency we do not think that the preparations were wasted. Landing at Gatwick Airport in an aircraft that had experienced an emergency, it was reassuring to see that fire engine, or one of its companions, following the plane. Thankfully it was not needed, but I am glad it was there. This approach could be useful in more situations. We need to be prepared to think the unthinkable more often and take action to prevent or lessen the consequences should it occur.

Efforts to anticipate potential problems and make advance preparations to deal with them, should they arise, is good practice. It is nothing new, but the temptation is to concentrate our resources on real problems, ones that trouble us today rather than those that may occur tomorrow. Unfortunately, the causes of today's problems often lie deep in the past, and because they have not been dealt with earlier they have often become more difficult and costly to solve. We cannot ignore current problems, but it would seem sensible to aim a proportion of our efforts at trying to anticipate the shape of new problems and taking preventive action to forestall them. It will be argued that such effort can never be proven to be effective because, by definition, a problem prevented does not occur. The expense of preventing it may appear to have been wasted. That is true, but our experience also tells us that early action is frequently easier and less costly. Only if we are prepared to gamble that the proportion of our problems that, without preventive action, will not develop into crises will outweigh those that will, are we justified in not attempting to pre-empt them. We do not spend money on insurance because we know our house is going to burn down, but because it might. If it is not burnt down, has that money been wasted? Technically yes, but we would think ourselves foolish not to take out insurance, particularly if it did!

Some changes can be foreseen, but not all. The certainty that we will fail sometimes—not anticipating things that do happen and anticipating things that do not—is not a good argument against the probability that we will succeed at others. If we do not try, we give up the benefits we could have gained in those areas where anticipation is possible. Waiting for problems to happen forces us to react to them. If we have not anticipated that they could occur, we will be surprised and our reaction either delayed while we think what to do, or instinctive. Reaction time can be critical and the need to react quickly can reduce the time we have to consider alternatives. Instinctive reactions, though sometimes successful, are immediate and do not allow for careful thought and the evaluation of alternatives. Emergency services are kept in readiness not because it is known that an accident is going to happen at a particular time but because one could happen at any time. We know that accidents happen but we do not know when they will happen or exactly what will happen. Anticipating the possibility enables the emergency services to respond quickly, reducing the delay arising from surprise. That accidents happen is not surprising; the surprise comes in their timing, but if we anticipate the likelihood of their occurrence the consequences can be minimised.

Reacting to changes we have not anticipated puts us at a disadvantage. We lose the initiative. Rather than being on top of events, we are forced on to the defensive, struggling to catch up. As a result, the future happens to us as events unfold. It continually bombards us with unexpected changes that we have to deal with the best we can. Such crisis-management, waiting until the problems hit us and then trying to manage, may be inevitable on some occasions and even acceptable where the consequences of doing so are limited and where the situation is redeemable without excessive cost and disruption. Unfortunately, with many of the issues facing the world and the types of accident that can happen in the late twentieth century, this may not be the case. Waiting until a crisis develops in the environment or in the application of a new technology may be too late. The potential impact of our activities suggests a need for much more careful anticipatory thinking than ever before. Jenkins (1993) provided a thought-provoking list of ten disasters waiting to happen in our modern world:

- a massive oil-tanker disaster
- a bomb on the Underground
- more Chernobyls
- a gas-tanker explosion
- computer error in an aircraft
- a nuclear weapons accident
- a major chemical disaster
- a fire in the Channel Tunnel
- a major rail crash caused by poor maintenance
- designer germs on the loose

Some of these have already happened—the Exxon Valdez and Bhopal disasters, for example—but could well occur again elsewhere. Some might best be avoided by not developing particular technologies, and the consequences of others could at least be reduced by taking precautionary measures or being alert to their possibility.

The disadvantages of crisis-management are easier to see in hindsight. We can frequently identify the events leading up to the crisis after it has happened. If only we had been more watchful, taken note of the warning signs, we could perhaps have prevented it. In 1982, there was much debate that the Falklands Crisis (as it was termed in Britain) could have been prevented if Argentine actions had been understood and different responses been made. Some credence is given to this assertion by the resignation of the then British Foreign Secretary, Lord Carrington, after the Argentine takeover of the islands. As the responsible minister he should have anticipated events and acted to forestall them. He failed to do so, accepted the responsibility, and resigned. The costs in lives and resources to both sides in the conflict might have been avoided had different actions been taken. There were claims that a similar situation had indeed been averted in the 1970s by preventive action. Similarly, it has been suggested that better understanding of intelligence reports might have enabled action to prevent the invasion of Kuwait that precipitated the Gulf War. Whether these particular suppositions are true is difficult to prove without access to secret papers, but it is possible to believe that it could have been the case that pre-emptive action in 1982 and 1990 could have averted the conflicts. In the Falklands/Malvinas case it would not have resolved the counter-claims over the islands but it might have avoided that particular conflict and not made their resolution more difficult.

One of the reasons why we do not attempt to avert crises may be that we actually enjoy them. There is a thrill of danger about them, a need for quick incisive action. Qualities of bravery and leadership are said to be tested by such adversity. At the time of the Falklands Crisis, Margaret Thatcher, then British Prime Minister, was reported to have said, 'When you have spent half your political life dealing with humdrum issues like the environment, it is exciting to have a real crisis on your hands' (M. Robinson 1992). Had action been taken to avert the crisis, that excitement would not have occurred. Ornstein and Ehrlich (1989) actually suggested that our sensory systems are wired up to encourage reaction and crisis-management. They were fixed to suit the circumstances in which we humans evolved. Quick reactions to attack by predators or enemies were vital to survival. Natural selection ensured that those with quick reactions prospered. In some circumstances such reactions are still necessary, but our world has changed so much, mainly as a result of our own actions, that Ornstein and Ehrlich argue we are now much less able to deal with the problems that face us by reaction alone. What is needed is 'sustained and complex effort' that will enable us to deal with gradual changes and anticipate their consequences before they become crises.

The necessary response to the contemporary condition is a proactive rather than a reactive one. As the military put it we need 'pre-emptive strikes' to deal with our problems. Renfro (1987) argued that by being proactive we can change the future from something that happens to us into something that happens for us. The influence we have over the future means that, in a sense, this is already true, but as yet we have not realised its significance. We still believe that we are passively experiencing the effects of so many events rather than realise that we are often the cause. If that is the case different actions on our part might have avoided the problem.

Part of our difficulty is that, while it is true that human kind collectively is affecting change, it is not always apparent to the individual. As individuals we frequently do not see our actions as significant and feel powerless to influence events. We are not responsible alone for what is happening and we are not able to influence events sufficiently on our own. This happens because many effects only arise from the interaction of numerous individual decisions. The useful phrase 'Think Globally, Act Locally' is favoured by environmentalists as a guide to achieving sustainable development, but it could equally be reversed to make more apparent the impact of individual actions when they interact: 'Acts Locally, Impact Globally'. Being unaware of this link may lead to actions that are apparently in the individual's own interest but are against the wider longer-term interest and may in turn affect our own and our children's interests adversely. Only if we feel a collective longer-term responsibility and understand how our actions impact upon future generations will we change what we do.

Increasingly the pattern of causation is circular. Our human actions affect the future, which in turn creates the situations we face. If all the time we are driven by problems which lead to crises, we can only react. We have little choice and therefore little control over the consequences of our actions, which will in turn be difficult to anticipate. If, on the other hand, we can begin to exert more influence by anticipating issues before they develop we can establish a much more constructive influence over events and the future becomes more manageable.

3.6. THE FUTURE AS A LEARNING PROCESS

Adopting a more positive attitude towards thinking about the future will not lead to a magical improvement in our situation. Futures-thinking is not a panacea for all our current ills, but thinking about the future more carefully has the potential to help us in dealing with the circumstances of the modern world. None of the difficulties of managing the future will go away, but careful thought will allow us better to understand our relationship to the future and learn how to approach it more constructively.

We know that in most circumstances single predictions and forecasts are likely to be wrong. If they were not there would be no gambling industry because there would be no profit in it. It is only because most punters make the wrong predictions that there is money to pay the few who get it right and profits for the operators. If we all guessed correctly no one would be prepared to run a gambling industry, and we would not be interested anyway because we could never win any more than anyone else. Yet we frequently expect to be able to obtain exact forecasts of what is going to happen in the future. We do so because we want to know what the future is going to be, even though realistically we cannot. The uncertainty of the future is unsettling, but it is inevitable unless we accept the idea of one fixed future that, with improved techniques, we can discover. Uncertainty about the future is inherent in the idea of alternative futures. It is further enhanced if we accept human choice as a significant influence on the future, because it is difficult to predict what individual choices will be and the consequences of the interaction of those choices. To deal with the prospect of alternative futures and human choice and their inherent unpredictability we need to develop ways of managing in uncertainty not ignoring it. Seeking spurious certainty about the future misleads us and encourages us to waste our efforts trying to achieve the unattainable, and discredits the exercise when forecasts prove inaccurate.

Uncertainty inevitably leads to mistakes. Some of our anticipations will be incorrect and our actions will not always produce the expected results. Traditional management approaches tend to criticise mistakes, but the only way to avoid them is to play safe, take no risks and do nothing. Creative approaches accept that success and failure go together. Playing safe may avoid mistakes but it inhibits success as well. Both success and failure are vital ingredients in the learning process of dealing sensibly with the future. We build on our successes and learn from our mistakes, using them as ways of eliminating unsuccessful approaches. Toffler (1990) argued that 'multitudes of bad ideas need to be floated and freely discussed in order to have a single good one', and that 'innovation . . . requires experimental failure to achieve success'. The dynamic nature of our situation also means that changing circumstances can quickly turn success into failure, as many a team that wins a championship one year and struggles to avoid the wooden spoon the next has found. The world, in this case the opposition, does not stand still, it throws up new challenges that need to be addressed with new responses.

Many forecasts and future images do not come true because the circumstances on which they were based change between the time they were made and the arrival of the time they were made. Two reactions are possible: to give up the impossible task and not bother, or to accept that forecasting and planning are continuing tasks in which our images of the future are continually adapted in the light of emerging information. No single forecast or vision may come true, but taken together they are our best and only guide to the unfolding present. Without them we are driving blind. New circumstances are taken into account in our assessment of the changing present without comment. They are equally important in the updating of our images of the future and the reworking of our ideas of what it will be like. We tend to think of forecasts and images of the future as blueprints, exact representations of how the future will look. Occasionally this may be true but more often they are more realistically seen as working drawings, a useful and vital stage in the process but not the final form.

This may raise concern about the impermanence of ideas about the future. If they are continually changing and particular images never come into being, what is the point in having them? This would be more worrying if ideas about the future were unique in this respect, but as Bronowski (1973) suggested, all knowledge is open to similar difficulties. 'We are always at the brink of the known, we always feel forward for what is to be hoped. . . .We have to cure ourselves of the itch for absolute knowledge.' The future is similar. We know, if we stop to think about it, that our current ideas, just like those we have held in the past, are likely to change as new information becomes available. We continue to use them nonetheless because they are the best we have and they serve to help us with our current problems. They may not be absolute, unchanging truth but that does not destroy their value. We use them until a better idea or theory is developed in the light of new knowledge. We may then reject old ideas as quaint old-fashioned notions, but future generations will regard our latest nostrums in the same way. 'Did they ever believe that?' they will remark with tears of laughter streaming down their cheeks. We think our newest notions are the ultimate, but they are not, just the latest in the continuing history of ideas. Forecasts and images of the future are not dissimilar.

Imagining or forecasting the future is not a task that can be undertaken once and the results used until that future becomes the present. It seldom does. The future moves ahead of us, tantalisingly out of reach but always drawing us forward. As in any moving situation, the image that we see changes. Our view is not a static one; we are on the move, and as we move new images become apparent to us. The world around us is changing too and our understanding of it is developing. In order to think realistically and creatively about the world and its future we need to update our image as the present advances. It may be frustrating, but as Alice discovered, 'It takes all the running you can do to stay in the same place. If you want to get somewhere else you must run twice as fast as that.' Thinking constructively about the future can help us obtain some of that extra speed.

Dealing with the future could be termed the ultimate learning experience, because there is always something else to be discovered or understood. The hole in the Earth's ozone layer was unknown until it was discovered in 1984. Research was then necessary to establish the cause and further action to reach agreement about the measures needed to address the problem. More work is needed to find alternatives to CFCs. It is unlikely that we will not discover other, similar problems in the future that require further action. They always have in the past. The learning process does not consist of acquiring a fixed body of knowledge that we can 'tick off' as we acquire it; it is a continually developing environment in which new ideas replace the old, and established views become redundant in the face of new developments. This makes dealing with the future exciting because it is continually new. New ideas are always emerging, new challenges to established approaches. We need to stay alert and question the adequacy of existing ideas in the evolving situation, to continue learning as the future unfolds in the continually evolving present.

3.7. THE NEED FOR DEMOCRATIC FUTURES-THINKING

The complexity of the task outlined may lead to the conclusion that we need some experts in Futures to whom it can be delegated, while the rest of us get on with our lives. Experts are indeed needed and it is one of the purposes of this book to argue for a more considered approach to the future to match the concern we show for the past and the present. This is far from a new idea. H. G. Wells called for Professors of Foresight in 1932:

> It seem an odd thing to me that though we have thousands and thousands of professors and hundreds of thousands of students working on the records of the past, there is not a single person anywhere who makes a whole-time job of estimating the future consequences of new inventions and devices. There is not a single Professor of Foresight in the world. But why shouldn't there be? All these new things, these new inventions and new powers, come crowding along; every one is fraught with consequences, and yet it is only after something has hit us hard that we set about dealing with it.

Much the same arguments could be made today.

There are many people, perhaps most of us, who have an interest in and impact on the future. The same was true in Wells's day, as his original broadcast made clear. He was concerned at how unprepared the world was for the new developments then being introduced. Then as now, discoveries and innovations were made and often introduced without consideration of their possible consequences. We are, perhaps, a little more circumspect these days, as a result of unpleasant experiences in the past—testing new drugs before they are put into use and preparing impact-assessments before carrying out developments—but it remains true that consideration of the future and its implications is an undeveloped field.

Necessary though they are, experts are not sufficient. As Benveniste (1973) argued,

> A dilemma of complex interdependent technological societies can be summarised by two opposing needs: 1) the need for technology, which implies increasing specialisation, interdependence, expertise and the funnelling of planning information through societal control systems that reduce the accessibility of decision makers; and 2) the need for individual and group self-expression and self-determination, which calls for higher levels of effective political participation.

We need experts, for without them most of the conveniences of our modern world would not exist, but the very fact that we may be considered an expert in one field means that we are a non-expert in most others. A nuclear physicist is unlikely to be an expert in financial planning and vice versa, but being an expert in one field makes us aware of the limitations of our expertise and perhaps sceptical about the expertise of others. We are less likely to be prepared to entrust our future to them. In our own field we are used to being respected and having our opinions taken seriously. In other areas of our lives we expect similar treatment. We resent being treated as idiots or pawns. We are used to asking questions. We want reasons and explanations, not orders. We want to be involved and consulted when issues we consider affect our interests arise. We are not prepared to let 'them' or the so-called experts decide for us. They have made too many mistakes in the past.

Without public involvement, the decisions of the experts can be nullified when people react unexpectedly or are not committed to the experts' programmes and take actions that nullify or undermine them. We need experts, but experts who are prepared to work with people rather than impose their own solutions on them, who can use their expertise to assist the processes of self-determination rather than hide behind technical complexity that excludes the non-expert. Many professions are facing these challenges. Their traditional mystique is no longer sufficient, and people will not do as they say just because they say it. They want to know why. Because I say so is not enough, they have to be convinced it is in their interests.

Being an expert in the future is not really possible in the traditional sense of expertise, because the future has yet to happen. There is no established body of knowledge that has to be mastered in order to become an expert in Futures. Instead, the expertise rests in the ability to deal with complex evolving issues that inherently entail considerable uncertainty. Much of that uncertainty arises from the human choices that influence the future. It is clear that Futures experts will need to be aware of the impact of such choices, but they should not make the choices for us. They can help in posing the choices and outlining the likely consequences of particular courses of action, but the outcomes concern us all and actions need to involve the whole population if they are to be effective.

They need to do so for two important reasons. First, we all have an interest in the future. It is where we will spend the rest of our lives. It is unlikely that we are going to be prepared for others to control it without any influence from us. Political theorists have argued for millennia about the best form of government, and democracy, literally people-power, has both its advocates and its critics. It is a messy and complicated process involving the expression of many differing interests and the working through of disputes, but as Winston

Churchill is said to have remarked, 'Democracy is the worst form of government . . . apart from all the rest.'

A democratic approach is also the most likely way to achieve a sustainable future. It is only with the support of the individuals whose actions are so crucial to the future of humanity and the planet that the necessary measures can be taken. Without such support the future will lack a crucial factor, a sustainable system of effective decision-making, because the disadvantaged will always have reason to undermine the system and its decisions. We have a long way to go; few current systems of government are truly democratic and many not at all, but involvement of people in their own future from an informed perspective is probably a necessary precondition for a sustainable future. The only other possibility seems to be a totally repressive benevolent dictatorship, which rigorously enforces sustainable policies. Unfortunately, though it may last for a long time it is unlikely to be sustainable in the long term itself and may even be self-defeating or contradictory in any event.

To be effective such a future must cope with the differences that divide humanity but make it so interesting. We need to develop systems of decision-making that can deal effectively with a multicultural and multi-ethnic world that, if it does not hang together, looks increasingly likely to be hung separately. The majority of people are still concerned with survival, unable to spare time or effort to think beyond their immediate needs. Those of us in a more fortunate position have a responsibility to do what we can to resolve these inequalities and to work towards a future that is more stable because everyone has a stake in it. Futures-thinking is not alone in this task but it can help us to explore the implications of different future situations in the search for solutions to some of the important issues of our time and others that will become more important in years to come. If we are to obtain the kind of future we want, more conscious and careful consideration of the future by all involved is vital.

Both history and the current sad state of the world clearly show that we have not yet obtained everyone's perfect world. Probably we never will, but if we are even going to attempt to move in that direction we need to imagine futures that are different from, and better than the past and the present. To do that effectively we need to develop our abilities to think constructively about the future, to imagine what has never been, and act to bring it about.

PART TWO
WAYS OF THINKING
ABOUT THE FUTURE

Introduction

When faced with the need to think about and deal with the future we often claim that we do not know how to do it. This is despite the fact that, as we have already seen, we do think about the future and routinely make decisions about it in everyday life, in business and in government, and have considerable experience of doing so. Most of this experience is informal and instinctive, we do not consciously 'engage future mode', and therefore do not realise that we are, in fact, so involved with the future. When we do make formal attempts to foresee the future we have varied success and it is the knowledge that we get it wrong from time to time, foreseeing futures that do not happen and failing to anticipate those that do, that can lead us to the conclusion that we are unable to do it. Then, both individually and collectively, we continue not only to try to foresee the future, but also to manage and create it in a range of circumstances and in a variety of ways.

One of the reasons we may believe that thinking about the future is difficult is that, in the Western perspective, we almost automatically think of the future as something that has yet to happen to us. That is indeed how most dictionaries define it. The implication of this is that we are locked in the present peering forward into the unknown future. We are like explorers entering unknown territory, discovering each part as we reach it. The past we know, since we have travelled through it and we have maps derived from historical observations, but the future is unexplored and uncharted. There are no maps, no one has been there; the best we can do is to peer out into the distance to try to discover what lies ahead. Occasionally we may get a better view, but usually the twists and turns of uncertainty ensure that only the immediate future can be seen, if that. Life is a journey of discovery into the unknown. Much formal forecasting takes this approach. It is even termed exploratory, attempting to look ahead to provide foreknowledge of what seems likely to happen before it does.

A number of assumptions about the future and our relationship to it underlie this exploratory approach. First, it is rooted in an image of time as linear and irreversible, passing at a steady pace from past to future. The present is the intervening period in which we exist, moving from the past towards, but never reaching, the future. To a Western mind this seems a perfectly logical approach that fits in with our normal perception of time, but it is not the only one. Indeed, since Einstein developed the Theory of Relativity this, essentially Newtonian, notion of time has been replaced in some areas of the quintessentially Western field of the natural sciences. Theories have been developed that see time as relative, circular, moving at different speeds, or even, in a black hole, coming to a halt. Intriguingly these theories reflect attitudes to time that are found in many non-Western cultures. They also relate to our own subjective experience. Time often appears to pass at different speeds, to drag when we are bored or fly past when we are enjoying ourselves. It may also appear cyclical, with day following night and the seasons rotating in a never-ending pattern.

Second, the exploratory approach implies that the future is *out there*, somewhere ahead of us. As Judge (1993) noted, metaphors are an important part of our approach to the understanding of reality and such images may help us examine some of the assumptions we sometimes make about the future. The metaphor of the explorer, travelling through unknown territory, suggests that the future already exists, like the land still to be discovered as we move towards it. If the future already exists, it is fixed. In moving into it we are either following a pre-ordained route or are restricted to choosing between already established alternative directions. We may choose to take one direction rather than another, but we cannot change the overall pattern of the future because it has already been fixed. Different personal futures may arise, as a result of our choices to take a particular route, but we can have no part in creating the terrain through which we are travelling. In this image the difficulties that we experience in foreseeing the future arise either from our inability to see far enough and clearly enough ahead, or, where choices are involved, to anticipate what they will be. Like the explorer we can usually see only a short distance ahead because of the nature of the terrain, the angle of the light and the limitations of our eyesight, although it is occasionally possible, from a particular vantage point, to see the way ahead set out before us.

Alternatively, the future may be regarded as yet to be created. There is nothing out there in the future in the form of a pre-ordained route or set of choices, but as we travel towards it, in the present, it is created. Like riding a wave into nothingness. Behind is the past, visible and known; in front the future, invisible and, in advance, unknowable. Dator (1993b) used the images of a surfer riding the wave in a turbulent sea and white-water rafters in the rapids of change without a paddle. Being able to see the past but not the future, he suggested, we face the rear of the boat while careering forward out of control. Forecasting in this environment would be little more than guesswork because we would have nothing to work on. The past is little use, except as a source of experience in surfing or rafting; all we can do is remain alert to the present and make decisions about our future as circumstances change. We need not be totally reactive to events, as may initially seem to be the case, because decisions we make now will affect our position in the future even if we cannot predict with any certainty exactly where we will be or what circumstances will accrue.

If, using a different analogy, we were to assume that our direction, like that of a supertanker steaming on the ocean, is largely determined by the momentum of our trajectory from the past, we will be carried forward in a constant direction with little room for manoeuvre. By steering on a particular heading we can gradually change our course even as the momentum carries us forward. This metaphor would suggest that by studying the past we can gain a fairly good impression of the future possibilities open to us, because in the short term at least, the possible changes are limited. If we understand the forces leading to our current course we should be able to project them and see the direction we are going and the extent to which we can alter it. As we can move further away from our existing track in the longer term only, relatively short-term forecasting is likely to be accurate, but the possibility of *determining* the future, particularly in the longer term, emerges.

Another view of the future as the unknown 'out there' sees it as completely random. Anything can happen. The present is only the coincidence of a multitude of events with no identifiable causes and no direction. We may impose a pattern on the past but it has no reality except in our imagination. From this perspective the future is equally random, and hence completely unpredictable and unknowable. The exploratory approach would have little value in this situation and it is doubtful whether we could effectively choose one future rather than another, because we could not predict what the effect of the choice would be.

Another feature of a present-centred perspective that concentrates on our attempting to foresee the future is its essentially passive approach. We may or may not be successful in foreseeing the future but there is little we can do about it. We may be presented with a number of choices as they appear to us, or we may be able to steer towards another heading in the long term, but we are not in a position effectively to create anything. Equally we may be locked in, just experiencing events as they happen to us, because they are either predetermined or completely unpredictable.

The examples in Chapter 1 suggest that this is not the only approach we take to the future. When we plan or decide to take particular actions we are not so much attempting to foresee the future as to manage or create it. As individuals we do this in everyday life, and governments and companies are probably more concerned with attempting to influence the future than simply forecast it. Rather than passively attempting to discover what the future might do to us we spend as much, if not more time trying to ensure that the future will be as we would like it to be, actively attempting to shape the future to our own image, to make it happen for us rather than just to us. That we do not always succeed does not stop us continuing to try—'Better luck next time'.

This more positive approach is based on the assumption that we can imagine things that have never happened and in our imagination place ourselves in the future, when what we are aiming for has been achieved. From that imagined position we then look back towards the present to work out what we need to do to get where we want to be. This is more like backcasting (a technique we shall meet later) than forecasting. Although we do not always realise it, it is an approach to the future that we often use. From this perspective, although we may be physically locked into the present our imagination allows us to move through time like an experienced time-traveller. We all do it, whether to the past as we remember past events in our lives or look for historical explanations of current situations, or to the future when we plan a holiday or speculate about the consequences of a policy or decision.

This normative approach is equally based on assumptions about our relationship to the future. It assumes, as did the exploratory approach, that the future has yet to happen, but that actions we take now can affect what will happen. The future cannot then be laid out in such a complete form as the exploratory approach might imply, because the element of choice increases the alternatives beyond one fixed future.

The two approaches can be linked. Our normative image of the future, the one we want to happen, has to be within the realms of the possible. There is no point in us imagining ourselves visiting Venus or becoming a brain surgeon next week if there is no means of our getting there or completing the necessary training in time. Equally, the very act of imagining and taking action to bring the image about can make things that seemed impossible, or that we would not have predicted, become realistic. We could decide to become a brain surgeon, go through the necessary lengthy training and in a number of years realise our ambition, or as President Kennedy did, we could set the goal of getting humans to the Moon by the end of the 1960s and take steps to achieve it. It is a two-way process of establishing an achievable desired future and working out how we can get there from where we are. Both may have to be adapted as we realise either that our aim in its original form is not possible or that our earlier predictions were too limited to envisage possible futures that we could achieve after all, if we tried. Once again we use forecasts, either implicitly or explicitly, to help us identify, evaluate and plan possible future situations that we either wish to encourage or act to avoid.

These two approaches suggest a method of classifying ways of thinking about the future (Table 5). Like any classification this one is not without its limitations, but it attempts to provide a broad view of the methods available for dealing with the future. Many of the methods included are not exclusive to Futures Studies but are in common use in business management and government. They are included because they are ways in which we deal with the future and therefore emphasise our experience of doing so, and because in some cases a Futures perspective may offer new insight into their application. Similarly, there are other methods that have not been included.

The classification attempts to arrange Futures methods on a continuum between those that are concerned with foreseeing the future and those that aim to help us actively create the future. In between are those which are concerned with the management of change as it arises en route to the future; useful in situations where it is difficult either to foresee the future or plan a route to a predetermined goal with any certainty. Stacey (1992) suggested that the business environment is often of this kind; uncertainty, particularly about the future, makes it impossible to predict either the future situation or the effect of particular actions on it. It becomes necessary in these circumstances to manage in the present without any clear idea of where we are going, or even, according to Stacey, how we arrived where we are.

Individual techniques often bridge a range of methods and even approaches, and depending upon the circumstances and the interpretation given could be located in a number of places on the continuum. No claims to perfection are made for the classification; it is just one way of examining the methods available that seems to offer some benefits. These methods are explained in more detail in chapters 4 and 5.

Table 5. Futures methods and techniques

Approach	Concept	Technique
Foreseeing	Prediction	• Prophecy • Astrology • Precognition
	Extrapolation	• Time series/trend-forecasting • S-curve • Precursor analysis • Cycles
	Analytical forecasting	• Causal models
	Speculation	• Science fiction and speculative writing
	Judgemental forecasting	• Delphi • Cross-impact • Content-analysis
Managing	Management	• Scenarios • Issues-management • Scanning/environmental scanning • Impact-Assessment • Cost–benefit analysis • Risk-Assessment • Role-play
Creating	Policy-making	• Planning • Strategy-formation • Problem-solving • Decision-making
	Imaging	• Brainstorming/brainwriting • Group Support Systems • Futures workshops • Visioning • Incasting • Backcasting • Relevance tree
	Innovation	• Creative imagery • Action • Politics

CHAPTER FOUR
FORESEEING THE FUTURE

To 'foresee' is defined as to 'see or be aware of beforehand' (Tulloch 1993). Synonyms include 'presage', 'envisage', 'predict', and 'prophesy'. All imply knowledge before the event, but generally do not suggest any influence over it. Such methods, then, are generally employed in the belief that they will provide advance information about a future over which we may have little or no influence; that we may gain foreknowledge about what is going to happen and prepare for it, but not change it.

4.1. PREDICTION

Masini (1993), quoting Jantsch, defined prediction as, 'a non-probabilistic statement on an absolute confidence level about the future', that is, an exact, categorical statement that something will happen: 'Manchester United will win the FA Cup.' There is no room for doubt, alternatives or probabilities. It *will* happen. In the natural sciences the ability to make predictions of this kind about future events is often interpreted as proof of scientific understanding. The ability to predict accurately what is going to happen is evidence that we possess understanding of the system that produces those effects (Johnston 1978). As such, prediction is the mirror image of explanation. Given full knowledge of the system and the ability to explain the causes of an event through physical laws, it is held that in similar circumstances, where those laws apply, the result will always be the same. It is possible therefore to predict future events with confidence so long as the same circumstances exist. For example, water heated under the appropriate similar conditions will always boil at 100° Celsius. Where variations from this are observed it is because the conditions, such as atmospheric pressure, are not the same. The importance of having the same conditions cannot be overemphasised. Any variation from them, however small, can affect the result, leading to a different outcome. The necessary conditions for the prediction to be fulfilled are much the same as assumptions made in other areas of forecasting. As long as they hold the forecast has a high probability of accuracy; if they do not hold the probability is reduced.

In astronomy our knowledge of the universe and its workings enables us to predict accurately the position of stars many years ahead and also to know where they were at any point in the past. In this sense, as Einstein observed, 'the distinction between past, present and future is only an illusion' (Coveney and Highfield 1990). The universe is a deterministic system, 'where time has no direction and the past and future are preordained'.

Such conclusions have led to the opinion that there is a distinction between the natural and human sciences, since such accurate prediction is seldom possible in the latter. For example, despite the considerable effort devoted to the development of complex economic models, which can be calibrated to fit past economic events, their success in producing accurate forecasts, even over a relatively short time span, is limited. Further examination, however, suggests that the difference may not be as great as is sometimes supposed. Although there are instances in the natural sciences where laws established from empirical observation enable accurate predictions to be made, as in astronomy, there are also much less predictable situations. Weather-forecasting is one. We know a great deal about weather systems and can make more accurate forecasts than we used to, but, particularly in the UK, where the weather is renowned for its variability, forecasting remains notoriously difficult. This is so because it is a requirement of accurate prediction in the natural sciences that precise knowledge of the system concerned and of the initial conditions is available. It is also necessary for there to be an absence of outside or random influences that may affect the system. Without these conditions predictability breaks down. Such conditions are unusual in social systems and often not present in the natural world either. We know that under certain conditions snow will fall because known physical laws can be applied, but it is more difficult, given the level of information that we have about particular weather systems, to predict the occurrence of the conditions themselves or the rate at which they will develop. Hence the introduction of probabilities and phrases such as 'during the afternoon', rather than 'at three o'clock' into the weather forecast. These indicate the difficulty of making exact predictions.

That does not prevent us making them. A considerable industry revolves around our willingness to gamble on predictions of sporting events and other happenings. The predicted results of forthcoming matches and tips identifying predicted winners of horse races are common features of the sports pages of most newspapers. The predictions are usually based on an analysis of form, how that team or horse has been performing lately, and an assessment, or judgement, of future performance based on it. Detailed data bases and sophisticated analytical systems may be used in reaching the conclusions, but they do not guarantee success.

Prediction has a long history. Two forms which have been in existence since early historical times are prophecy and astrology, and both retain a following today. More recently there has also been a growing interest in another form, precognition.

4.1.1. Prophecy

The Oracle at Delphi, the Old Testament prophets, Nostradamus and Mother Shipton are among the most well-known historical prophets. Similar prophecies are still made; in 1994, for example, advertisements appeared in UK newspapers prophesying catastrophe following the collision of a comet with Jupiter. The oracles and Old Testament prophets usually claimed revelation from the gods or God as the source of their inspiration. In the cultural circumstances of the time, this must have given their prophecies credibility in the eyes of the public and the many powerful people who consulted them. An element of self-fulfilment may have been present if they then acted in ways that increased the chances of the prophecies coming true, further enhancing the reputation of the oracle. Some examples of more recent prophecies were cited by Gattey (1989), including predictions of the rise of Hitler, the case of an adviser to Stalin who predicted the course of events in Second World War, and the Aberfan disaster in 1966, in which a coal mine's slag heap engulfed a school in the Welsh village, killing 144 people.

Whether or not the provision of correct prophecies is greater than would occur by chance is the subject of continuing debate, but Ellis (1973) noted that the ambiguity of the predictions of the Delphic Oracle could cover a range of eventualities, and that at least one well-known prophet of the second century AD was an accomplished trickster. Examples can be quoted to 'prove' the issue either way, and conclusions are probably more a matter of belief than absolute proof.

Considerable interest has been shown in the prophecies of the sixteenth-century prophet Nostradamus (see for example Hewitt and Lorie 1991). It is not clear how he derived his prophecies, which are contained in quatrains, short verses of four lines, but much effort has been given to their interpretation. The prophecies cover 7,000 years (Hewitt and Lorie 1991) or the period 1555 to 3797 (Ellis 1973). It is claimed that several have been proven by events over the last 400 years, such as the reigns of Elizabeth I in England and Napoleon in France, and more recently the death of Pope John Paul I and Mikhail Gorbachev's leadership of the Soviet Union. Other prophecies are said to predict imminent happenings. As the work of Hewitt and Lorie makes clear, the interpretation of the quatrains via a complex system of modernising the language, anagrams, rearrangement of word order, inference and dating, is crucial. Several questions can be raised about the way it is carried out. Prophecies for the period 1991–4 show some errors, such as the coronation of Prince Charles, the re-election of George Bush and a major earthquake in California in May 1993. There was an earthquake in early 1994—a false prediction, or a timing error? Another near miss was the consecration of the first women priests in the Church of England, which was prophesied for 1995, but actually occurred in March 1994.

Is it all nonsense? Certainly most scientists, academics and futurists think so, but there are people who take the prophecies of Nostradamus and others much more seriously. Clearly there is no known mechanism by which such prophecies could be made, although various methods of prophecy are claimed by those who believe in psychic powers. Gibson and Gibson (1974), for example, described several forms of divination, including the I Ching, tasseomancy (reading tea-leaves), the Tarot, playing cards and palm-reading. There is continuing interest in these ideas despite the lack of scientific proof to support them. To accept them would appear to imply a predetermined future that is revealed in some way to particular individuals, but that most of us do not possess the ability to comprehend.

4.1.2. Astrology

Another area that attracts much scepticism but also has a considerable following is astrology. It has been reported that 55 per cent of Americans believe in astrology (Radford 1994a) and many popular newspapers and magazines regularly publish horoscopes. Astrologers believe that the position of the stars at the moment of a person's birth has an important influence over their life and can be used to identify tendencies rather than make exact predictions of events (Ellis 1973). In a book examining the role of astrology in management, Alexander (1992) suggested that 'the natal chart is like a blueprint for the construction of the "self"—how we go about building our "self" is, for better or worse, up to us'. Radford (1994b) reported research that reveals that soccer players in The Netherlands and England are twice as likely to have been born between August and November than at any other time of the year. Is this evidence of astrological influence, or is it explained by the division of school groups, which means that those born in this period are the eldest, and probably the biggest, in their group, and therefore able to dominate in such sports?

Are we influenced by the cosmos? In some aspects of our lives we are. Generally we are active during the day, when the sun is in the sky, and sleep at night when it is not. Our physiology is actually adapted to this diurnal cycle of light and dark. Our lives are also affected by the seasons, around which we organise many of our activities. If this is the case, why is it not possible for other astronomical happenings to influence us? In the absence of proof to the contrary it is possible, but it is a further unproven step to ascribe causality, to show that our actions can be influenced and predicted from our personal horoscope.

The claims of astrology are sufficiently real to some—including, apparently, former President Reagan (Alexander 1992)—to convince them of its value. To others they are pure rubbish. Ellis (1973) concluded that the case is unproven; no conclusive scientific evidence can be produced to prove that astrology can predict events, but neither can some people's belief in it and examples of claimed 'successful' predictions be denied or proven false.

4.1.3. Precognition

How many times have you woken up just before the alarm rings, or thought about contacting a friend just before they phone you? Do such events have any significance, or are they just chance? Perhaps we only take note of them because of the coincidence of thought and event, while we forget the other cases where there was no such connection.

Precognition, '(supposed) foreknowledge, especially of a supernatural kind' (Tulloch 1993), or 'the mind crossing time' (Pedler 1981), requires some means by which such knowledge can be obtained. Several examples of dreams appearing to foretell future events, including air crashes, the Aberfan disaster and Abraham Lincoln's assassination, were quoted by Zohar (1983). Dreams are seen as a way for the mind to become disconnected from 'normal' reality as we experience it from day to day, and to tune into a wider reality, rather like Einstein's notion of time in which past, present and future all exist. Zohar also gave examples of waking precognitive experiences, which included predictive stories, trances and auditory examples. She suggests two interpretations for such occurrences. First, that the examples do foretell an actual event, either one that has already occurred, but not yet been experienced by us, or one that is waiting to occur. Both imply predetermination, either in the sense that all events that will ever occur have already happened—Einstein again—or that the fixed future is gradually being revealed as we move through time. Second, that they are a 'future perception of a possible future event' over which we may have some influence. This would account for those situations in which people have foreseen events and taken action to avoid being involved: for example, the case of a woman who dreamed of an air crash and decided not to go on the trip on which many of her friends and neighbours were killed. Whether this could be extended to cases where the event itself has been forestalled is not clear, because such situations would effectively invalidate the precognition.

In this latter situation the result may not be noticeably different from our imagining possible futures and then acting in order to bring them about or prevent them from occurring. If this was the case it might imply the existence of a means by which on particular occasions alternative futures become apparent to a few, although they normally remain hidden from the majority. Unlikely though this may seem, some of the theories of modern physics would not necessarily prohibit such a possibility.

4.2. EXTRAPOLATION

Extrapolation is probably the most commonly used and easily understood form of forecasting. It is based on the assumption that once a pattern has been identified in the past it can be extended, or extrapolated, into the future to give a picture of what is likely to happen. The method does not attempt to provide an explanation of the pattern observed in the past but assumes that the factors that brought it about will continue to operate and have the same effect for the period of the forecast. The future will, it is assumed, be a continuation of the past. For this reason it is sometimes called a 'naive' or 'black-box' approach.

4.2.1. Time Series

The basis of extrapolative forecasting is the time series. Information, usually in the form of quantitative data, is collected for a period of time and then analysed to determine whether it exhibits any recognisable patterns. Makridakis and Wheelwright (1989) suggested four different patterns that might be identified:

- *horizontal*, where there may be small variations up and down, but the general pattern is stable, without any identifiable direction of change;

- *seasonal*, where there is a regular variation related to different seasons of the year, days of the week, or times of the day, e.g. traffic flow or retail sales;
- *cyclical*, where regular variations over a longer period are observed, as in the business cycle or the long-wave theory of economic activity first identified by Kondratiev (1935); and
- *trend*, where 'a pattern of general increase or decrease in the value of a variable over time' can be seen.

Firth (1977) added

- *fluctuating or random*, where again there is no recognisable pattern of change.

Some time series may exhibit a combination of patterns. Within an overall increasing trend, traffic growth, for example, may show marked seasonal variations.

4.2.2. Making a Time-Series Forecast

Step 1. Data collection

The first step in preparing a time-series forecast is to collect information over a period of time. There is no hard and fast rule about how long a period the data should cover, but it is unlikely that two or three readings on their own, or very intermittent data will be sufficient to establish a clear trend. For example, comparisons are often made between censuses, which are taken every ten years, to identify the trends in population in a given area over that period. The conclusion may be reasonable but, as Fig. 6 shows, the intervening years could hide a variety of patterns. Extrapolating those would give very different forecasts.

It would also be unwise to extrapolate a pattern over a period longer than the period of observation. Again, there is no absolute requirement, but a useful rule of thumb is to have past data for a period at least twice the length of time to be forecast. Other problems apply to time-series data, such as the need to ensure comparability and consistency. If these are lacking the pattern which emerges will be invalid. Table 6 gives a data set that would normally be considered suitable.

Table 6. Live births in the UK 1951–1990 ('000s)

1951	797	1971	902
1952	793	1972	834
1953	804	1973	780
1954	795	1974	737
1955	789	1975	698
1956	825	1976	676
1957	851	1977	657
1958	871	1978	687
1959	879	1979	735
1960	918	1980	754
1961	944	1981	731
1962	976	1982	719
1963	990	1983	721
1964	1015	1984	730
1965	997	1985	751
1966	980	1986	755
1967	962	1987	776
1968	947	1988	788
1969	920	1989	777
1970	904	1990	799

Source: *Annual Abstract of Statistics*, various years.

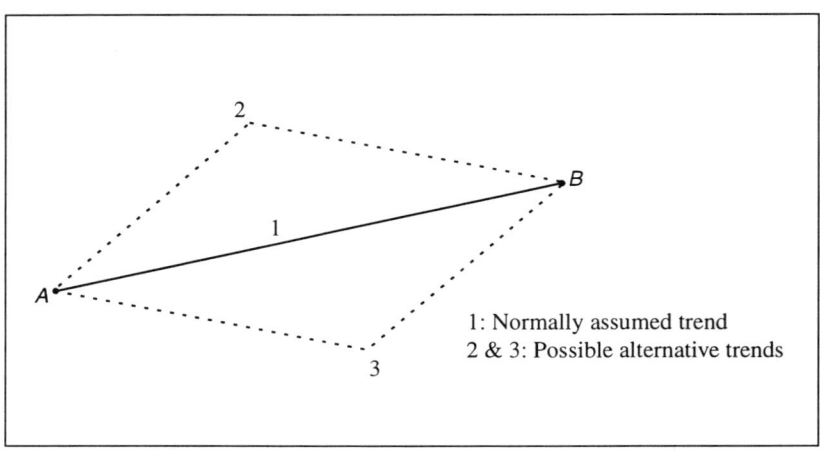

Fig. 6. Possible trends between two points

Step 2. Plot the data

Having collected the data the next step is to plot it (Fig. 7). This provides a picture of the past and helps identify any pattern within the time series. It can be done manually, but is more easily achieved using a spreadsheet or statistical package, of which there are many available.

Step 3. Identify the pattern

Pattern-recognition has its own difficulties. Apart from questions about the influence of the attitudinal perspective of the observer on the pattern observed, it is not always a simple matter to identify a pattern in data. Consider Fig. 7, which depicts a typical time series. Depending upon our opinion about which part of the data provides the best indication of any pattern, and when we observe the time series, we could reach very different conclusions.

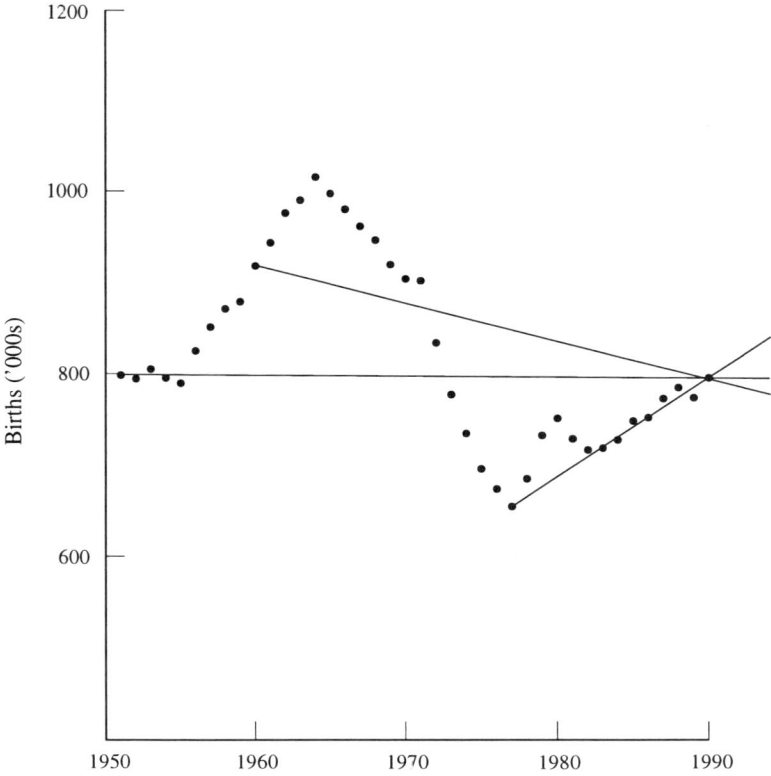

Fig. 7. Plot of live births in the UK 1951–1990

Taking the whole of the data available suggests that there is no recognisable single trend, but that the level varies around the horizontal (1). If we were to assume that the more recent data give a better indication of the way things are likely to change in the future we might either consider the thirty years from 1960 and identify a slightly declining trend (2), or seeing an up turn since the mid-1970s regard this as an indication of a new trend (3). Our choice might be influenced by what we wanted to see. Those who are concerned about the growth of world population would probably be worried by the apparent increase in births, while those who see the problem of the ageing of the population as a major concern would welcome it. Similarly, if this was a graph of unemployment it is likely that the government would concentrate on the medium term as evidence of a reduction in unemployment, while its critics would emphasise the most recent figures, which could suggest an increase.

The example also emphasises the value of collecting data over a longer time period. If all we had available were the figures for the last ten years we would be likely to reach a very different conclusion than if we had the last twenty, the last thirty, or the whole of the data. Since it is the pattern we identify that is extrapolated to create the forecast, the identification of that pattern is critical. The pattern we draw out from the data effectively determines the forecast, and inaccuracies can often be traced back to the identification of what was later revealed to be a misleading pattern. Having more data does not guarantee a more accurate forecast—the most recent readings may indicate a new trend that will continue, or a short-term variation—but it does make the judgement involved in selecting the trend to be forecast more apparent and should increase our caution in leaping to 'obvious' conclusions, or relying on apparently 'scientific' methods when they are not appropriate to the circumstances.

So far we have only considered the identification of patterns by eye from a graph. In some circumstances this can be a useful quick guide but there are a wide range of more sophisticated statistical methods available. Their general intention is to 'smooth' the data by eliminating the most significant variations in it to produce a recognisable pattern in the underlying trend.

One of the simplest is the *moving average*. The data is divided into a series of small blocks of, for example, three or five readings. The average for the first block is calculated and plotted. The second block is obtained by dropping the first reading from the group and replacing it with the next—in the case of a three-period moving average, the fourth reading—in order to calculate the next point in the moving average. This can be expressed mathematically as

$$\frac{Y_1 + Y_2 + Y_3}{3}, \quad \frac{Y_2 + Y_3 + Y_4}{3} \quad \text{to} \quad \frac{Y_{n-2} + Y_{n-1} + Y_n}{3}$$

where the data set is represented by Y and the last number in the set by n. In the case of the live births in the UK from 1970–90, the three- and five-year moving averages are shown in Table 7.

Working progressively through the data in this way gives a series of averages that move through the data set. This has the effect of reducing the extremes of the raw data and producing, when the points of the moving average are linked up, a smoother curve. The larger the groups used the smoother the curve tends to become, but the fewer the points obtained, because not so many large blocks can be created from the data as small ones. The result may be a more easily recognised pattern. If it is considered that the more recent data should be given more importance the averages can be statistically weighted to increase their value in the calculation. In worked examples both Makridakis and Wheelwright (1989) and Firth (1977) used the average of each group of readings as the forecast for the next reading, the average of the first three being

Table 7. Three- and five-year moving averages for the UK birth data

Date	Number of of births	3-year moving average	5-year moving average
1970	904	—	—
1971	902	880	—
1972	834	839	831
1973	780	784	790
1974	737	738	745
1975	698	704	710
1976	676	677	691
1977	657	673	691
1978	687	693	702
1979	735	725	713
1980	754	740	725
1981	731	735	732
1982	719	724	731
1983	721	723	730
1984	730	734	735
1985	751	745	747
1986	755	760	760
1987	776	773	769
1988	788	780	779
1989	777	788	—
1990	799	—	—

plotted at point four, and so on. This has the advantage of giving a one-point forecast beyond the latest available reading but it is statistically questionable. It is more usual to consider the average of each group of data points as referring to the mid-point of the group rather than to a time outside the group altogether. Using this convention, the line of moving-average points will end some distance before the last-available actual reading and can only approach the date of the last reading, let alone provide a forecast, if extrapolated.

More credibility is usually attached to more mathematically sophisticated methods that provide a curve that more closely fits the data in the statistical sense. The *line of best fit* is the line that statistically most closely follows the actual data. It can be obtained by minimising the divergence between the recorded data points and the statistically calculated line. There are a wide range of techniques of varying sophistication available for the smoothing of data. Two of the most common are exponential smoothing and linear regression.

Exponential smoothing is a technique that reduces the extremes in the data, making it easier to identify any underlying pattern. Using the recorded data it produces a series of new points that creates a flatter line. Unlike the moving average, which treats all the data points equally, exponential smoothing gives more weight to the more recent information. This is achieved by calculating each new point from a combination of the previous actual and smoothed values so that the next calculated value is equal to the current calculated, or smoothed, value plus or minus the difference between the current actual and calculated values. The two current values can be given different weights by inserting a smoothing factor into the calculation. Expressed mathematically:

$$F_{t+1} = F_t + a(X_t - F_t)$$

where F_{t+1} is the next calculated value, F_t is the current calculated value, a is the smoothing factor used to vary the weight given to the actual and calculated values, and X_t is the current actual value.

The lower the value given to the smoothing factor, a, the greater the smoothing that results, because this gives more weight to the calculated values than the observed ones. A higher value for a has the opposite effect. It is a matter of judgement in each case as to which value gives the best indication of the underlying pattern. Too much smoothing may remove the pattern as well as the variations from it, whereas too little may leave too much variation for the pattern to emerge. Table 8 gives an example based on the live births in the UK between 1970 and 1990. (See Makridakis and Wheelwright (1989) for guidance in the use of the technique.)

With hindsight we can see that in this example the higher smoothing factor would have given closer forecasts in more than half of the years listed, but apart from the years 1972–7 there is no extended period when relying on one

Table 8. Exponential smoothing for the UK birth data

Date	Number of births	Exponential Smoothing		
		$a = 0.1$	$a = 0.5$	$a = 0.9$
1970	904	—	—	—
1971	902	904	904	904
1972	834	904	903	902
1973	780	897	868	826
1974	737	885	824	785
1975	698	870	780	742
1976	676	853	739	702
1977	657	835	707	679
1978	687	817	682	659
1979	735	804	685	684
1980	754	797	710	730
1981	731	793	732	752
1982	719	787	731	733
1983	721	780	725	720
1984	730	774	723	721
1985	751	770	727	729
1986	755	768	739	749
1987	776	767	747	754
1988	788	768	762	774
1989	777	770	775	787
1990	799	771	776	779
1991	—	774	788	797

value rather than another would have guaranteed greater accuracy. The number of recorded births in 1991, incidentally, was 793.

Linear regression approaches the problem from a different direction. Rather than attempting to smooth the curve of the actual data points, as the moving average and exponential smoothing techniques do, it produces a straight line which statistically fits the data with the minimum of divergence between the line and the actual readings. One of the most frequently used techniques is the *method of least squares*, which minimises the square of the distance between the line of best fit and the actual data points. It is found using the equation:

$$y = a + bx$$

where y is the value of the matter under consideration, x is the year, a the point at which the line of best fit crosses the y-axis, and b the slope of the line. The necessary points can be calculated using the following formulae:

$$b = \frac{n\sum xy - \sum x \sum y}{n\sum x^2 - (\sum x)^2}$$

and

$$a = \frac{\sum y}{n} - \frac{b\sum x}{n}$$

where n is the number of readings in the data.

The two parts of Fig. 8 illustrate linear regression using the live births data. One limitation of the method is immediately apparent: it only works well where there is a clear linear trend. The data from 1970 to 1990 is not linear, neither is the extended data from 1950, but that from 1977 to 1990 is much

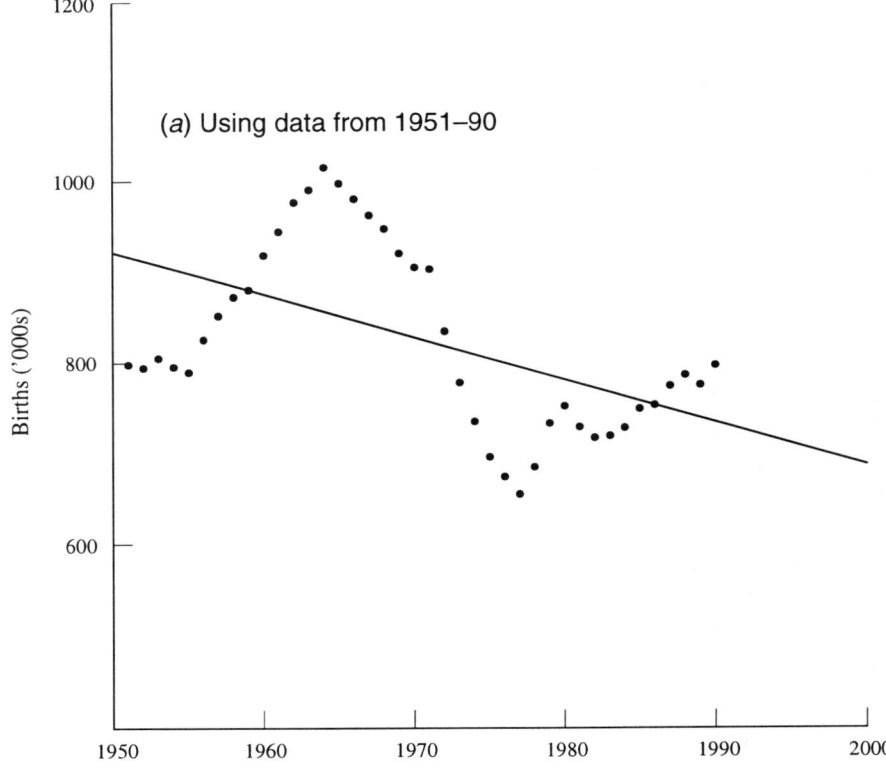

Fig. 8. Linear regression by the method of least squares

more linear. Statistically the method works better over this shorter period, but whether it produces an accurate forecast is an open question.

If the data is not linear there are other statistical methods that can be used to describe it and identify patterns. Simple calculations can be carried out manually, though there are computer packages available to calculate these and much more complex methods. They are considered in much greater detail in most statistical textbooks and in a forecasting context by Makridakis and Wheelwright (1989), Firth (1977), Lewis (1982) and Martino (1993), among others.

The techniques described above work best where there is a clear trend in the data. Where other patterns such as seasonality or random variation are present it is necessary to remove them from the data before such techniques can be used. Retail sales and unemployment data, for example, are notoriously seasonal, peaking at certain times of year and falling at others. To establish the longer-term trend in them it is necessary to *deseasonalise* them.

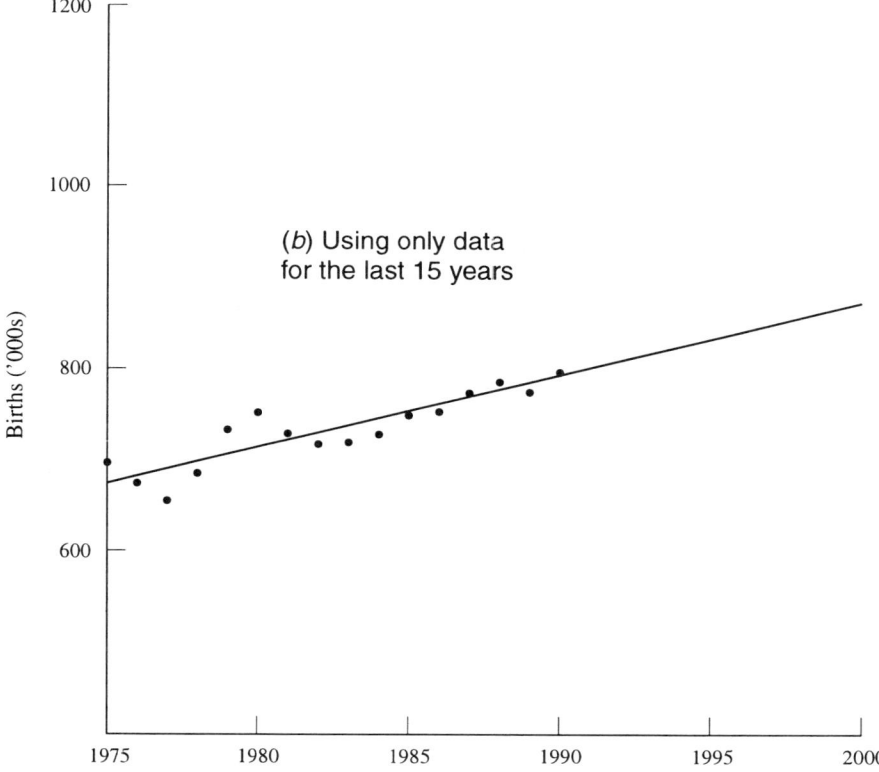

Fig. 8. (*cont.*)

This can be achieved by calculating the average for each season or month over the period of years for which information is available and then expressing each actual reading as a percentage, or index out of one hundred, of that average. This has the effect of producing a smoother curve with the seasonal variations removed. At the forecasting stage the factors that have been removed by this decomposition have to be built back in.

The extensive discussion by Makridakis and Wheelwright of the various statistical methods of trend-identification confirms the view that establishing the pattern in the data is probably the most crucial part of extrapolative forecasting, because it is the pattern that is extrapolated.

Step 4. Project the Trend

Depending upon the methods used to describe the trend, the projection may be based on advanced statistical techniques or simple observation. Although the former are statistically more accurate in describing the trend in the historic data, they may not offer a better forecast if the underlying assumption of extrapolative forecasting, that the pattern or trend will continue, does not hold. It will be a matter of judgement in each case whether the increased sophistication obtained from the more complex methods is worthwhile. As Yeomans (1968) points out, 'There is no guarantee the relationship will continue', for

> A trend is a trend is a trend,
> But where and when will it bend,
> Will it shoot to the sky,
> Turn over and die,
> Or asymptote off to the end.
>
> Twiss (1981)

(An asymptote is defined as 'a line that continually approaches a given curve but does not meet it' Tulloch 1993.) This emphasises the difference between fitting a line to historic data, which can be done mathematically, and forecasting, where there is no data until it is generated by the forecast on the assumption that past patterns will continue. That, of course, is the point of the exercise—the generation of data about the future for which none is yet available. But that is 'imaginary', whereas past data is 'real'.

Extrapolation is a much used method of forecasting. Its main advantages are that it is relatively simple and easily understood. Depending upon the methods used it can be easily carried out by hand or using readily available computer packages. Its disadvantages are that, although its limitations are usually understood by the forecasters themselves, they are less likely to be considered by the users of the forecasts, who welcome the apparent clarity and certainty of the results without appreciating the limitations. The apparent accuracy of such forecasts is comforting, but it is also spurious, because it is invented rather than real information. We may well prefer to approach the future with knowledge of what is going to happen, but if that knowledge is wrong, because it has no basis in reality, we may be worse off than if we accepted the uncertainty. Extrapolative methods of forecasting are useful, they should not be dismissed, but it is important to remember that they can only provide a picture of the future if—and that is a big if—it is a continuation of the past. As such they are often used to provide a base forecast on the assumption that past trends will continue. Other forecasts can then be produced by varying that assumption.

4.2.3. Non-quantitative Trends

Most applications of extrapolation tend to be based on quantitative data and its projection to obtain quantitative estimates of future levels of the issue of concern, but an essentially similar process may be used to examine and project qualitative trends for which numerical data are not available. It might also be argued that most quantitative data is only a measure of some quality in any event: retail sales, for example, are used as an indication of the health of the economy and temperature a measure of warmth.

Kahn (1978), for example, identified a Long-term Multifold Trend made up of sixteen sub-trends, 'which together seem to us to represent the most basic tendencies in the evolution of Western culture', on which he based his projections for the next twenty years. Subsequently Naisbitt (1984), Naisbitt and Aburdene (1990) and Popcorn (1992) each identified trends occurring in, mainly American, society and proposed these as themes likely to continue into the future.

The basis of Naisbitt's work is *content analysis*, the study of trends through the issues reported in local newspapers and the media. This, he argues, yields a good indication of the direction of events and the development of issues. From this trends can be identified and projected into the future. Popcorn used a similar approach, scanning over 300 newspapers and magazines, monitoring the top twenty television shows, films, books and music and monitoring new products. She termed this 'brailling the culture'. Coates *et al.* (1986) described a similar technique, which they call *media analysis*. It involves the analysis of the column inches in newspapers and the length of time on television news reports devoted to particular topics. Over time this provides a measure of the changing significance of issues and can be used to identify emergent concerns.

Slaughter (1993) criticised many of these attempts to identify Megatrends (as Naisbitt calls them) as superficial and lacking in substance. He pointed out that the identification of trends is subjective, being influenced by the stance of the observer, which itself is a product of several influences, including personal background, institutional orientation, culture and ideological stance. All these examples above are from a Western, Anglo-Saxon, market-orientated perspective. They identify and project trends, therefore, that are relevant and sympathetic to that perspective. There are other perspectives, but they seldom receive similar publicity.

As with the use of quantitative trends, it is not only the projection of the trend that is critical, but the selection of the information and the identification of the trends from which the projections are made. It is the assumptions within the process that have a determining impact upon the forecasts produced. If they are inaccurate or biased, then the forecast is unlikely to be accurate. In making such forecasts, quantitative or qualitative, it is important to examine carefully the assumptions made at all stages of the process—collecting information, identifying the trend, projecting the trend and interpreting its significance. Similar care needs to be taken in using the forecasts prepared by others; they should not be taken at face value but critically examined to establish the assumptions on which they are based. If these are not apparent, as is often the case, treat them with care, you do not know where they have been!

4.2.4. Non-linear Trends

Trends are not always linear, as we have assumed so far. Linear trends increase or decrease by a constant amount for each unit of time. This pattern is, in fact, quite unusual. Trends are much more often measured in percentage terms, such as a growth of 2 per cent or a decline of 5 per cent. Constant percentage change means that the amount of change varies, increasing in a growing trend and decreasing in a declining trend. For example, if we have a constant 10 per cent growth per year from a starting point of 100, the next year the value would be 110, but the one after is 121, because 10 per cent of 110 is 11. This is exponential growth, which we met earlier when discussing the work of Meadows *et al.* (1972, 1992) on global population growth and other issues. When plotted on ordinary graph paper, exponential growth or decline appears as a curve. However, by using a logarithmic scale on the vertical axis it can be converted into a straight line. Transforming the data in this way makes it possible to use the techniques already discussed to identify the pattern and project it.

As Meadows *et al.* (1972) argued, exponential trends are unlikely to be able to continue for ever, but will eventually approach a limit and begin to slow down. This can be depicted in terms of the growth curve often observed in nature. Initially growth is fairly slow because it is starting from a low level, but beyond a certain point the continued growth explodes until it reaches another point at which it begins to decrease and tail off towards its limit. Animals, plants and other natural phenomena tend to follow this pattern. This is represented by the *growth* or *S-curve* shown in Fig. 9, which grows exponentially for a time but then slows as it approaches its natural limit.

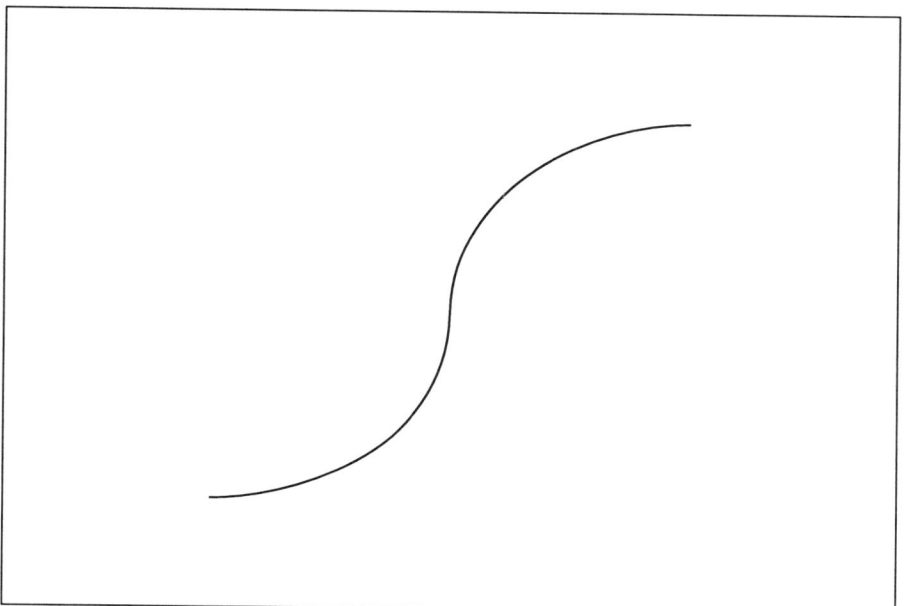

Fig. 9. The S-curve

The pattern can also be found in human affairs such as markets and the population of cities. For example, sales of colour television sets grew at an exponential rate when they were first introduced into the UK, but when most households had replaced their old black-and-white sets with colour the sales began to tail off. Although there was initially a large potential market in the replacement of black-and-white sets, once this had been achieved there were a smaller number of continuing sales to be made to new households and for second and replacement sets. Given this eventuality the pattern of sales would follow a different pattern in which it built up to a peak and then fell away to a lower, steadier level. In other circumstances it might even tail away to nothing as the market became saturated or other products became available. There is some evidence to suggest that the producers did not appreciate this pattern at the time and invested in the belief that exponential growth would continue (Twiss 1981).

In forecasting and planning in a situation where an S-curve is involved, it is critical to know where on the curve we are. Initially we may expect a fairly slow growth, but there will then be a period of rapid expansion followed by a decline to a steadier but continuing level, unless further developments occur to bring about another growth spurt—such as personal computers, which use essentially the same technology as televisions for computer screens. Unfortunately, it is not always easy to establish where on the curve we are, or even if the S-curve offers a good guide to the future. Fig. 10 shows how it is possible to obtain a variety of forecasts from an S-curve depending where on the curve we believe we are and how it will develop from that point on.

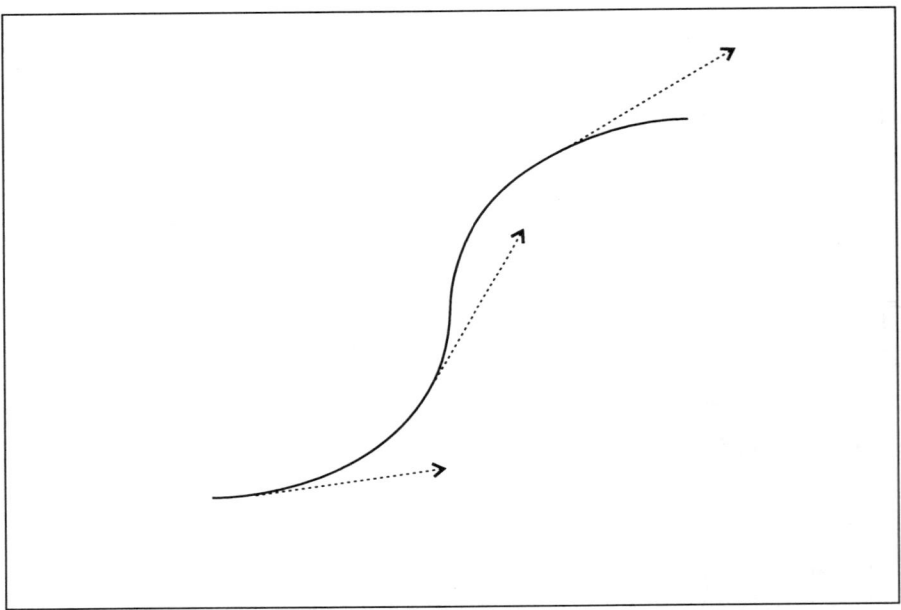

Fig. 10. Varied forecasts from an S-curve

An interesting example of data which tends to follow the S-curve pattern is found in the availability of selected durable goods in households in the UK. The information, collected for the General Household Survey, is published as percentages of all households having the selected goods; it therefore has a limit in each case of 100. As new products become available they are added to the list and as others reach saturation, where the majority of households have them, they are omitted. As Fig. 11 shows, all the selected goods tend to follow some form of S-curve. Closer inspection reveals that different products have penetrated the market at significantly different rates. Video players, which were not included until 1983, have been taken up very quickly, while dishwashers, which have been included for much longer, have not. To examine the usefulness of this information in predicting markets for the products listed, it would first be necessary to relate it to the pattern of actual sales. If they follow the expected pattern in a particular market there is some evidence to work on.

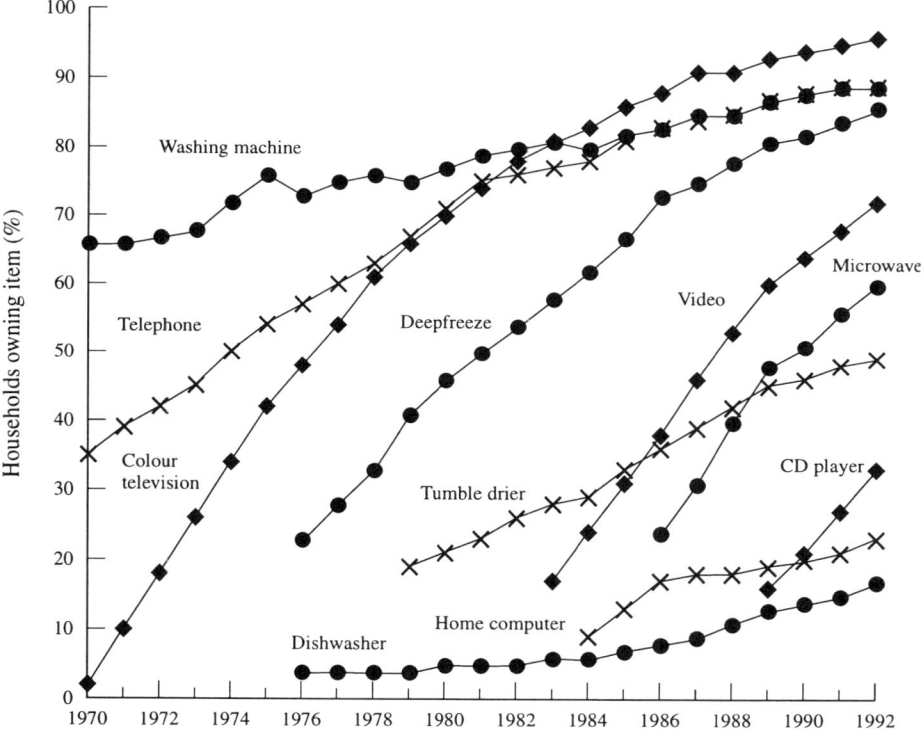

Fig. 11. Availability of selected household goods

Stewart (1989, 1991) maintained that the S-curve can provide a very useful guide to the future both in the substitution of one technology by another, as in the case of colour television, and in the adoption of new technologies, as with the General Household Survey. Using a technique developed by Fisher and Pry, which he termed the *Growth–Ungrowth curve*, he showed that the S-curve has described the pattern of growth in many situations in the USA. His examples include the adoption of cars and their substitution for horse-drawn carriages between 1900 and 1925, substitution of air travel for rail, substitution of manmade for natural fibres and the growing importance of the service industries in the economy. He asserted that it would have been possible to forecast the level of market penetration by the automobile in 1925 from information that was available in 1906. Writing at a time when the latest sales data for compact discs gave them 20 per cent of the market in 1986, he predicted almost total substitution for LP records by 1990, which was not far out.

His approach is based on the ratio between the proportion of the market which has already switched to or purchased a new product and the proportion still to do so. Mathematically this can be expressed as:

$$Y_t = F_t / (1 - F_t)$$

where Y_t is the level at time t and F_t the percentage of the market which has already switched to or purchased the new product. Once a small number of points have been observed, Stewart maintained, it becomes possible to project the continuing penetration of the market accurately.

Jones and Twiss (1978) remained sceptical. They pointed out that the cases used to 'prove' the theory are always historic, and that assuming similar patterns can be applied to emerging technologies encounters the same problems as other methods making the same assumption. Many factors that are not considered within the calculation may affect the way the market develops.

S-curves may also be combined to reflect the way in which successive developments have extended the capability of a particular technology. Examples include the valve, transistor and chip, which have successively extended the capability of electronics, and developments in transport, where improvements in engine technology have increased the speed of travel. Applied as a forecast, these *envelope curves*, so called because they enclose a series of S-curves, assume that further technological developments will continue the process (see Fig. 12).

4.2.5. Precursor-Analysis

Some observers have suggested that the observation of trends in particular countries, states or firms provides a guide to similar developments elsewhere later. Naisbitt, for example, (Coates *et al.* 1986) monitored social developments in five 'Bellwether' states to provide an indication of ideas that he believed would subsequently spread to the rest of the USA. Others have identified certain countries as leaders in particular areas of activity—Sweden, for example, in social policy and developments in car safety—suggesting that

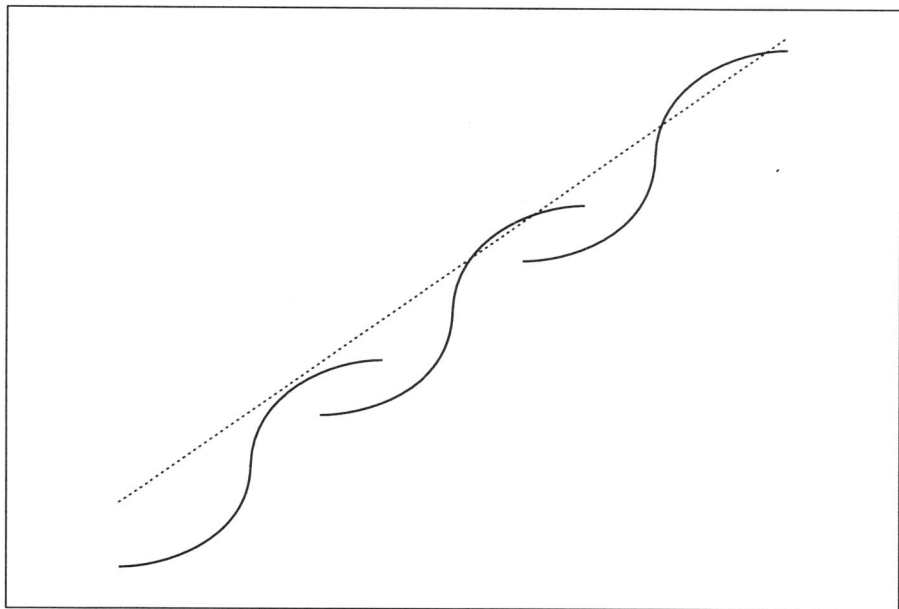

Fig. 12. The envelope curve

monitoring them will provide foresight into developments elsewhere. There is some historic evidence to support these ideas, but in forecasting they also rely on the future continuing to be like the past and the bellwethers continuing to predict changes elsewhere. Picking the bellwethers is crucial.

4.2.6. Cycles

Cyclical patterns are a common feature of everyday life. The daily cycle of day and night, the lunar cycle, the seasons and the life-cycle from birth to death are all examples of cyclical processes that recur at intervals. Some are regular, some less so. The power of the priests in Ancient Egypt is often attributed to their understanding of the seasonal cycle and their use of it to predict the onset of the Nile floods. Cyclical processes have also been perceived in human affairs, in the rise and fall of empires and in business activity. Such ups and downs may be considered random, fluctuating with events to no apparent pattern, or regular and explainable. The birth data used earlier in Table 6 are a good example, as are the UK retail prices index, mortgage rates and bank base rate, depicted in Fig. 13. They may be interpreted as random, with the RPI indicating a declining trend, or alternatively, by noting the peaks and troughs, as a cyclical pattern.

136 WAYS OF THINKING ABOUT THE FUTURE

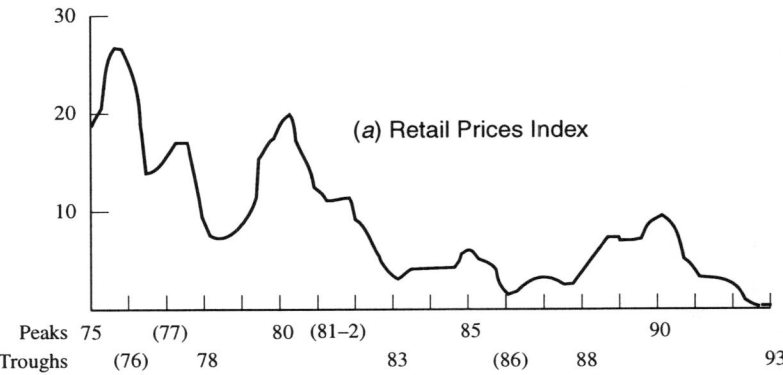

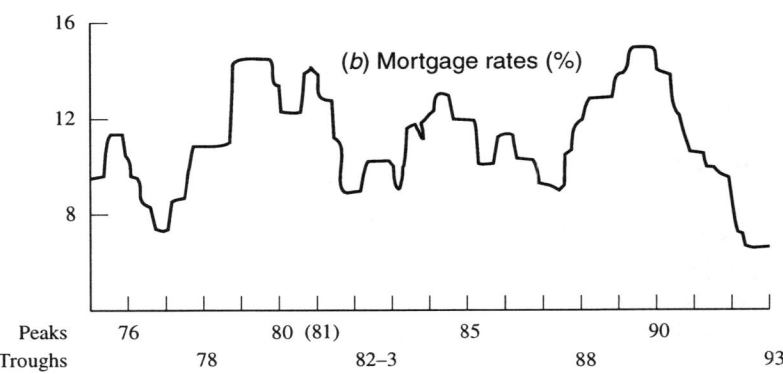

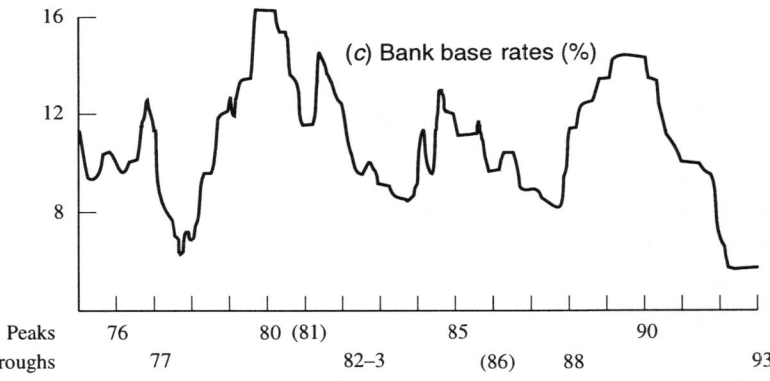

Fig. 13. Random or cyclical?

While it is not completely regular it could be argued that there is a pattern of peaks and troughs that tends to occur at approximately five-year intervals; peaks occurring in 1975/6, 1980, 1985 and 1990, with troughs in 1977/8, 1982–4, 1988 and 1993. Again, the interpretation is crucial. If the cyclical pattern is accepted, and it is assumed that it will continue into the future, we would forecast a new peak in 1995 followed by a trough in 1998 and a further peak in 2000. Predicting the levels that might be reached is more problematic because past peaks and troughs have varied quite markedly.

Makridakis (1990) suggested that three different lengths of cycle have been identified:

- economic cycles of about four years' duration, similar to those noted above;
- nine- to eleven-year 'jugular cycles'; and
- long-wave cycles of fifty to sixty years in length.

Some commentators have also suggested the existence of 500-year cycles in which the dominant global power moves from the Eastern hemisphere to the Western and back over a period of five centuries.

The existence of long-wave cycles was first proposed by Kondratiev (1935), who identified a regular pattern of prosperity and depression in the capitalist economies of France, England and the USA between 1780 and 1920 (Fig. 14). This has subsequently been extended by other authors to produce a pattern of cycles of approximately 55-year duration (for example F. M. Smith 1982, Beckman 1988, Stewart 1989). If this pattern, which is itself subject to some-

	Prosperity	Recession	Depression	Revival	
I	1787	1800	1813	1827	1842
II	1843	1857	1869	1885	1897
III	1898	1911	1925	1939	1953
IV	1954	1965	1979	1994	2009

Fig. 14. The pattern of long waves

considerable debate, continues into the future, there will be a new period of prosperity around the turn of the century. Both Beckman and Stewart confidently predicted this.

We have noted that, in most cases, extrapolative forecasts are based on the continuation of a past pattern without any attempt to explain why that pattern has occurred or why it should continue. Cycles, particularly the long-wave theory, are an exception and can consequently be regarded as possessing some of the characteristics of analytical forecasting. Given the identification of cyclical patterns, the obvious question is, why? During the 1980s renewed interest in the long-wave theory, itself perhaps cyclical, led to several explanations.

Mensch (1979) suggested that successive waves of prosperity were each based on preceding technological innovations, which themselves tended to occur periodically and created the capacity for the next wave of prosperity to develop. Stewart (1989) argued that periods of innovation can be identified around the following dates, linked to particular industries that formed the foundation of the subsequent period of prosperity:

- around 1770 inventions in textiles led to prosperity in the late eighteenth century
- around 1825 inventions in steel, steam engines and railways led to prosperity in the middle of the nineteenth century
- around 1880 inventions in chemicals, electricals and cars led to prosperity in the early twentieth century
- around 1935 inventions in polymers, television and jet aircraft led to prosperity in the 1950s and 1960s

He further argued that the coming period of prosperity between 2000 and 2020 will be based on innovations that have occurred since 1980 in digital communications, space travel, biotechnology and new materials.

The most frequently quoted alternative explanation of the long wave relates to the existence of lags in the economy, the limited information available to decision-makers and bounded rationality, according to which we are unable to make completely rational decisions because we lack the information, particularly about future states, that we would need to do so. The effect is to create oscillations in the economy that are reinforced by the self-reinforcing tendencies within the capitalist system (Steerman 1985). According to Stewart (1989), this leads to periods of rapid growth, market saturation and over-expansion followed by retrenchment. Graham and Senge (1980) brought these two approaches together, suggesting that during prosperity there is little pressure to invest in innovation because sales are buoyant. Capital-producing industries consequently begin to decline and obsolescence sets in. The decline is enhanced as markets are saturated. Eventually new investment by a new generation of entrepreneurs, emerging countries, or government (often instigated for military reasons) occurs, developing new technologies that have become available but not previously been taken up. These form the basis for the next period of prosperity.

The long-wave theory appears to offer an elegant explanation for some of the perceived variations in the economy in the past, but does it provide a reliable forecasting technique? If the future continues to exhibit the same pattern as the past, it does; if not, it does not. The very identification of the pattern might be thought to lead to actions to prevent its continuation as it would surely be considered preferable to maintain prosperity rather than oscillate between booms and slumps. Interest in the theory itself seems to be cyclical, waning during periods of prosperity when it does not seem relevant, only to be rekindled during economically less successful times. It was popular in the 1930s and again in the 1980s but less so in between. However elegant an explanation of the past cycles may provide, Makridakis (1990) was in no doubt that 'cycle forecasting is not within our present abilities'.

4.3. ANALYTICAL FORECASTING

4.3.1. Causal Models

'A model is simply a way of representing reality in which real world objects are expressed, either physically or in the abstract, in some way relevant to their characteristics' (Field and MacGregor 1987). Models are familiar to most of us from childhood in the form of a model car, Barbie Doll, teddy bear, train or, more recently, computer game. Each has certain features that mimic characteristics of the real world. They are not complete replicas, but by representing selected aspects of the original, are recognisable as an approximation.

Models also have more serious uses. Testing of new aircraft and new cars involves the use of models in wind tunnels; new ships, models in water tanks, and new buildings, architectural models. Increasingly these physical scale-models are being replaced by computer simulations that even allow designers to 'walk' through their proposals in virtual reality. Such models are useful because they can be constructed to behave like the real thing. Pilots can be trained to fly on simulators before they are let loose on expensive real aircraft. They can also 'experience' situations, like total engine-failure, that it would be impractical to test in reality. Computer models can also be made of the economy, cities, traffic-growth, population, the global climate and many other things. Many of these could not be effectively modelled before computers became available, though as Meadows, Richardson and Bruckmann (1982) noted, we have always used mental models of reality in order to comprehend and talk about it. That is essentially what theories are. Computer models provide a much advanced capability both in the development and testing of such theories.

The use of models in forecasting has made it possible to introduce more complex approaches. Instead of relying on the extrapolation of unexplained past trends, it has been possible to model historic change and examine how the changes in different aspects of the model interrelate to reach conclusions about the factors causing particular events and use this understanding to forecast future patterns.

For example, a simple model of population change within an area over the last thirty years can be constructed if we have the following information:

- total population at the start and finish of the thirty years,
- the number of births in the area during that time,
- the number of deaths in the area during the period, and
- the number of people who have moved into, or out of, the area during the thirty years.

This must be the case because the only way that the population of an area can change is by people being born, dying or moving into or out of it. The model can be expressed mathematically as:

$$P_{t+n} = P_{(t)} + B^{t+n} - D^{t+n} \pm M^{t+n}$$

where P is population, B is births, D is deaths, M is net migration, the balance between movement in and out, t is the start of the period, and $t + n$ is the end of the period. Where the information on births, deaths and migration is known the model can be used to replicate population change in the area over the period in question.

It can also be used to forecast the future population, except for the fact that we do not have information on the number of births, deaths and migrants in the future. To obtain them it would be necessary to make forecasts of each to feed into the model as we fed in the historic data. Where would these forecasts themselves be obtained? It would be possible to build further models to explain the patterns of births, deaths and migration in the past. The pattern of births, for example, is affected by a number of factors including the number of women in the population, the proportion of them that is of childbearing age, the proportion of that group that is sexually active, the availability of methods of birth control, their social and economic circumstances, their personal

Box 2. A population model

For example, if we assume a present population of 100,000, a birth rate of 13 per 1,000 population, a death rate of 12 per 1,000 population, and zero net migration (that is that the total number of people moving into the area will be the same as the total moving out), the population in 10 years time will be:

$$100,000 + ((13 \times 10) \times (100,000 / 1,000)) - ((12 \times 10) \times (100,000 / 1,000))$$
$$= 100,000 + (130 \times 100) - (120 \times 100)$$
$$= 100,000 + 13,000 - 12,000$$
$$= 101,000$$

(Statistically this is not quite correct, because the annual population increase arising from the birth and death rates used is 0.1%. In the first year this would amount to 100, but from then on the increase should be slightly larger each year. As we cannot have fractions of a person we can ignore this difference, but over the 10-year period, using the statistically correct compound interest formula, the difference would add up to 4.5 people. Given the room for error in the assumptions made in adopting the birth and death rates, such a variation can probably be safely ignored. Where the rates of increase or decrease are significantly larger, or we are not dealing in whole numbers, it may not be safe to do so.)

One of the advantages of using models becomes apparent if we change the assumptions about births, deaths and migration. To illustrate this we will assume a higher birth rate of 13.5 per 1,000 and a net in-migration of 100 per year. Using these assumptions in the model gives a significantly different result:

$$100,000 + ((13.5 \times 10) \times (100,000 / 1,000)) - ((12 \times 10) \times (100,000 / 1,000))$$
$$+ (100 \times 10)$$
$$= 100,000 + (135 \times 100) - (120 \times 100) + 1,000$$
$$= 100,000 + 13,500 - 12,000 + 1,000$$
$$= 102,500$$

(The statistical inaccuracies would be slightly more significant because the numbers are slightly larger—but again for our purposes we can ignore them.)

We can see immediately that making these different assumptions leads to a different result, a population increase that is significantly larger than in the first example. If we were using these forecasts to estimate the number of new dwellings needed to house the increased population the difference could be important. Making a further assumption that the occupancy rate, the number of people living in each house averages out at 3, we would have two different estimates of housing need: 333.3 and 833.3 over the ten years. The advantage of the model is that we can test out the different future situations that would arise if these different assumptions were to occur. It provides a useful means by which we can examine some of the uncertainties of the future.

decisions, and so on. Much of this information would be difficult to obtain and would still only provide a model of past change, useful though that might be to our understanding of changes in the pattern of births. Again, each factor could itself be the subject of another model. It is rather like those Russian dolls—open one and there is always another one inside.

Forecasters usually overcome this problem by making assumptions about future levels; effectively using their judgement to predict what the future will be. In our original population model this would mean assuming future birth, death and migration rates over the period we wish to forecast. Common assumptions would be that current rates will continue in the future or, if there is a clear increasing or decreasing trend, that it may reasonably be projected. Other information—if we know, for example, that the population is ageing—could also be taken into account. The assumptions can then be built into the model in order to allow us to make the forecast (see Box 2).

In this very simple model the relationships between the births, deaths and migration variables are clear. This is not always the case. In the following example, used by Firth (1977), it is suggested that sales are affected by the level of advertising, price, the number of sales staff and the discounts given. The importance of each factor in the end result is far from obvious; we do not immediately know, though we may have our own ideas, which is the most important. For the model to be useful it has to be calibrated; that is, past records must be fed in and weighted statistically until the model gives a close match between its results and what actually happened. This is quite reasonable because it is unlikely that each factor is equally important. It is quite possible, for example, that price could account for more of the past variation than the number of sales assistants, or vice versa. The process involved is similar to linear regression, in which a line is fitted to explain historical data. Indeed, the approach is sometimes called *multiple regression* because it is the same process working in more than one dimension (see Box 3). Statistically this model can be expressed as:

$$S = aAD + bRP + cSA + dDI$$

where S is sales, AD is advertising, RP is price, SA is the number of sales assistants, and DI is the discount; a, b, c, and d are constants or weights calculated for each factor so that the model replicates the observed data as closely as possible. Assuming that the model gives a close replication of past data, it seems reasonable to use it to forecast future sales. To do so, however, we would again need to make assumptions about the independent variables (advertising, price, the number of assistants and discounts) and their continuing relative importance. Assuming that we are the managers of the firm in question we are in a position to influence these things. The model could be

> **Box 3. Developing a model**
>
> Makridakis and Wheelwright (1989) set out nine steps in the development of a model using multiple regression.
>
> 1. Clear formulation of the problem and the matter to be forecast
> 2. Selecting and collecting the relevant data
> 3. Testing the model with the data in different forms in case the relationships are not linear ones. Mathematical transformation of the data can convert some non-linear relationships to linear
> 4. Studying the relationships between the independent variables to select those which best 'explain' the variation in the dependent variable. This should result in 'five or six alternative equations that seem promising'
> 5. Deciding among the alternatives and developing the final equation
> 6. Checking that the selected equation explains statistically sufficient of the variation in the dependent variable
> 7. Checking that the equation meets certain statistical criteria, otherwise it will be invalid
> 8. Making the forecast
> 9. Using the equation to increase understanding of the situation modelled
>
> Makridakis and Wheelright suggest that the biggest benefit from using models may often be in understanding rather than forecasting. Given a computer, developing a model is not as daunting as it sounds, but it is important to understand what the model produces and what it does not.

useful in helping us decide how to alter these variables in order to achieve the level of sales we want. Other factors would, of course, influence our decisions, such as what we could afford and the activities of competitors. But the model could be a most useful tool in helping us reach conclusions about what would be our best course of action. As such it becomes less a passive forecast of what we think will happen and more a tool in helping us deal with the uncertainties of the future and make what we hope will be better decisions.

Models are a very useful tool, but we need to understand that they contain at least one other set of assumptions about the relationships between the variables incorporated in them. Our sales example assumes that the relationship between the variables will remain the same as it has been in the past; that if we vary the price by a given amount the model will give us an accurate picture of the impact of that move on our sales. That may not be the case if events not considered by our model have created a different situation—if, for example, a change in the level of taxation has made consumers more or less likely to spend their money on our product. An example of changing relationships that invalidated the forecasts obtained from a model can be found in the field of energy. It used to be assumed, because there was evidence to indicate it, that an increase in production in an economy, as measured by the Gross National Product, could only be achieved by increasing the amount of energy used (Barney 1980). Forecasts of economic growth were therefore used as the basis for forecasts of increasing energy demand, assuming that a particular percentage increase in GNP would necessitate a certain increase in energy use. The forecasts proved to be overestimates, because other influences changed the relationship between GNP growth and energy demand. In particular the increased price of oil in 1973 led to a more efficient use of energy (Foley 1981) and the changing economic structure of Western economies, as they moved from goods-producing to service-producing, reduced the amount of energy required per unit of GNP. That the GNP forecasts were often overoptimistic did not help in obtaining accurate forecasts either.

The problems that have been experienced with forecasting models in the past should not cause us to doubt their value or the major advances that improving computer models can make to our understanding of events. They enable us to manage the information that is now becoming available and to relate factors together in previously impossible ways. Given the right circumstances models can help in the development of theories that explain situations that have occurred and indicate the probable causes of particular events. In forecasting they can be used to investigate the anticipated consequences of different courses of action, as Meadows *et al.* (1992) clearly showed. These and similar explorations of 'what will happen if' are invaluable, but as forecasters we should not forget that they are dependent both on the 'if' and on the continuation of the relationships enshrined in the model. Variation from the assumed future circumstances or the pattern of relationships embedded in the model will invalidate the forecasts; but the models themselves contain the ability to vary both the assumptions and the relationships, and to modify the forecasts accordingly.

The availability of greater computing power has greatly advanced the use of models in forecasting and it seems likely that they will continue to play an important role. They have been particularly popular in economics, transport and global systems. Economists use them to compare the anticipated economic effect of alternative policies such as interest rate or tax changes. Transport-planners use them to forecast future traffic levels, and given the construction of new roads, the distribution of traffic on the road system. Global models have been used to examine the impact of global warming on climatic patterns and, in the World 3 Model developed by Meadows *et al.* (1992), the future of the planet. The complexity of the World 3 Model is clear from the description in Meadows *et al.* (1992), itself a précis of a 637-page technical report. With varied success, models have been used to examine and test issues and policies in urban development (Klosterman *et al.* 1994). In this field an indication of their potential is the commercial success of computer games like 'Sim City', 'Civilisation' and 'Transport Tycoon'.

Meadows, Richardson and Bruckmann (1982) argued that although computer models

- are sometimes too complicated to be understood even by the modellers,
- may be too specialised for users to understand them,
- may leave out important factors that cannot be easily quantified, and
- suffer from other human mistakes,

they are also

- rigorous, precise and consistent,
- written out explicitly in order to be understood and criticised by anyone,
- able to contain many more variables (than other methods) and keep track of them all simultaneously,
- able to draw error-free conclusions from their assumptions, and
- able to be changed and tested very quickly.

As such they form a very important tool in our collection of methods of thinking about the future.

This discussion has dealt almost exclusively with regression-based models, but other mathematical techniques are also used in appropriate circumstances. In an examination of forecasting techniques in the area of urban and regional planning, Field and MacGregor (1989) discussed *matrices* and *gravity models*, while Martino (1993) included an examination of *probabilistic methods*. It is not appropriate to consider these methods in detail here, but we should note that they can be useful in forecasting as long as the application is made in the full knowledge of the mathematical technique on which they are based.

4.4. SPECULATION

Literary, and more recently film and television speculation about the future plays a considerable role in entertainment. Although many examples are no more than a means to tell a story that is not limited by historical or contemporary circumstances, there are others which set out to examine important issues in a thought-provoking manner. Slaughter (1984) notes that this enables science fiction, through its popularity, to make ideas about the future available to a wider audience. Films like 'Jurassic Park', presented in an entertaining way, examine some of the issues raised in genetics. The 'Back to the Future' trilogy explored the relationship between past, present and future, through the medium of time-travel. The effect of the past on the present, and of both on the future was central to their plots, and while this may have been incidental to the main purpose of entertainment, it may serve to increase awareness in the audience of such relationships and of how actions today may have future consequences.

It is not clear whether science fiction writers are among the first to raise questions about new developments, particularly in technology, or whether they popularise current concerns (Miles 1993), but their work has had a role in bringing such concerns to a wider audience. In raising such 'What if?' questions, science fiction challenges the notions of both an inevitable future and an empty future. The role of human action in influencing future events, even if often portrayed in the unlikely person of a super-hero, comes through clearly. Even in the face of apparently overwhelming odds, changes can be made, and individual actions count. The future does not just happen to us, but can be made to happen for us. It is neither inevitable nor empty, but contingent upon our actions in the present.

It is often suggested that science fiction is not actually about the future as much as a device that uses the future to cast light upon present issues. For example, George Orwell's *1984*, which was apparently about a society thirty-five years in the future from its date of publication, is often said to have been inspired by the author's concern for developments occurring in 1948; '84' being only a device, the inverting of '48'. Whether this is true or not, this type of fiction frequently extends current concerns into an imagined future that could occur if present developments are extrapolated in a particular direction. Their intention may then be similar to the forecasts in *The Limits to Growth*—to alert a wider public to the potential opportunities and risks associated with the developments of new technologies or the continuation of present trends, and in so doing to question whether that is what we really want.

The very extent of our perceived current problems may, in part, explain trends in science fiction. Although there has been a tradition of warnings about the future implications of current trends, much writing in the early twentieth century was optimistic. *Utopianism*, positive images of a better future, often resulting from scientific and technological advance, was common. Since the middle of the century the mood has been more sombre, dominated by generally pessimistic or even apocalyptic views of the future. At one level, these dystopian images may be useful, acting as warnings and encouraging avoiding action, but at another they may contribute to feelings of helplessness in the face of overwhelming problems. Some commentators have identified a further trend suggesting that science fiction writing has now become little more than escapist fantasy. Our contemporary world has become too frightening, horrific and complex for us to cope; the only rational thing we can do is to escape into fantasy or manic humour. Even the development of Cyberpunk could be seen in a similar light, escaping the real world into a virtual, anarchic alternative. Is this a prophetic view of potential trends in society or does it do no more than reflect changing moods, from optimism in the potential of science and technology in the early twentieth century, through pessimism associated with the realisation that technology has enhanced humanity's ability to inflict damage on itself and the planet, to postmodern confusion?

Not all speculative writing is science fiction. Many of the references quoted in this book are examples of speculative writing that would not normally be classified as fiction, despite the definition of fiction as 'an invented idea or statement or narrative, an imaginary thing' (Tulloch 1993). Kahn, Toffler, Meadows, Drexler, Beckman, Hall, Kennedy, Masser, Handy, Robertson and many others who have written about future developments as they saw them have been concerned to speculate about the future. That their work included more formal forecasts, scenarios and proposals does not mean that they were not speculating about the future in written form.

Such speculation is often trend-based, arising from the observation of change and its extension into the future, but it can also include new, discontinuous ideas and innovative thinking, and different ways of doing things that would imply practices quite different from those to which we are accustomed. For example, Robertson (1985) originated the concept of 'ownwork'. It is unusual for us to rely on others to provide opportunities for us in the way we rely on employers to provide work, so Robertson suggested that we would gain freedom and responsibility by taking control of our own work.

The value of such works is to encourage the questioning of established wisdom and generate new ideas for the future.

4.5. JUDGEMENTAL FORECASTING

Separating out a particular group of forecasting and futures methods as judgemental is only a matter of convenience and degree. Judgement is clearly needed in applying most methods, however objective they may appear. Whether a trend is likely to continue or the relationships enshrined within a model develop in a certain way are matters of judgement. Neither the trend nor the model provide certain guidance about the future, but the basis of the techniques in statistics and computing is sometimes regarded as providing a scientific approach to the future that excludes the need for judgement. It does not, but neither does it invalidate their usefulness so long as the role of judgement is appreciated. But just as judgement is necessary in statistically based forecasting methods, so trend-extrapolation and models can be useful in enhancing judgemental approaches. In that sense our classification is false, but it serves to emphasise the differences between the approaches. Judgemental methods are based on the assumption that judgement is the most significant factor in Futures and forecasting methods and that better results can be obtained using this approach. Not surprisingly this is the subject of considerable debate.

Armstrong (1978) suggested that the most serious problem in judgemental forecasting is bias. Those making the forecasts 'confuse their desires for the future with the forecast'. Evans (1987) noted that 'the preservation of theories in the face of conflicting evidence is, of course, a commonplace observation in science and in social science'. He suggested that in human affairs like economics, where theories are closely linked to personal and political beliefs, the likelihood of belief-maintenance is much greater. Because they are operating in the real world where control experiments are not possible it is relatively easy to accept apparent inaccuracy in forecasts as being caused by rogue factors outside the control of the forecaster. For example, economic forecasts can be invalidated by natural disasters or political events beyond the scope of even the most complex models. In the opinion of those committed to the particular theory on which the model is based, such events do not invalidate the theory, the model or the forecast. Evans also noted that an 'accurate' forecast may be no more convincing, because it may be said to have occurred by chance or because other factors have changed. The decline in recorded crime in the UK in the first quarter of 1994 was interpreted by the Home Secretary (the minister responsible for law and order) as confirmation of his belief that putting more criminals in prison would lead to a reduction in crime. His opponents, in contrast, pointed to information that suggests that 'Of all offences committed, only 50% are reported, 30% are recorded, 7% are cleared up, 3% draw a caution and 2% result in a conviction' (Phillips 1994). They suggest that this completely invalidates such predictions because the impact of imprisonment is so small in relation to the number of crimes committed. Makridakis and Wheelright (1989) related this to the common tendency for people to look for evidence to support the idea that they have already decided upon, rather than for information that would invalidate it. Only in the proven absence of evidence to invalidate the judgement should it be maintained, they argued.

Makridakis and Wheelright also noted the tendency of individuals to be overconfident in their judgement. Contrary to accepted wisdom, psychological research shows that far from improving judgement, additional information only serves to confirm existing opinions. Armstrong (1978) suggested that, in forecasting, these opinions are too often conservative and tradition-bound. Quoting work by Janis, Makridakis and Wheelright pointed out that this is a particular problem of groups, which are subject to pressure to conform. The result is groupthink, the tendency for members of a group to isolate themselves from outside opinion and pursue their own particular view of the world, whatever the evidence to the contrary and the consequences.

Beach, Christensen-Szalanski and Barnes (1987) questioned the validity of much of this research on judgement, suggesting that it concentrates on the negative and gives little attention to examples of good performance. They also suggested that because experiments to test judgement are usually laboratory-based, they are therefore unlike real-life situations; that the subjects have a different perception of the tasks contained in the experiments from the experimenters, and that appropriate criteria to evaluate the research are difficult to establish. They argued that as a consequence the research into judgement is itself questionable and that a much more important issue than how good or bad our minds are is how best to integrate judgement and the advanced technologies now at our disposal into making better decisions. In that vein Armstrong (1978) offered a number of suggestions designed to overcome some of the problems he identified, including selecting the judges, formulating questions, obtaining the forecasts and assessing uncertainty.

There is evidently a division between those who believe in analytical approaches to forecasting and those who favour judgemental methods. The former dismiss the latter methods as little better than crystal ball-gazing, while the latter note that however good sophisticated models are at explaining the past they cannot guarantee that the same relationships will continue into the future. It is difficult not to conclude that the argument is between Crystal Balls and Silicon Balls, and that though the methods may be different there is a danger that the result could be the only common theme between them, Balls! In the face of the difficulties that we have in dealing with the future we would probably be better advised to use both approaches, as belt and braces, to obtain as much insight into the future as we can.

4.5.1. Delphi

One of the most written about, derided and defended judgemental methods is Delphi, a technique developed by Helmer and Gordon at the RAND Corporation in the 1950s and 1960s. Opinions about the method are sharply divided.

Sackman (1974) called it 'basically unreliable and scientifically invalidated', concluding that it was little more than, 'fortune-tellers using new versions of old crystal balls'. Martino (1993) by contrast suggested that there are particular circumstances in which the basis of the technique, expert judgement, is either superior to 'objective' methods, or all there is available. Where little or no historical data exists, where external factors such as political decisions are likely to have a determining effect, and where ethical or moral arguments may dominate economic or technical considerations, he contended, the Delphi method is valuable. Linstone (1978) summarised such situations as those 'where a problem does not lend itself to precise analytical techniques but can benefit from subjective judgement on a collective basis'.

Delphi is based on the assumption that collective expert judgement is a valuable method of forecasting in these circumstances. The technique aims to derive the benefit of bringing together a group of experts without the disadvantages of a committee situation. Besides the practical problems of the cost and the difficulty of assembling a group of busy experts, there are the difficulties of group dynamics. Deference to recognised leading opinion, persuasion by dominant members, dismissal of minority views and groupthink are all characteristics of committee situations. Delphi attempts to overcome these by a series of questionnaires interspersed by controlled opinion-feedback. Anonymity is maintained throughout.

Delphi is not a method to be adopted without considerable care; even its defenders have termed it a technique of the last resort. Where there is insufficient data, no reliable time series or a high probability that existing patterns will change, Delphi comes into its own. These are the circumstances in which it offers most, mainly because other techniques are of little use. Given that when thinking about the future, particularly beyond the short term, these characteristics are reasonably common, the users of the technique have a case. Many Delphi studies have been reported in the literature and few are exactly the same in their methodology, although there is general agreement that the basics revolve around a panel of experts responding to a series of questionnaires with interspersed feedback.

Setting up the panel is a crucial first step. In this connection, there is some dispute as to whether experts are better than non-experts. Armstrong (1978), for example, contended that they make no difference. Personal experience suggests that in comparison to students, experts may be more conservative and less prepared to contemplate situations removed from the current orthodoxy, and may be very tentative when asked about matters they regard as outside their field. One of the criticisms of Delphi studies is that they seldom make clear how or why the panel was selected. Care is therefore needed in recruiting the panel and the criteria for selection should be clearly set out. The purpose of the Delphi should be clear; is it to produce a consensus forecast, to gain a wide spectrum of views from individuals who would not normally communicate with each other, to act as the basis for alternative future scenarios or to evaluate policy alternatives? This may influence the composition of the panel. Before they agree to take part, the purpose of the Delphi and the commitment required needs to be understood by the members of the panel. One of the difficulties of Delphi arises from the iterative nature of the questionnaires. If the exercise is to maintain its credibility the tendency for panel members to drop out after the first round has to be minimised. The fact that the exercise requires completion of more than one questionnaire must therefore be made clear and agreement to take part on that basis obtained. Jones and Twiss (1978) suggested that a panel smaller than ten is unlikely to be credible but that one larger than fifty is likely to be unmanageable. It is worth allowing for some reduction in the number of participants if it is intended to have three or four rounds, but necessary to maintain a credible number throughout.

Depending on the purpose of the exercise the first round can take one of two main forms. It may either pose certain defined questions, such as the date by which particular developments or events are expected to occur, or be completely open, asking the panel, for example, what are the most likely changes they anticipate in the area of concern in the next twenty-five or fifty years. In the first instance the results will be a series of dates. These are traditionally analysed by calculating the median, or middle date of the range, and the interquartile range, the middle half of the range outside which lie the upper and lower 25 per cent, or quarters, of the range. This information then forms the basis of the second round, in which the panel are asked to review their estimates in the light of the group opinion. In the latter case, in which the answers will be in prose form, the responses are grouped and tallied to analyse the frequency with which particular events or developments have been identified by the members of the panel. Depending on the amount of information, the moderator who is running the Delphi may decide to recirculate all of the responses or just the more common ones for further comment in the second round. In the second round the panel are asked to consider the list generated by the group and to say whether they think the items listed are likely to occur, or if the aim is to obtain an idea of when the developments may occur, to provide dates. The value of circulating the list comes from the much wider set of ideas generated by the group as opposed to each individual.

The second-round responses will then either be a revised set of dates or a weighted set of events. In the former case those panel members who maintain an estimate outside the interquartile range are asked to provide a brief justification for their opinion. A new median and interquartile range can then be calculated and either used as the final forecast or circulated again for further refinement. The idea behind this iteration is that the forecast will converge, most probably around the median, and that this refined collective estimate is likely to be a better judgement. A similar result, with certain events or developments identified as more likely than others, will emerge from the second approach. Whether this produces any benefit is again doubted by the method's critics.

To date it has been difficult to test the accuracy of the forecasts in many Delphi studies because they have by nature been long-term and cannot yet be proved, and because in the light of subsequent developments the forecasts often seem to have been imprecisely worded. For example, a RAND Corporation study on scientific breakthroughs (quoted by Linstone 1978) included a forecast of 'effective fertility control by oral contraceptive or other simple and inexpensive means', between 1970 (lower quartile and median) and 1983 (upper quartile). The definitions of 'effective', 'fertility control', 'simple' and 'inexpensive' are crucial in any assessment, although at the time they may have seemed sufficient. At one level this prediction seems to have been correct, but at a more critical level it is less easy to be so certain.

Martino (1993) suggests that the quantitative-style Delphi should continue for four rounds or until the forecasts have reached stability, though personal experience with the non-quantitative style indicates a sharp reduction in participation by the third round. This may be overcome if each round is given a clear function; merely re-estimating earlier forecasts seems unlikely to hold the attention of the panel without very strong commitment or an incentive to continue. Further details of the method can be found in Delbecq, Van De Vem and Gustafson (1975), Linstone (1978), Jones and Twiss (1978) and Martino (1993). Reports in the literature indicate that the technique has been used in assessing the future of nuclear power (Davis and Fitzsimmons 1991), the risks associated with the application of sewage sludge to farmland (Webler et al. 1991), future office construction (Eger and Smith 1987), the future of a local economy (Masser and Foley 1987) and the future use of information and microtechnology in road transport (Svidén 1988). Assessments of its value are found in Rowe, Wright and Bolger (1991) and Woudenberg (1991). The latter concluded negatively; the method does not overcome pressure to group conformity and 'is in no way superior to other (simpler, faster and cheaper) judgemental methods'. While repeating many of the same criticisms, Rowe, Wright and Bolger concluded that 'Delphi does have potential as a judgement aided technique', but that there is a need for improvement and greater understanding of the processes involved.

One obvious criticism of the technique is the influence the moderator may have on the process and therefore the result. The decision to adopt the approach, the selection of the panel, the form that the questionnaire will take and the interpretation of the responses are all subject to the control of the moderator. Clearly this raises questions of potential bias. Although the Delphi technique is clearly open to such abuse it is not alone in this; all of the methods described here rely on the integrity of the operators. It may, in fact, be harder to hide bias in a Delphi than in a complex computer model that only the experts can understand. All methods are fallible; use them carefully.

The majority of Delphi exercises conducted to date have been paper-based, the questionnaires being sent by post to and from the panel. This means that the process, particularly if it entails a number of rounds, can be quite lengthy and sufficient response times need to be built in. Modern telecommunication and computer technology now raise the possibility of much quicker responses, which may enable participants to interact on-line rather than through the formalised round structure.

Delphi is clearly not a 'scientific' method and has been resoundingly criticised as a result. Whether or not judgement is a good basis for forecasting—or perhaps more significantly, whether forecasting is an adequate approach to the future—is a continuing debate. Sackman (1974) argued that 'the future is far too important to be left to fortune-tellers using new versions of old crystal balls. It is time for the oracle to move out and science to move in'. Parente and Anderson-Parente (1987), on the other hand, maintained that Delphi is 'a valuable technological forecasting tool', and that 'it may be the only way to predict emerging technologies where there is no empirical database'. They also contended that there is little evidence that more conventional quantitative methods provide more accurate long-range forecasts anyway.

4.5.2. Cross-Impact

Most of the methods discussed so far have been concerned with attempts to forecast single events or developments, or groups of them, without taking into account that they may be linked; that one event may affect the chances of another occurring. A technique that attempts to account for such interactions is cross-impact analysis. In its simplest form the technique takes the form of a matrix of interactions between a list of occurrences. As such it can help clarify the interactions between possible future events. In more complex forms it involves the calculation of interlinked probabilities of events through which possible future pathways can be traced. It has, for example, been used to examine alternative developments in space technology (Martino 1993).

The starting point for cross-impact analysis is to compile a list of possible future events. This is obviously crucial, because exclusion of important events would reduce the value of any conclusions, while inclusion of unimportant events would unnecessarily complicate the procedure. A Delphi exercise is suggested as one way of obtaining the list. When the list has been agreed it is set out as a matrix as in Table 9. In this example an index between + 10 and − 10 has been used to indicate whether the occurrence of one event is considered likely to increase or decrease, and by how much, the likelihood of each other event occurring.

Table 9. A cross-impact matrix

If this event occurs	The effect on this event would be				
	[A]	[B]	[C]	[D]	[E]
[A] Scientific proof of global warming	—	+9	+3	+5	−6
[B] Imposition of a carbon tax	0	—	+7	+8	−9
[C] Increased energy conservation	0	−4	—	−5	−4
[D] Solar energy development	0	−7	−4	—	−4
[E] Demand for coal	0	+2	+3	−2	—

The relationships suggested in this example may seem fairly obvious, even if the exact values allocated are disputed. It suggests that proof of global warming would be very likely to lead to the imposition of a carbon tax and boost the development of solar energy. Scientific proof is not regarded as so effective a stimulus to change as the price incentive given by the imposition of the carbon tax, which would lead to a major impetus to both energy conservation and the development of solar energy. All of these events would have a downward impact on the demand for coal, but again the price mechanism is regarded as the most effective. Energy conservation measures and the development of solar energy would both reduce the pressure for a carbon tax and the demand for coal, but each would have the effect of reducing the need for the other. An increased demand for coal could have some effect on moves towards a carbon tax and on conservation, but would tend to reduce the development of solar power.

In its simplest form the matrix is used to give just positive enhancing (+), negative inhibiting (−) or unrelated (0) estimates of impact, though it is more normal to indicate the strength of the influence by assigning an index, as here, or a probability. Using probabilities can quickly become complicated. Each event is given its own individual probability of occurrence. The matrix is then completed to provide estimates of the probability of each event given the prior occurrence of the other events listed. Porter *et al.* (1991) recommended the preparation of a non-occurrence matrix at the same time, because 'just as the occurrence of an event can affect the probability that another will occur, its non-occurrence can have an impact as well'.

Further developments of the technique include the use of computer programs to assess the probability of strings of events. Details of these and other developments are given in Stover and Gordon (1978), Jones and Twiss (1978) and Martino (1993). The cross-impact method can also be used to evaluate the effect of policy decisions by comparing the estimated consequences of alternative actions and to determine important stages in the achievement of particular objectives, if certain steps are considered likely to increase the chances of success. It can therefore be regarded as a transitional technique between foreseeing and managing the future, with uses in both situations.

The advantage of the technique is that, unlike most others, it does attempt to link future events together and examine the interactions between them. It suffers the same disadvantages as other methods that rely on judgement and rapidly becomes very complex as it moves into the mathematics of probability and interpreting the results of computer-based calculations.

4.6. CONCLUSIONS

Attempts to preguess the future by foreseeing what is going to happen have their uses, particularly where we wish to examine what would appear likely to happen if certain assumptions hold; but as we have already argued that is not the only approach we adopt. We also believe that we can influence what happens in the future and it is to techniques which help here that we turn in the next chapter.

CHAPTER FIVE
MANAGING, PLANNING AND CREATING THE FUTURE

'The best way to predict the future is to invent it' Kay (1994).

Forecasting is prone to error and may imply an essentially passive approach to the future, but can we cut the Gordian knot and create the future, as Kay suggests?

Believing that we can invent or create the future relies on certain assumptions about the future and our relationship to it, just as forecasting does. To believe that we can invent the future we must assume that we can influence the course of events by our actions; that what we do matters; that the future is not fixed but open and subject to human choice and intervention—what Polak (1973) called influence optimism. This is a significant assumption. As individuals we are only one among some six billion human beings on the planet, and only one among many lifeforms. Even if humans are alone in being able to make decisions and take actions that affect the course of history, it is bold to presume that what we, as individuals, do is significant, particularly when we are often inclined to think that we are helpless in the face of forces much more powerful than ourselves. The impact of humanity as a whole or the combined effects of large sections of it are perhaps more significant than our individual actions, but this collective impact still results from the sum of our individual actions. To change the overall impact would appear to require changes in the behaviour of individuals. If so, our individual actions do matter, even if they are the same as everyone else's.

If six billion people are all making their own individual decisions and acting on them, can we predict how those decisions will interact? If we cannot, we may be able to make decisions but can have no idea what their effect will be, little or no control over events and no real basis on which to prefer one action to another. To believe that we can effectively influence the future in directions that we prefer requires the assumption that there is a reasonable probability of our being able not only to influence the course of events, but also to assess the future implications of alternative actions, including the reactions of others to our actions, with some reliability. Choice, particularly when available to so many, introduces randomness into the situation. Even if everyone has only two alternatives the possible interactions rapidly become unimaginable. How can we cope with all the possibilities? Within the relatively contained world of our everyday lives the number of interactions and the number of alternatives may be limited to enable us to make reasonably informed and reliable judgements in many situations, and to make the assumption reasonable. On the broader scale, Asimov's (1960) concept of *Psychohistory* may offer some potential. He suggested that while it may not be possible to predict the actions of so many individuals, the overall impact of many individual choices may be predictable. Developments in computer modelling are essentially based on the assumption that, taken together, there are tendencies in human behaviour that can be identified, modelled and used to predict probable futures.

If our actions do matter, then their significance is probably greater in our immediate situation, mostly affecting ourselves and those around us. Interpretations of history and current events, on the other hand, would suggest that certain powerful individuals have a wider impact. It seems quite reasonable to interpret our current circumstances as the result of decisions and actions made by ourselves and by previous generations in the past, and further, to conclude that this process will continue, that in effect we, both individually and collectively, make the future for ourselves and our successors. Nonetheless it is an assumption, however reasonable or desirable it may seem.

The approach also assumes that humanity, individually, in groups and as a whole, is a significant force within the cosmos. Considering how long we believe the universe has been in existence, the forces involved in its creation and its scale, to regard ourselves as significant may seem presumptuous. Criticisms are made, for example, of the environmentalists, who believe that human activity is the cause of such climatic changes as the Greenhouse Effect, by those who suggest that human activity is insignificant in comparison to the natural processes of variations in the Sun's radiation, the orbit of the Earth and volcanic eruptions and that it is these that are the cause of any observed changes. If this is so then human activity, even in total, could be considered insignificant. If that is the case we can do nothing about it, except perhaps look for another planet to live on if this one changes too much, or find ways to create artificial environments that suit us. But that, of course, assumes that we can make decisions and act on them. Perhaps even that is beyond us.

It may be that what we do does not, in fact, have any impact; that the future is fixed and our action predetermined. Some people believe this to be the case, others insist that such an attitude is far too fatalistic and what we do does matter. We cannot prove either case absolutely. Evidence can be assembled for either side, and positions in between, but it seems likely that however powerless we all feel on occasion we still like to believe that there are occasions when what we do counts. If that is the case it seems preferable and more responsible to manage and invent the future by taking considered action in the present rather than letting it happen by default. Futures, as an activity, clearly makes such assumptions. It is based on the belief that what we do has an effect, that we can make effective choices to manage and create the future and that we have both the opportunity and the responsibility to do so.

5.1. MANAGEMENT

Management is an age-old art that has been developed in recent years into a major industry in itself. It has become a subject of study and research, with a wide range of methods and techniques, from simple to very sophisticated, at its disposal. Different perspectives from that taken here would regard forecasting, decision-making, planning and creativity as part of an all-encompassing management process. The approach here is to regard managing for the future as part of the range of ways of approaching the future. From this perspective it becomes a means of organising and administering events that have future consequences, in the present. The image of the surfer, which we have encountered before, is, perhaps, the most apt. The central concern is riding the wave, being alert to circumstances as they change and modifying our behaviour to make the best of the ever-changing situation.

The idea of management rests on the assumption that we can influence the course of events as they occur. Whereas solely relying on foreseeing the future might imply that all we are able to do is attempt to preguess what is going to happen, managing the future suggests that we are in a position to affect the outcome and at least choose between alternatives to steer the course of events in a preferred direction. In doing this we are moving from attempting to foresee possible and probable futures into steering towards a preferable one. The two are not mutually exclusive, because in order to be able to choose preferable futures it is useful to be able to have an idea of what may be possible. The concept of preferable futures raises significant issues that can easily be overlooked in our enthusiasm for imagining and working towards a future we favour.

A future that we prefer may not find favour with others. It may, for example, give us advantages to the disadvantage of others—at least in their opinion.

Western people generally assume that their ways are best and that the rest of the world, which currently lacks the advantages of the Western standard of life, wishes to obtain it. Perhaps it does, but concerns are also expressed about the problems of Western societies that may be seen as outweighing any potential advantages.

Even if we did all share the same vision of what a preferable future would be, it would be difficult to achieve, because there would most probably be argument over the best way to attain it and because of the constraints of our environment. Different individuals, nations and cultures frequently have different or competing preferences. In our increasingly global world these may well be incompatible; not everyone will be able to have what they want without preventing others from obtaining their wishes. How such conflicts are to be resolved and how we might move towards a collectively preferable future on a global scale is likely to remain a major concern. A shared vision of the preferable future is not self-evident and cannot be imposed by one set of interests on another. If such a future is to be developed it will require a great deal of debate and tolerance on all sides.

An important theme in management literature is the management of change. Change is a normal process; we live in a world that is constantly changing both naturally and at our instigation. In the 1950s and 1960s it seems to have been generally assumed that we were following a steady, growing economic trajectory. Assuming that steady progress will continue means that traditional forecasting methods aimed at foreseeing the future will give adequate guidance about what is coming. The task of management in those circumstances is to prepare for the future as forecast and make decisions that it is believed will bring the most benefit. It is widely agreed that in the 1970s this pattern broke down and the assumption of continuing progress was invalidated. The future as forecast failed to arrive. Change came to be seen as a more complicated process and the future as more difficult, if not impossible, to predict. To manage in these circumstances required new methods and techniques that could enable us to make decisions in the absence of knowing what the future would be.

Stacey (1992) contended that the traditional approaches adopted by most managers remain essentially extrapolative, and as such are inappropriate to our present circumstances. Basing his approach in Chaos Theory, he argued that because the future is open-ended, it is essentially unpredictable. Change and choice have too great an effect to enable correct predictions to be made. Both traditional forecasting, which attempts to foresee, and strategic planning, which attempts to set goals and work out paths to attain them, are impractical because it is not possible either to foresee the future or to establish with any certainty in advance what steps will lead to a given future. This does not imply that consideration of the future should be abandoned but that learning in the present is the most realistic approach to adopt. He recommends an approach in which:

- we would start from the here and now, with challenging aspirations and ambitions, determination and initiative
- we would go forward from where we are, without trying to work out in advance what will happen
- we would use intuition, reasoning by analogy, reflection upon experience, to design innovative and creative actions to deal with issues we have detected now; issues we know will have important long-term consequences even if we cannot say what those consequences will be
- we would act and see how that turns out, dealing with the consequences as they occur. In short we would learn in real time
- we will be concerned, not with adapting to a given world out there, but with making that world different from the way it would have been
- we will be concerned with creating conditions within which people can learn and act spontaneously, using their own initiative.

Traditional forecasting methods of the kind examined in the last chapter are of limited use in these circumstances. What methods are there, then, to help us?

5.1.1. Scenarios

Scenarios are often classified as a form of judgemental forecasting, and in certain situations they can be used as such. But as Schwartz (1992) noted, they are also used in a more positive way as a tool of management. In other circumstances they may be used in a creative form, where normative scenarios depicting preferred future developments are prepared, and ways to achieve them devised. This emphasises the difficulty of allocating methods that can be used in a number of situations to a particular place in any classification.

The term scenario has become more common in recent years, particularly in relation to the direction of future events. It was used, for example, by the UK Minister of Defence, Malcolm Rifkind, in an interview on a BBC Radio news programme on 13 May 1994 in respect of possible future developments in Bosnia. He acknowledged that the future was unpredictable and that it could develop in a number of ways, depending on the actions of the parties involved. The inclusion in the dictionary of this second meaning of scenario, 'a postulated sequence of future events' (Tulloch 1993), recognises this increasingly common usage. It is a recognition of the impact of Futures concepts on everyday life. The original meaning of scenario comes from the field of theatre, 'an outline of the plot of a play, film, opera, etc., with details of the scenes, situations, etc.' (Tulloch 1993). The definition is useful in making clear an important characteristic of scenarios as used in both situations—they are outlines or sketches of major developments, not detailed accounts.

As a Futures technique, the scenario again owes its origin to the RAND Corporation, and in particular the work of Herman Kahn (Kahn and Wiener 1967). Since then scenarios have been used by several major multinational companies, notably Royal Dutch Shell (Wack 1985, Schwartz 1992) and Southern California Edison (1988), and in national future studies, for example *Norway 2000* (Nore and Osmundsen 1988) and *Britain in 2010* (Northcott 1991), and they form a central part of Godet's *Prospective approach* (Godet 1993), which has been employed in a range of consultancy situations.

Schwartz categorically stated that 'Scenarios are not predictions. It is simply not possible to predict the future with certainty.' Indeed it is suggested that scenarios were adopted by businesses as a direct consequence of the failure of traditional forecasting methods in the 1970s. The traditional extrapolative methods that they had been using relied on the assumption that present trends would continue. During the 1960s these gave reasonably reliable guidance, but in the 1970s trends, particularly in the oil business, did not continue. Major disruption in the supply of oil at stable prices occurred as a result of both the Arab–Israeli conflict and the decisions of the Organization of Petroleum Exporting Countries (OPEC). The oil industry was directly affected, and consequently the Western economies entered a recession; a major discontinuity from the trends of the 1960s that extrapolative forecasting methods did not, and could not, foresee. They do not foresee discontinuities because they are not designed to look for them. Neither do they usually incorporate the broad non-quantifiable areas of political, regulatory, social, economic and technological developments that are frequently the source of major discontinuities. These are more easily built into computer simulations, but if they cannot be quantified it can be difficult to incorporate them.

The scenario method begins from a recognition of the unpredictability of the future, but acknowledges that we need to take decisions in the present that will have future implications. Its intention is to help us make better decisions about the future in the presence of this uncertainty. Schwartz (1992) defined scenarios as 'a tool for ordering one's perceptions about future environments in which one's decisions might be played out' and Hirschorn (1980) succinctly called them 'Histories of the future'. Fuller definitions are offered by Kahn and Wiener, and by Warfield. Kahn and Wiener (1967) defined a scenario as 'a hypothetical sequence of events constructed for the purpose of focusing attention on causal processes and decision points', and Warfield (quoted in Coates *et al*. 1986) as 'a narrative description of a possible state of affairs or development over time. It can be useful to communicate speculative thoughts about future developments, to elicit discussion and feedback, and to stimulate the imagination. Scenarios are generally based on qualitative expert information, but may include quantitative information as well.'

Schwartz (1992) was clear that 'The purpose of scenarios is to help you change your view of reality—to match it up more closely with reality as it is, and as it is going to be. The end result, however, is not an accurate picture of tomorrow, but better decisions about the future.' Scenarios, then are a means to help us cope with the uncertainty of the future and make better decisions than we would otherwise do, in the present, about matters that have long-term future consequences. This is a pretty big claim and as Armstrong (1978) noted, 'little research of any kind has been done on scenarios'. He did acknowledge, however, that there is a reasonable possibility that they can contribute to the implementation process. An examination by Vlek and Otten (1987) of scenarios used in an energy-policy debate in The Netherlands suggested caution. They found that drawing up scenarios is a difficult task; that it is prone to questions about the validity of the assumptions on which the scenarios are based, the plausibility of the development processes involved and the comparability between the scenarios. The use of scenarios by decision-makers may also be questioned by the findings of Vlek and Otten's research with an experimental panel. They found that different scenarios varied in the ease with which they were memorised and in their plausibility and attractiveness to the panel. The difficulties may be compounded by the absence of an agreed methodology for constructing scenarios. Like many of the methods used to consider the future, the construction of scenarios is not an exact science.

Despite these difficulties scenarios have many supporters. Masser, Svidén and Wegener (1992) believed them to be 'superior to more rigorous forecasting methods such a statistical extrapolation or mathematical models if the number of factors to be considered and the degree of uncertainty about the future is high', and Millett (1988) quotes a survey of 1,500 major companies which concluded that 'scenarios were the most used technique for "conjectural forecasting"'. Reviewing his experience of scenarios, Godet (1993) concluded that they contributed to 'stimulating strategic thought and communication within companies; improving internal flexibility of response to environmental uncertainty, and providing better preparation for possible system breakdowns; reorienting policy options according to the future context on which their consequences would impinge'. Martino (1993) also saw scenarios as a means to combine individual forecasts into a composite whole.

To be useful, and to be given serious consideration, scenarios must be credible, useful and intelligible. One recommended way of increasing their value is to involve the users in the development of the scenarios, rather than present them with a finished product to which they have no commitment. To be credible scenarios must be internally consistent and logical; the inclusion of situations that the users believe could not coexist will understandably destroy their confidence in them. This can create difficulties, because one of the claimed benefits of scenarios is their ability to change peoples views. To get people to consider eventualities that they would normally dismiss out of hand can be difficult. It emphasises the need to anticipate the disbelief of the users and stresses the advantages of involving them in the development of the scenarios. Involvement should also enhance the chances of ensuring that the scenarios address the issues that are important to the users and that they are intelligible to them.

Scenarios are normally prepared in multiples in order to stress the alternative futures that could occur depending upon the direction of decisions, actions and events, and the uncertainty inherent in dealing with the future. Although this reflects the accepted view, that the future is difficult to predict, it runs counter to our wish to know what *is* going to happen. The traditional view of an expert is someone who is able to provide clear unambiguous advice based on their expertise. A forecaster might be expected, therefore, to provide clear forecasts. If they cannot, or will not do that, but only point out the uncertainties involved, what is the point of employing them? As Schwartz (1992) notes, 'Often, managers prefer the illusion of certainty to understanding risk and realities.' They are not alone in that, but convincing the users of scenarios that, as they already know, the future is uncertain, and that a range of scenarios may in fact be more useful than spurious precise forecasts is not always easy. It again emphasises the advantages of building up commitment by involvement in the development of the scenarios.

There is no firm agreement on the number of scenarios that should be prepared. Southern California Edison (1988), for example, considered twelve, but to provide alternatives there must be more than one and to avoid overload there cannot be too many. Zentner (1975) noted that in a situation where six were developed, three were ignored and only one used. He suggested that even four may be too many and concluded that three is about right. Three is a common number, used by Schwartz (1992), Northcott (1991), Masser, Svidén and Wegener (1992) and Wagar (1992). McNulty (1992) preferred two, to provide the extremes of the range of possible futures. This was intended to develop awareness while avoiding the danger that with three, unless they are very carefully constructed, one will be seen as the middle, most likely, and the other two rejected as extremes, in which case the purpose of developing the scenarios is lost. The best advice seems to be that the number will depend on the circumstances, but that between two and four is most likely to realise the potential of the technique by emphasising the uncertainty of the future but

Box 4. Preparing scenarios

1. Identify the central concerns of the users of the scenarios. What are the key decisions that will need to be made or the key issues involved?

2. Identify the developments or driving forces that are likely to have the most important influences on these central concerns in the future. This could include scientific or technological developments, political or social changes or anything that could have a major impact on the central concerns.

3. Analyse these important driving forces. Where can they be reasonably predicted, like an ageing population, and where are the main uncertainties? This step is useful in identifying the areas where more research is needed into the factors affecting the central concerns and where major unknowns remain and uncertainty is unavoidable. Schwartz stresses the need to look for the main trends and the trend breaks, which are particularly difficult to find but are often critical.

4. Assess the importance and the uncertainty of the driving forces for the central concerns. The identification of two or three such critical factors is useful in the next stage of defining the central themes of the scenarios, since they could be important in bringing about quite different futures.

5. Selection of the scenario logics, the main themes or assumptions around which the scenarios are to be constructed, is crucial. Schwartz suggests that it is important to end up with 'a few scenarios whose differences make a difference to decision-makers'. Themes that seem likely to lead to clearly different future situations are the most useful. Northcott (1991) used three policy-based scenarios, market, interventionist and environmentalist, to examine possible futures for Britain, while Wagar (1992) centred his world futures around different ideological stances or paradigms, technoliberal, radical and counterculturalist.

6. Develop the scenarios, usually in the form of narratives that present a plausible sequence of events. They should centre around the impact of each of the scenario themes on the driving forces identified earlier. A balance needs to be struck between detail and ease of understanding. As outlines scenarios are not intended to cover all events and one or two pages should therefore be sufficient. Anything longer is difficult for users to understand.

7. Analyse the impact of the scenarios on the key concerns with which the process began. This may reveal common themes that seem likely in the different circumstances envisaged by the scenarios, help identify robust decisions that will probably remain relevant in different situations, or stress the need to monitor a highly volatile and uncertain situation.

8. Analyse the implications for policy and identify indicators that will help monitor changes as they occur. A series of questions can be useful at this stage, such as 'Do certain decisions seem more likely to be successful in different circumstances while others appear to depend on only one set of circumstances?'

avoiding the confusion of too many alternatives. There is, of course, no guarantee that the eventual future will be like any of the chosen scenarios, but to think that it will be is to miss the point of preparing scenarios in the first place. They are not intended as accurate forecasts, but as tools to help us deal with the inherent uncertainty of the future.

Scenarios are generally viewed as a means of examining longer-term issues that are less amenable to extrapolative methods. According to circumstances this may mean ten to fifteen years in the case of Shell (Zentner 1975), or fifteen to thirty according to Cross (1982). A useful guide is that they should be 'short enough to be a reasonably foreseeable future, but long enough to encompass significant changes that are expected to impinge on the area of concern' (Cross 1982). In certain rapidly changing or unstable situations, such as military campaigns or taking precautions against disasters that could happen at any time, they could be useful in the analysis of relatively short-term issues.

There is no one correct way of preparing scenarios, though common themes do appear in the literature. Comparisons of different methods were made by Schnaars (1987) and Huss and Honton (1987). Box 4 details a procedure based on that developed by SRI International and described by Huss and Honton (1987) and Schwartz (1992). It sets out a series of eight steps in the development and use of the scenarios.

Although this discussion has emphasised the narrative nature of scenarios, the method does not exclude the use of quantitative forecasts. It is also often combined at different stages with other Futures methods, such as Delphi (to identify driving forces), cross-impact (to analyse interrelationships) and computer models (to examine the consequences of particular events or policy choices). Meadows et al. (1992) used the World 3 Model to examine the different consequences of thirteen scenarios based on a variety of assumptions about technology, resource availability and policy responses. Only the use of the computer model makes this possible.

The discussion of scenarios so far may suggest that they can only be prepared by experts with access to large budgets. It is true that the method was developed by a think-tank and has been used by several major companies, but as the examples in Box 5 indicate, scenarios can be prepared quite simply to examine different possible futures—in this case two alternative views of the future of a small town in northern England. The scenarios provided local people with alternative visions of the possible future of their area, making connections between a number of events that could occur to give a picture of the future resulting from different decisions. Different perspectives could be gained on issues and opportunities seen where only problems were visible before.

Box 5. Scenarios for Ilkley

Scenario 1

Since the bypass was built Ilkley has been a much pleasanter place. It was not easy persuading the Department of Transport to build the tunnel but the effort was worthwhile. Church Street, without the through traffic, has become a lively shopping street, the buildings on either side have been refurbished and pedestrians can move about without fear of mortal injury. People can now get to the Manor House and the river, and the open air cafe in Castle Yard was an inspired move. Of course, there is traffic in the centre, but the traffic-calming schemes mean that pedestrians have priority and drivers are forced to drive slowly through the heart of the town. It is amazing to think, when you look at those old photographs of Brook Street in the early 1990s, that people put up for so long with all that tarmac and a space that was mostly road with dangerous, crowded, narrow footpaths. What a waste it was and how marvellous to see people reclaim it from the cars.

Car-parking was always a problem and it remains one today, even if the new electric- and hydrogen-powered vehicles are not so polluting as the petrol-driven ones were. We still like to drive when possible. Parking has been carefully managed, particularly in the controlled parking-house on the western side of Rombalds Square. By clever use of the levels, a part-below-ground, part-above-ground facility providing about 400 spaces could be constructed. When it was first suggested there was uproar against the idea of a multi-storey car park in Ilkley, but when the design of the facades became clear, matching as they do the shops on the rest of the Square, support grew. Even the Civic Society recommended the scheme for a national Civic Trust award. Later, the redevelopment of the old car park—a real eyesore, as some of you will remember—into Rombalds Square, won a major European Environmental Award as an example of how to create a new town square from a dead heart. Bradford Council, as the responsible authority, was overjoyed at the publicity it brought to the district and even more by the international tourists who spend their money here.

Ilkley has grown slowly over the years, with some new housing, but most of mid-Wharfedale is now protected from development by its status as a European Landscape Protection Area. This enables local groups working to enhance the area by repairing stone walls, laying paths, replanting and so on to obtain grants to help with the work. Yes, Ilkley is a great place to live and to visit; more people can do so now by West Yorks Electric, the electrified rail service that links all the main centres of the conurbation together. Actually it is better than it was twenty-five years ago, much to many people's surprise.

Scenario 2

As many people thought twenty-five years ago, despite the consistent denials, the M65 through mid-Wharfedale was completed a couple of years ago. It has been a major factor in the transformation of Ilkley into a twenty-first-century town. Once the dual carriageways were built round Burley and at Manor Park, the bottleneck of Ilkley was the only major delay between the M6 and the A1. Local opposition, which was very fierce, even to suspected sabotage of the road building equipment, never stood a chance. Once the route was built, only a little widening was needed to convert it to full motorway standard for the designated Stranraer to Hull Euroway. It cut through the north slope of the valley below Middleton and once the service area was allowed on the old hospital site, the rural view from the Moor, on the south of the valley, was completely lost.

Initially there was some reduction in the traffic in the town but levels soon grew again. Church Street and Leeds Road are as busy as they ever were and most of the shops have closed, being replaced by all night take-aways, amusement arcades and virtual-reality entertainment complexes. The centre of town is one big traffic circus. There are parking restrictions, but that just means people spend ages driving round looking for somewhere to park. All the streets around the old town centre are either race tracks or car parks. The remaining Victorian buildings and the Manor House are now devoted to the booming heritage industry with international tourists coming to see how Britain was in the 'Good Old Days'.

Ilkley has grown a great deal recently. There is only a small amount of open land now in the Wharfe Valley, between Addingham and Pool. First, there was the research complex to the east of the town followed by big expansion of house-building in the late 1990s. Then the Wharfedale Leisure–Shop complex just east of Burley was built to serve the growing population. North Yorkshire has restricted development on the north side of the motorway, which falls within the Nidderdale Area of Outstanding Natural Beauty, but the land to the south of the river is mostly urbanised. The combination of good access by road and rail, the airport only fifteen minutes' drive away, and nearby open country has been a major attraction to investment as the plans of the early 1990s anticipated.

Old photographs of Ilkley from the 1990s show a small town set in the mainly rural Wharfe Valley; now most of that valley is built up. It is a prosperous area, people are keen to move to Wharfevale, as the area is known by the property press. As the cities of Leeds and Bradford have decentralised, places like Ilkley have become more attractive. As always there have been those who have opposed the changes, but you can't stop progress, can you?

5.1.2. Issues-Management

Like a number of the methods discussed in this section, issues-management may more accurately be regarded as a package drawing on a range of techniques. This is apparent in Coates *et al.* (1986), which includes an introduction to more than twenty methods and techniques.

Issues-management was developed as a tool for the commercial sector. Coates *et al.* and Renfro (1993), in particular, saw it as a means by which companies can benefit by responding to emerging issues before they reach critical proportions. A particular concern is to anticipate issues likely to result in new legislation that will impact on the operations of the company. Choucri (1991), for example, argued that companies that anticipate environmental issues and act voluntarily in advance of legal requirements will gain an advantage over those that wait until they are forced to take action. That the technique may have applications over a wider field is indicated by the report of an application in education by Renfro and Morrison (1982).

Coates *et al.* listed a number of assumptions on which issues-management is based, including the ability to identify emerging issues before they become mainstream, and the belief that this early identification is beneficial. The benefits claimed include the opportunity to study issues in greater depth before having to respond to them and the opportunity this provides to consider a wider range of possible options than reacting in a crisis allows. Coates *et al.* also suggested that anticipation of emerging issues enables an organisation to take a more positive approach to them whereas waiting until they become problems limits us to a reactive response. Quoting a personal communication from Molitor he suggested that issues tend to follow a common pattern from an original idea—often in fringe media, science fiction or art—through detailed research and specialised journals before they are taken up as public concerns that eventually lead to legislation or changes of behaviour. This suggests what Renfro (1993) called the Issues Life Cycle, which follows an S-curve-like pattern from birth through definition, naming (such as 'Greenhouse Effect'), and group involvement to media attention and action. If this is the case, and it is possible to identify such issues at an early stage, then the basic premiss of issues-management, 'Forewarned is forearmed', seems valid.

Renfro (1993) suggested that the issues-management process has four main stages:

- identifying potential issues by environmental scanning,
- researching the background and assessing the potential impacts of issues,
- evaluating the issues and selecting those to be considered further, and
- developing strategies.

5.1.3. Scanning

The initial stage of the issues-management process, the identification of issues, uses a technique, *environmental scanning*, with which it sometimes appears synonymous, but which also exists in its own right. The Quick Environmental Scanning Technique (QUEST) described by Nanus (1982) and Slaughter (1990) covers essentially the same process, moving from the identification of issues to strategy. Scanning also has similarities with content-analysis (mentioned in the last chapter). Both are concerned with monitoring events in order to identify changes, though scanning and issues-management are, perhaps, more focused and purposeful. It is generally acknowledged that we all indulge in passive scanning, reading newspapers, magazines and periodicals relevant to our interests and watching television, without really thinking about it. It is how we keep up to date, with the stock market, the football results, fashion or whatever is our particular concern. Taking scanning more seriously means *actively scanning* particular sources regularly, perhaps making an effort to extend the scope beyond the area we normally cover, while *directed scanning* as part of a team implies a much more organised and selective approach for particular purposes. Guidance on setting up a scanning system was given by Renfro (1993) and Pflaum and Delmont (1987), and on running the QUEST process by Nanus (1982).

QUEST is a self-contained package of workshops and intervening activities, while scanning tends to be a more continuous process. QUEST begins with a preparation phase, organising the process and providing basic information to the participants, who then come together for a scanning workshop to identify changes with potential importance for their organisation. As with all scanning activity, a wide-ranging and speculative approach is recommended before the most important issues revealed are selected for further consideration. Further development work will probably be necessary before a second workshop to consider scenarios focused around the main themes identified. The scenarios are used to help develop strategic options. The QUEST technique could be used to raise consciousness of change or be incorporated into the planning process.

Scanning usually involves a longer-term commitment, since it is a continuing process of monitoring change. It is important, at the outset, to be clear why the scanning system is to be set up, the level of involvement required and how the results are to be used. Is it to increase the awareness of change by updating information, provide early warning of potential problems, minimise surprise, or feed into planning and strategic thinking? Answers to these questions will influence the form of the system, its place within the organisation and how the products of scanning are disseminated.

Neufeld (1985) suggested four types of indicators that can be useful in indicating emerging issues. *Lone signals* are the one-off items that may indicate new developments. An example might be the observation in mid-1994 that the number of women in management in the UK had declined for the first time in recent years, reversing a previous gradually increasing trend. By contrast, the number of small businesses run by women continued to increase. Various explanations were floated, but one of the most interesting was the conclusion that women were reacting against the macho culture of big firms in favour of their own control. If this were to continue it would be shown up in further *statistical descriptions*, which could indicate a growing trend with significant implications. Regular statistical series are important indicators of change, though by definition they only measure those things that we have already recognised as important. Decisions to begin monitoring particular changes are important indicators in themselves. *Landmark events* or *Breakthroughs* in science and technology and in social and political affairs can be particularly important. They are, like many developments, more easily recognised in retrospect; but events like the discovery of a new drug or the breaching of the Berlin Wall form critical stages in the evolution of events and require new thinking to deal with their consequences. The *forecasts of experts* and informed speculation about the future are also, Neufeld suggested, worth monitoring.

Scanning, Marien (1991) contended, is a normal, healthy and absolutely necessary activity 'for the intelligent guidance of our individual and collective affairs', but it 'is and always will be . . . imperfect'. Its imperfections arise from choices we have to make in order to cope with the amount of information we would need to scan to even approach perfection. These choices were summarised by Marien (1991) as a preference for secondary over primary sources; the present over the recent past (which might counsel caution); print over non-print; non-electronic over electronic; for English speakers, English over non-English (which, as Godet (1993) pointed out, excludes most of the world's writing); non-fiction over fiction; periodicals and books over the 'grey literature' of reports and government documents; views that concur with our ideology, prejudices, world-view, background and orientation over those that do not; and trends over opportunities for human betterment. Recognising biases like these may help us expand the scope of our scanning and reduce our exposure to surprise.

In isolation, scanning may be regarded as a form of trend-identification but it is clear that its practitioners see it as much more than that. Cook (1986), for example, stated that the 'primary purpose of most . . . scanning programmes is continually to search out new issues of potential importance . . . and, when appropriate, refer them to the policy management mechanisms that already exist'. Its use is in informing the management process and enabling it to consider issues at an early stage, rather than reacting to them when they become critical.

5.1.4. Impact-assessment

The second stage of the issues-management process concerns background research and the assessment of the potential impacts of the issues identified. This relates closely to an area which has itself developed into a major activity since 1970, impact-assessment. Several variants exist, including technology-assessment, environmental-impact-assessment and social-impact-assessment. Coates (1978) defined technology-assessment as 'a class of policy studies which systematically examine the effects on society that may occur when a technology is introduced, extended or modified'. Clark *et al.* (1980) saw environmental-impact-assessment as the 'systematic examination of environmental consequences of projects, policies and programmes. Its main objective is to provide decision-makers with an account of the implications of alternative courses of action before a decision is made'. The future-orientation of impact-assessment is made clear by the reference to *effects that may occur* and *action before a decision*. This, as Westman (1985) noted, has propelled impact practitioners 'into what has at times seemed a murky world of futurology', which, according to Rossini and Porter (1983), has set them apart from most of their scientific compatriots, who are not used to making predictions.

As Carley and Derow (1983) pointed out, impact-assessment rests on two assumptions:

1) that the future can be predicted, or guessed at, with enough reliability to make it worthwhile considering potential changes which might be caused by the introduction of new projects or new technology, [and] 2) that policy-makers will understand the assessment and respond by modifying the decisions that they might otherwise have made.

As a forecast, impact-assessment is subject to the difficulties of prediction. The little research that has been done comparing impact-assessments prepared before the event with evaluations made afterwards confirms that the two are not always the same.

An important area of the debate about such assessments is their political significance. They are most frequently used to assess particular proposals, for example the environmental impact of a toxic-waste incinerator or road proposal, or a new technology. As such they are concerned with issues of major local, national or even wider significance about which there are a range of different, and often opposed opinions. The debate between the pro- and anti-lobbies is unlikely to be influenced greatly by an environmental assessment of a particular proposal. As a quasi-scientific technique to try to assess the impact of a certain development, an impact-assessment cannot be separated from the value positions of the protagonists, however much those preparing it try to be objective and impartial. Within the technique evaluations are made that can have a determining effect on the conclusions reached. A particular environment that its protectors believe should be preserved unaltered for future generations cannot, in their eyes, be valued against the benefit to be gained by using it for some other purpose. The question is meaningless. It is equally difficult for their opponents, who see the benefits, such as jobs to be created or the savings to be made, as important gains outweighing other considerations. Such situations raise important issues about who should undertake impact-assessments, how they should be used and what considerations should be included. It is not surprising that such assessment procedures have often been regarded unfavourably by both the proponents and the opponents of the proposal under consideration. The supporters may regard them as a way of delaying necessary progress, while the opposition sees them as a whitewash, giving the appearance of fairness but in reality only justifying decisions that have already been made.

The case for impact-assessment arose from the experience of past technologies and activities in the environment. The environmental and human consequences of past activities have been such as to encourage the view that similar problems could be avoided in future if prior consideration was given to the possible outcome of a development or technology. More informed decisions could then be made about proceeding or incorporating modifications to alleviate some of the undesirable effects in preference to attempting to clean up after the event. Coates (1974) gave a useful list of the possible consequences of a successful assessment, including making modifications, defining a programme for monitoring the effects as the development occurs, stimulating research into areas requiring further information, identifying regulatory and legislative needs, delaying or preventing development and, where appropriate, identifying ways to implement the proposal incrementally. As the scale of the impact of both technologies and particular proposals has grown, the case for prior assessments has increased and formal arrangements for them have been incorporated into law. Environmental-impact-assessment, which was first introduced in the USA by the National Environmental Policy Act of 1969 and subsequently in the European Community and other countries, is a case in point.

The details and the particular techniques employed at different stages will vary according to the requirements of each case, but Coates insisted that it is unlikely to be a linear, once-only study. He recommended working through the process three times, once to understand the problem, a second time to get it right and once more to check and polish the results. Many of the techniques discussed in this volume were listed by Coates (1978) as being useful in technology-assessment. A general procedure for impact-assessments, into which particular techniques can be incorporated as appropriate, is set out in Box 6.

Box 6. General procedure for impact-assessments

1. Clearly establish the nature of the issue to be considered and the purpose of the assessment. In some circumstances this will be obvious but it is necessary to be clear, for example, whether alternatives are to be considered or not. Where they are considered the intention may be to illuminate the choice between them to assist in adopting the least damaging. Where they are not, the concern may be with exploring ways to minimise or alleviate the impact of a chosen development by modifications. This first stage should include a clear description of the proposal.

2. Decide the scope of the assessment to be made and the major factors to be included. Where a legally laid-down or established procedure is being followed this may be apparent, but, if not, because the list of possible considerations is almost endless, it is important to establish the boundaries before proceeding. The issues included, the time scale (how far into the future the impacts are to be assessed), whose interests are to be considered and the spatial scale are all matters of potential debate that will affect the perceived validity of the assessment.

3. Identify the relevant features. Techniques like checklists, brainstorming, Delphi or intuition may be useful here in identifying the range of possible impacts and selecting among them. This is clearly a crucial stage of the assessment but also one of the most difficult because it requires the identification of impacts that have yet to occur. Cross (1982) wondered, for example, whether a social-impact-assessment of the car in its early days would have identified the wide back seat as relevant to courtship patterns, and White (1974) doubted that the significant social consequences of the chimney could have been forecast by a technology-assessment exercise in the Middle Ages.

4. Identify the different social groups that will be affected by the project or technology. This is because the effects are seldom the same for all involved. For example, the 'dash for gas' in the UK electricity-generation industry in the early 1990s had a direct effect on the coalminers who lost their jobs and the gas-workers who gained jobs, and beyond that was the impact upon the suppliers to the mines and the gas industry and the communities in the different localities affected. Loss of the coal traffic also reduced the need for rail-freight from the mines to the power stations, affecting the jobs of the railway workers and the

viability of that section of the rail-freight industry. A wide general benefit that was claimed for the shift was the potential reduction in sulphur and carbon emissions. This could work to the advantage of communities as far away as Scandinavia, who had previously suffered from Britain's reliance on coal-fired power stations, and contribute to the UK's commitment to reduce emissions following the Rio environmental summit. How far such impacts should be traced socially, spatially and temporally (how many future generations should be considered?) are important decisions that will affect the assessment.

5. The occurrence of the impacts across the social groups then needs to be identified. An effective way of achieving this is to use a matrix to clarify which groups are likely to experience which impacts. It may be important to the final conclusions to attempt to assess the size of each group and the intensity of the impacts upon them, because they are unlikely to be equally felt by the same number of people. This will lead to a need to make judgements between, for example, low-level impacts that affect a large number and high-level impacts that affect a few—in the case of a road proposal, the few who will lose their houses against the many who may gain a few minutes by using the new road.

6. An analysis of the impacts as they are likely to affect the groups is the culmination of the assessment, and is fed into the decision-making process. Within the field of environmental-impact-assessment Clark *et al.* (1980) listed a number of methods that can be used, including checklists, matrices, networks and models. Where complex issues are under consideration the presentation of the results of the impact study can be a problem in itself. To deal effectively with the issues may require lengthy and detailed technical discussion that the decision-makers and interested public have neither the time nor the background to assimilate. For example, a study of the environmental impact of road schemes identified six major themes of impact over three geographical scales. These were then divided into eighteen subsections and 103 different impacts, several of which were themselves further subdivided. Differential social impacts were not included (SACTRA 1992). Summarising details of this nature into a form usable by decision-makers raises many issues that require considerable judgement and are capable of widely differing interpretation. There seems to be value in producing a full report of the impacts and a summary for those without the time or interest to study the full document.

Source: adapted from Cross (1982).

Harman (1983) set out necessary—though not sufficient—requirements for a competent impact-assessment:

1) The purpose which guides it should be to contribute to the public dialogue, to clarify questions and to raise issues, not to tell a particular 'decision maker' what is his 'best' decision;

2) It should be carried out with integrity in the sense of a desire to clarify, not obscure and defend. There should not be, for example, a preoccupation with the quantifiable which may favourably impress critics but becloud important qualitative features. Where intuitive insight plays a role this should be acknowledged openly, not hidden behind an after-the-fact synthetic bridge of logic;

3) The IA requires a holistic paradigm, which is to say a comparison of whole-system scenarios or the equivalent;

4) It requires a teleological outlook; that is to say it must take into account the purposes of the actors involved. Meanings, values, and attitudes are of central importance.

5.1.5. Cost–Benefit Analysis

Cost–benefit analysis was an early form of impact-assessment. Originally it was an attempt to assess the costs and benefits of proposed developments before the decision to proceed was made. Since it was derived from economics, it was based upon the idea of converting the costs and benefits into a single common measurement, money. This, it was argued, would provide a clear yardstick by which to assess a project. If the benefits outweighed the costs, it would be justified; if the reverse was true, it would not. The criticisms of the technique centred around the ease with which important factors could be given a monetary value. Estimates of the construction costs of a project are relatively easily determined, but it is much more difficult to ascribe a value to a piece of landscape that would be destroyed or affected by the proposal. Too often these imponderables were set to one side in the calculation, and were consequently given much less weight than things that were given a monetary value. Similar problems occurred in attempts to value the benefits to be gained. The benefits of road proposals in the UK were based on calculations of the forecast savings from prevented accidents and reduced travel time, both of which depended on a series of assumptions about the number of accidents prevented and their costs and the value of time saved by drivers. During studies for the location of a third airport for London, the difficulties were summed up in the phrase 'And how much for your grandmother?' and in the valuation of an eleventh-century church, an irreplaceable asset, at its insurance value in the cost–benefit calculations undertaken.

5.1.6. Risk-Assessment

Another set of techniques that could also be useful in identifying which issues to pursue is risk-assessment. It, too, has developed into an area of expertise in its own right but it has a relevance to Futures because its central concern is to identify, assess and where possible reduce or avoid risks *before* they become reality. Risk has been defined as 'exposure to the possibility of economic or financial loss or gain, physical damage or injury, or delay, as a consequence of the uncertainty associated with pursuing a particular course of action' (Cooper and Chapman 1987). We all live with risk, whether in the form of potential accidents, breakdowns and losses of various sorts or, as Cooper and Chapman pointed out, potential benefit. In arranging a holiday, for example, we effectively discount the risk that we will not be able to take it for any reason or not enjoy it when we get there. The risk exists in the form of any of the potential events that could occur between the time of our decision to take the holiday and the time of the holiday itself, and unknowns about the location, weather and so on.

Taking out insurance against the occurrence of situations that would prevent us going on holiday, or other unpleasant events, is the way we normally deal with such matters. In setting their premiums, the insurance companies assess the risk of particular events over the number of policy holders they have and charge rates in relation to the estimates made. In doing so they will be relying on their experience of the past relationship between the income from premiums and the expenditure on claims extended in some way into the future. That they are not always successful in their forecasts is indicated by the £7 billion losses made by Lloyd's of London between 1988 and 1991 (Springett 1994). The cause seems to have been unanticipated claims associated with environmental accidents and liability for past environmental damage, sometimes relating to policies written more than thirty years before, when the likelihood of claims being made was assessed as much lower than has transpired. For those involved in covering the loss, the so-called 'Names', this is a graphic and painful illustration of the uncertainty of the future. During the mid-1980s the industry was producing good profits and attracted several investors on the assumption that this would continue. Unfortunately for them it did not.

Risk-assessment has become more important as it has become apparent that accidents and system-failures can cost a great deal of money. Dickson (1991) noted that the cost of material damage alone from fire in the UK in 1988 amounted to £645.9 million. For both companies and individuals reducing risk can be beneficial. The task of risk-analysis is to assess the risk and to assist in the decision about taking measures to reduce or protect against its occurrence. Dickson suggested that it is important in four main situations: identifying new potential risks that have not yet occurred, assessing known risks, evaluating the impact of risk, and ensuring that all potential risks are identified. Looking essentially to the assessment of risk in an industrial situation, he recommended the use of techniques such as *checklists*, statistical techniques of the kind already discussed, *fault trees* and *probability trees*. A fault tree is 'a diagrammatic representation of all the events which may give rise to some major event. It shows the way in which individual events can combine together to produce potentially dangerous situations.' It can be used to gain some estimate of the likelihood of the occurrence of the major event from an analysis of the chances of the causal events occurring together. The probability tree works in the opposite direction, beginning with a major event and breaking it down into more detailed possible occurrences, for each of which a probability is estimated. At each succeeding level more tightly defined events are identified so that the probability of any one occurring reduces as the tree branches. Estimates of the probability of any particular event can therefore be made.

One of the issues to be considered in risk-assessment is the varying perception of risk by individuals. Travelling by car is statistically more dangerous than flying, but people are more likely to be afraid of flying than of travelling by car. Some people regularly engage in risky activities like hang-gliding or caving, while others would never consider doing so. Public perception of risk can be influenced by publicity or propaganda and may often be quite different from the assessment of risks by experts. A debate of this kind surrounds the use of nuclear power to generate electricity. There are other issues involved but an important part of the public reaction to nuclear power has been formed by the events at Chernobyl and Three Mile Island. These, actual or nearly, catastrophic events cause much greater impact than the more gradual problems associated with coal-fired power, such as air pollution, the contribution to the Greenhouse Effect and accidents to miners, even though some experts assess the risks of nuclear power as lower than those of more conventional means of electricity-generation. As a result the evaluation of risk becomes a very complex matter, particularly where issues of public policy are concerned. Rational assessment of the risks can assist the decision-making process but cannot completely eliminate the uncertainty of the future and therefore a residual element of risk.

5.1.7. Role-playing, Simulation and Gaming

Playing and games are frequently associated with childhood and not considered appropriate to serious adult issues. On the other hand, the recognition of the importance of play in the development of children and the establishment of war-gaming as a training mechanism and a means of examining potential conflict situations has encouraged the growth of a related set of methods involving simulation, gaming and role-playing. Duke (1978) was clear that gaming is not predictive but can be useful 'for gaining perspective on complex systems particularly for guiding speculation about future circumstances'. Gaming, he claimed, can be future-oriented and convey complex and rapidly changing situations in a more effective way than more conventional methods. In particular it provides a way of examining complex situations that does not rely on the sequential nature of language. In order to describe situations through the written or spoken word we have to break them down into segments that can be communicated one after another in a sequence. Duke claimed that this is not necessary in a simulation game, where more sophisticated, interactive approaches can be employed in what he termed a *multilogue*, a series of simultaneous and parallel interactions. This gives a much closer representation of reality. It can therefore be a useful Futures technique for exploring the consequences of different decisions. He quoted the example of a Simulated Nutrition System Game, used by the United Nations, where players adopt a series of different roles to examine the problem from a number of perspectives. Gaming can be especially useful, according to Porter *et al.* (1991), in situations characterised by:

- numerous interacting variables,
- variables and their interactions that are difficult or impossible to quantify,
- the absence of a conceptual model for decision making, [and]
- decision making in a socio-political context in which the players may be idiosyncratic and unpredictable.

Armstrong (1987) suggested that role-play can also be an effective predictor of future outcomes and often provides superior forecasts to other methods, particularly in conflict situations. He presented a number of examples to illustrate his claim. Armstrong set out guidelines for role-playing in forecasting situations that also have application to circumstances where the examination of alternatives, rather than accurate prediction, is the aim. Providing a clear but brief description of the circumstances of the simulation so that the participants understand the situation is an important first step. In some circumstances, where they are themselves directly involved in the issue, the participants could themselves draw up the brief; elsewhere this will be the responsibility of the facilitator. Two pages is usually quite sufficient. Unless the purpose of the simulation is to allow participants to play out their real-life roles it will also be necessary to cast the roles in the game. Armstrong suggests that for the purposes of prediction it is best to find subjects 'somewhat similar' to the actual participants, but the random allocation to roles has usually been adequate.

Where the participants are not familiar with the circumstances or the roles they are to play, it is necessary to provide them with detailed descriptions, to enable them to understand and play the role. One page is enough in most circumstances. Having done this it is vital that the participants understand the need to stay within the role and improvise within it during the simulation, whether they are instructed to act as they themselves would act or as they believe the person being played would act. The setting for the simulation should be as realistic as possible, with participants being encouraged, for example, to dress in their role. A brief period (about ten minutes) should be allowed for preparation before the session itself, which should not be overextended. About an hour is usually sufficient for the session itself. A debriefing session discussing the results and insights obtained during the simulation should follow, either immediately or after time for reflection. There is a temptation to curtail this evaluation but in many respects it is the most important part of the process, where the value of the simulation, in terms of the insights and lessons gained, is either realised or not.

In designing gaming simulations there is often a trade-off to be made between the attempt to replicate reality and the need to produce a 'playable' game. Reality can be highly complex, requiring many differing roles and complicated situations. If they become too complex and the roles require vastly different levels of involvement by different players, those who may have only a few opportunities for intervention may lose commitment and fail to remain involved even at those points in the game where their part is important. Consequently the 'reality' of the simulation can be lost.

Advances in computing have added another dimension to gaming and simulation. Increasingly sophisticated computer games simulate a wide variety of situations. Many are purely fictional and designed for enjoyment, but others provide opportunities to explore the future implications of alternative decisions and allow for interaction between several players. They will undoubtedly become more important in assisting the decision-making process as they evolve to become more realistic both in their presentation and construction. It will be important to remember, however, that they remain a replication of reality based on particular perceptions and ideas of how reality works and will evolve, rather than reality itself. Competing, equally valid or even better perceptions may be excluded if reliance is placed on one model alone. We have already argued that reliance on single forecasts is generally unwise because it assumes the future is predictable. Reliance on one simulation could be equally unwise when the aim is to gain insight into the future. It might, then, be advisable to create more than one game, based on different theoretical interpretations of reality, or to repeat the original game with different players and/or by varying the roles.

5.2. POLICY-MAKING

5.2.1. Planning, Policy, Decision-Making, Strategy-Development and Problem-Solving

Whole libraries have been written on each of these topics individually. To consider them together is not to devalue the ideas that have been developed, but to acknowledge that they also have similarities. Essentially they are all future-oriented, as two of the following quotes make clear and the others imply. They are all concerned with making a difference, bringing about circumstances that do not currently exist. The only time-scale in which that can be achieved is the future, whether in the short, medium or long term.

- 'Planning is that process of making rational decisions about future goals and future courses of action' (M. M. Webber, quoted in Kenney 1988). It is, as Branch (1990) noted, 'a fundamental element of conscious human activity', which exists in a wide range of situations from individuals and households to government and business. To illustrate its role in government and business Branch listed over 200 job titles that include the words 'Planning' or 'Planner'.
- Policy, 'A deliberate course of action or inaction taken . . . on the way resources are to be used in the pursuit of objectives or in support of other policies' (B. Smith 1976).
- Decision, 'a conclusion or resolution reached, especially as to future action, after consideration' (Tulloch 1993).
- Strategy, 'a plan of action or policy" (Tulloch 1993).
- Problem-solving techniques, 'formal, structured approaches that have been developed . . . to aid in solving . . . problems' (Van Gundy 1988).

An essential feature of planning, policy, strategy, decision-making and problem-solving is intention, the desire to achieve particular ends. Planning is undertaken because it is thought to be a more effective means to achieve these ends than not planning. Individuals and companies plan as a matter of course, but in certain situations, notably at the level of government, planning can be a very contentious issue. Some people hold that planning is the most effective means for society to achieve its ends, while others believe that free, unregulated markets are better. The demise of the 'Planned Economies' and the triumph of Capitalism are frequently taken as proof of the market approach, but examination of the most successful market economies, such as Japan, reveals a significant element of planning behind the success. Paradoxically, it seems possible that both approaches are useful in different circumstances and that some combination of both may work best. Even if that is accepted, how much of each will remain a matter of debate. Policy is often associated with government, as in phrases like 'economic policy' or 'transport policy'. These are sets of measures designed to bring about desired situations. Integral to both planning and policy-making are strategies and decisions about how the aims may best be attained. Frequently the need for decisions, plans or policy is based on the identification of problems that are perceived to require solutions.

Planning and policy-making assume that we can affect the future by making decisions in the present that will lead to circumstances different from, and preferable to those that would have occurred without our intervention. Like many other such assumptions, this one is unprovable in a wholly scientific way. We cannot both intervene and not intervene in the same circumstances, at the same time, in the real world. We can draw evidence from comparable situations that are removed in space and/or time from our current concern, or simulate different actions and observe their results, but however convincing this may be it is not absolute proof that intervention will be best. Equally, it is impossible to prove that not intervening is superior, though the liberalism that dominates Western thought generally assumes that non-intervention is preferable at the level of government and society, though not the firm.

Decision-making, problem-solving and strategy rest on similar assumptions. If our decisions could have no effect on events then they would not be worth making. If our actions did not have any influence over the problems we identify, the effort that we put into attempting to solve them would be wasted. If attempts to move towards preferred aims made no difference they would be futile. It is because we believe that our efforts do make a difference that we undertake them. Where people are convinced that they cannot exert effective influence over what happens, because mere humans cannot affect natural forces or because they lack the power to influence those who make decisions that affect them, they may give up any attempt to do so and become fatalistic. One of the aims of Futures is to encourage people to become more involved in the belief that their opinions do matter and that they can and should affect society's decisions and actions.

Intervention of this kind also assumes that we can compare the probable outcomes of a number of courses of action and decide between them. This implies a belief that when we compare decisions or policies we are able to foresee their likely effects and in consequence make meaningful comparisons between them. Stacey (1992) contended that this is often not possible because the future is inherently unpredictable. Such is the variation among the many possible futures that may occur as a result of the interaction of the many forces involved that 'There is no point in trying to simulate this future because you would have to know all this precise detail in advance to get anywhere near the future which will emerge.' To make a rational comparison between policy options we would need to do this for as many different futures as we have alternative policies. But this is often not possible because of the 'inevitable unpredictability and irregularity of the innovative, the creative and the new'. Decision-making in these circumstances, while centred in the changing present, becomes a learning process with important future significance.

The processes of planning, policy-making, problem-solving and decision-making are basically similar. They are all intentional approaches that aim to improve the responses made to issues. In their pure form they adopt a rational approach, assuming that it is possible to identify issues and design and implement the best solutions. That is no bad aim, but it is seldom achievable in social situations where different opinions, attitudes and values are brought to bear on the issues and uncertainty is inherent. The main steps in a typical process are depicted in Fig. 15. It begins from observation of the real world, from which we identify either a problem or a desire, a divergence between what we would like the situation to be and what exists. In order to move towards our preferred situation alternative means that we believe will solve the problem, or achieve our desire, are generated. The alternatives are then compared in terms of their anticipated ability to produce the preferred situation and the one we believe will have the best chance of creating the situation we

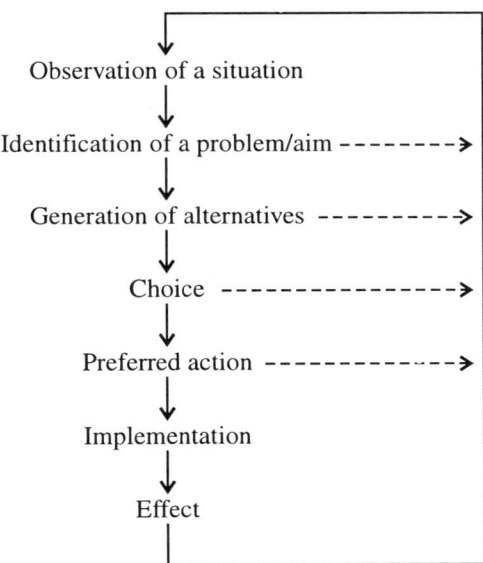

Fig. 15. The planning/policy-making process

want is selected. The decision is then put into action and leads to effects in the real world. The effect may be as we predicted or not, but whatever the result the new situation may lead to the identification of new problems or desires and encourage us to start the process all over again. The steps are often not as clear-cut as this suggests—they often overlap, occur all at once, come in a different order, feed back on each other, or are skipped or assumed. We may also be working on several issues at once, each perhaps influencing the other in some way, while the solution to one problem, or the achievement of one desire, may well result in the creation or recognition of others.

5.2.2. Problem-Identification

A problem exists when the current situation is seen to differ from what we consider acceptable or desirable. We have an unemployment problem, for example, because so many people are without jobs in a society in which having a job is regarded as important both for the individual and for the society as a whole. If the number of people unemployed declined or we came to the conclusion that there were better ways of organising society and spending our time than by having a job, the problem would disappear: in the first case because there were no longer so many unemployed, but in the second because our perception of the desirable situation had changed. What had been considered a problem would no longer be considered one, even if the number of people without jobs actually increased. (This may appear a shocking idea but only because we have become used to the notion of employment as central to society. It did not occupy such a position before the Industrial Revolution and might not again. There are other ways of filling our time and circulating wealth. Perhaps in time we will develop them and look back on the idea of employment as an outdated and even shocking notion, like slavery.) Problems do not just exist but are identified and defined by observers who compare the observed circumstances with those that they wish to see. A problem is not a problem until we recognise it as such, and the recognition of problems can be a matter of considerable debate.

Not all problems are of equal importance. The severity of a problem and opinions about whether it is one that should attract concern are influenced by our attitudes, different people identifying and prioritising different problems and considering particular problems of varying importance. Like most things, problems change, either because the situation changes or our perception of it alters in response to changes in our environment. New problems emerge and existing ones may seem less significant or worsen in relation to others. It is often suggested, for example, that the attention given to environmental issues varies more with the state of the economy and the attention given to them in the media than with their innate significance. When the economy is doing well attention turns to environmental issues, but during a recession they are pushed off the agenda by what are seen as more pressing economic concerns.

Problem-identification, then, is frequently a social and political process. Scanning and related methods can be useful in identifying new problems, but political action may be necessary to attract attention to them. Campaigning through publicity and exerting pressure on the decision-makers will often be necessary to get issues on to the agenda and keep them there long enough for action to be taken.

There is an argument that to be worth consideration an issue should be regarded as a problem. Such an opinion may be based on the reasoning that with limited resources we should concentrate on alleviating real problems, issues that are causing difficulties and are clearly not as we would wish. On the other hand, it can be argued that to restrict ourselves to the solution of problems constrains our field of action and discounts the possibility that there might be situations in which, although there is no problem as such, we can envisage circumstances that are clearly preferable to those that exist at the moment and that it would be worth trying to achieve. The difference is neatly summed up in the phrase, variously attributed to Robert Kennedy and Bernard Shaw among others, 'Some see things as they are and ask why; I see things that never were and ask why not.' The former is essentially a problem-solving approach, while the latter is opportunity- or goal-centred, raising the prospect of improvement not as a solution to a perceived problem but as an end in itself.

Only where we can imagine circumstances that are better than those that currently exist are we in a position to take action. Several words in English convey this idea: 'invention', 'innovation' and 'creation' are three of them. All suggest the new, the different; bringing into existence something that has not existed before. That we can imagine situations and things that have not previously existed ties in with our experience. That we have not visited a particular place before does not prevent us from imagining that we could do so and making arrangements to make our visit possible. That a particular product does not exist does not stop a designer imagining it and working to create it. That there is gap in the market is an incentive, rather than a problem, to the entrepreneur. In each case, these situations require an ability to imagine what does not exist, to make decisions about what to do, possibly by comparing alternatives, and to take action to bring the chosen image into effect.

The incentive to action can arise from either side of the comparison, the identification of a current situation that we find unsatisfactory or a mental image that seems worth working towards because it is preferable to the current situation, even though that may not be unpleasant. Much technological innovation can be regarded as arising from the latter approach. Sometimes technological advances are developed in answer to perceived problems, but others arise from curiosity or a good idea. The video, for example, was not developed to solve particular problems as much as because it created opportunities for new markets to be opened up.

5.3. CREATIVITY

There is growing interest in the mental process that we go through in creating images of things that do not exist, and in ways of enhancing these images. The creative process can be divided into four interrelated parts (Rickards 1990):

- Preparation
- Incubation
- Insight
- Validation

Particular attention is paid to the core of the process, incubation and insight, the 'A-ha' or 'Eureka' moment. Most writers suggest that this relies on the intuitive processes of the right brain as much as, or more than the logical abilities of the left brain. They contend that creativity is often blocked by our everyday left-brain logical attitudes and search for ways of reducing its dominance and freeing up the more intuitive processes of the right brain, as the key to enhancing our creativity.

On the other hand, ideas seldom develop out of thin air. Our brains need to be prepared. Writers who approach creativity from a problem-solving perspective regard preparation as defining the problem. Van Gundy (1988) saw this as a process of focusing in on the problem to be considered by analysing it and breaking it down into its component parts. But limiting creativity to problem-solving ignores the power of what Land and Jarman (1992) called *Future Pull*, the yearning for things that have never previously existed. Nystrom (1979) suggested that 'This involves a conscious effort to open up the universe of discourse and broaden the problem perspective', rather than narrow it down. Which approach is appropriate may depend on the nature of the problem or issue being considered. Where the concern is to solve a known problem and re-establish a situation that is thought to have existed before the problem developed—what Parnes (1992) called 'bringing things back to normal'—a convergent, analytical approach is probably suitable. We have a clear idea of where we want to be; the problem arises because that is not where we are.

MANAGING, PLANNING AND CREATING THE FUTURE

Creativity may be involved in the development of new ways of solving such problems, but considering the amazing creativity of humans the problem-solving approach alone seems unnecessarily restricted.

Not all creative situations are problem-oriented. The Wright Brother's achievement of heavier-than-air flight was not a solution to a problem in the 'back to normal' sense, but the realisation of a dream. They probably encountered and solved many problems in achieving their aim, but there was nothing of a return to normal in the idea of human beings flying; it was an extraordinary notion, one that many people thought preposterous. Watching a jumbo jet take off is still pretty amazing, even though it is an everyday occurrence. Believing it could be possible when nothing like it had ever happened required some imagination. Dreams of that kind are more likely to come from a divergent approach that considers all sorts of unlikely possibilities. Preparation in this context requires the creation of images of situations, things and events that do not exist and never have existed. Creativity is involved not just in finding the solution but in conceptualising the dream as well.

It is often argued that the issues that concern the future are almost by definition ill-defined. They lack an easily identifiable and agreed situation that could be seen as a solution.

Futures problems are ill-structured. We do not know what information is needed; we have few comprehensive models and no prescription for how to process the information we have. . . . Most people like to believe they are working on well-structured, 'under control' problems. We can apply rational methods to well-structured problems and get well-defined, permanent answers. But nonrational thinking has to be employed to solve ill-structured problems and this scares people. So people treat futures problems as well-structured and dither over how to improve our methodologies, rather than how to improve our intuition and creativity. This represents an elemental misconception. (Mendell 1978)

Futures issues have to be developed and explored as much as defined and analysed, which requires both divergent and convergent thinking at different times.

It was suggested earlier that one of the shortcomings of modern societies is their inability to create images that are different and better than the present, which provide the incentive for society to move on. Such images were seen by Parnes (1992) as 'opportunity problem solving', which works towards the realisation of desired images rather than merely the solution of problems. Parnes suggested that we create new images of three kinds or levels. First, there are images that arise from experience, which we share with others to whom they provide new ideas. Second are the images that arise when we 'Deliberately combine, rearrange or adapt ideas . . . in new ways'. These provide us with new ideas that are different from those we held before. The third level are images that occur 'As in a dream, without the imager trying to deliberately change or transform them. One must surrender to the images. It happens spontaneously [as] artists, writers and other creative people [find] when the material flows from their minds without conscious effort.' For this to occur we may need considerable preparation, either in years of experience or training in the activity or in knowledge of the issue of concern.

Whether the process is problem- or opportunity-based, or both, it is useful to have a clear definition of the issue under consideration—what our aims are, why we are interested in the issue and what we hope to achieve. Van Gundy (1988) offered a number of techniques, including boundary-examinations, goal-orientation and progressive abstractions, to assist the process of issue-definition. Although different in detail, many of them consist of a series of steps or questions designed to deepen understanding of the initial concern. Boundary-examination, for example, has four basic steps:

1. An initial statement of the issue
2. Identification of the key words and phrases and an examination of them for the assumptions behind them
3. Identification of any implications arising from the assumptions, and
4. A redefinition of the issue in the light of the implications.

Goal-orientation is similar, but combines steps 3 and 4 into a series of questions about what the aims are, what obstacles are preventing their achievement and what constraints must be accepted in finding a solution. This is not always as easy as it seems because the process may involve people with very different views of the issue and what should be done about it.

Disputes may also occur in the next stage, the analysis of the issue. Simply to identify an issue is not enough for ideas of action to emerge. It is necessary to investigate both the nature and causes of the situation, establish how it is changing and generally increase our understanding of it. To argue that we do not know enough and need more research before proceeding can be a classic delaying tactic, but understanding an issue is an important part of taking successful action. Agreement about the nature and causes of a situation is not always possible. Competing explanations are often given by different individuals or groups. Is unemployment caused by high wages, which price people out of jobs in a competitive market, or inadequate skills, which mean that individuals and companies are not able to take the opportunities available? Is global warming the result of human activity or variations in the level of solar radiation? Acceptance of any one factor as the cause of the problem will clearly influence the recommended solutions. Such disagreements indicate the presence of uncertainty in the past and present as well as where we more readily accept it—in the future. Disturbing though this may at first appear, the acceptance of different interpretations can be helpful. It can, for example, caution us not to 'put all our eggs in one basket', and persuade us to take a range of measures rather than rely on one. If it is true that it is unwise to rely on a single forecast in the presence of future uncertainty, it is equally unlikely that, without a great deal of luck, reliance on one policy will produce the future we desire.

As Prime Minister of the UK, Margaret Thatcher was apt to say that 'There is no alternative.' Only one course of action would achieve the desired results, and considering or looking for other options was not worthwhile. Those with strong convictions, who believe that they are right and 'know' what should be done, will always be disinclined to listen to alternatives. But if we are inclined to accept the idea of alternative futures, it seems probable that we should consider the likelihood of alternative courses of action and a number of possible solutions to a problem. That we may instinctively not like some of them need not mean that they should not be considered. Formal techniques for analysing problems, such as *decomposition, input–output* and *dimension analysis*, were discussed by Van Gundy (1988). They are generally based on breaking down the problem into its component parts as an aid to analysis.

Opinions about the generation of courses of action differ. Some people hold that solutions emerge from the deeper analysis of the issue; others that the processes of analysing issues and generating solutions are essentially different. The latter argue that although an understanding of the issue is important, the generation of solutions is a creative process that calls on different abilities. Van Gundy (1988) argued that analysis requires convergent thinking, while creativity depends on divergent thought.

Preparation and analysis do not guarantee new ideas, but they are usually important prerequisites for effective innovation. Unless we are ready to consider new approaches and look at things in different ways, it may only serve to confirm us in our existing opinions and hinder the processes of incubation and insight. Rickards (1990) used the term *stuckness* for situations in which we are unable to break through into new ways of thinking. Established ways of doing things or thinking about them, what Rickards called *mind-sets* and others *world-views* or *paradigms*, tend to inhibit new ideas. For new ideas to arise we need to be open to them. Most creativity-theorists agree that an important part of this process is the combined operation of the two halves of the brain, in which the more intuitive right brain is able to work with or take over from the normally dominant analytical left brain. Three main ways of achieving this are suggested: standing back from the issue to allow the intuitive part of the brain to mull it over, jolting our creative powers into operation, and suppressing normal consciousness through methods of guided imagery and hypnosis, which tap other capacities of the brain.

Quite often ideas occur when we least expect them. Perhaps we have been wrestling with a problem but getting nowhere. Suddenly while doing the washing-up or cutting the lawn an idea just comes to us. It does not arise from conscious thought, because we have been concentrating on our immediate task, but from our subconscious, which has been reviewing the matter, without our realising it, all the time. Hence the commonsense advice to 'sleep on it'. As Smith and Ainsworth (1989) noted, sleep can be a productive source of ideas, particularly the 'periods on the edge of sleep, either "drifting off" or semi awake in the morning'. Keeping a notebook or a small tape-recorder handy is the best way to make use of these unintended insights. Recording them as they occur can provide an ideas bank to draw from, and it avoids that annoying inability to remember such good ideas later.

Just letting it happen by 'sleeping on it' is haphazard at best, but the observation of this kind of creativity has led to the development of ways of tricking the mind out of its normal modes of thinking into modes that are similar to the subconscious. Creativity can sometimes be triggered by seeking out novel situations or surroundings, consciously seeking out different experiences that encourage new perspectives or just doing something different. Such new ways of examining an issue can often trigger useful metaphors, ideas from different situations that break through the blockage when applied to our concern. Smith and Ainsworth (1989) suggested going for a walk somewhere different, reading a magazine you don't normally look at or visiting a shop you would not normally go into, and Rickards (1990) noted the value of distracting the overactive left brain through physical exercise.

A wide range of methods of triggering creativity, generating ideas or blockbusting has been developed. One of the fullest collection of techniques was presented by Van Gundy (1988), who gave details of sixty-one idea-generation techniques, thirty aimed at individuals and thirty-one at groups. Among the most popular techniques for assisting individual creativity are *checklists*, *lateral thinking* and *reversal*. Checklists can take many different forms depending on the circumstances, but among those most frequently noted are:

- Osborn's key questions: Adapt? Modify? Magnify? Minify? Substitute? Rearrange? Reverse? Combine? (which was devised for product innovation)
- SCAMPER: Substitute, Combine, Adapt, Modify, Put to other uses, Eliminate, Reverse
- CREATIVITY: Combine, Reverse, Enlarge, Adapt, Tinier, Instead of, Viewpoint change, In other ways, To other uses, Yes! Yes!

Rickards contended that such a positive 'yes and' attitude to ideas, rather than the more usual 'yes but', provides a much more productive approach to creativity, particularly in other individuals. He suggested that an atmosphere that encourages rather than inhibits creativity, which is so often the case, may be an important prerequisite. Makridakis (1990) supported this approach, arguing that a willingness to take risks, to be different and to take pleasure in being a 'rebel' is conducive to creativity.

Lateral thinking is usually associated with Edward de Bono, who first put forward his ideas in the 1960s and 1970s. In his view, creativity depends upon new ways of looking at things that are not simply vertical extensions of current patterns. Rickards (1990) selected three of de Bono's techniques: the *intermediate impossible*, *random juxtaposition* and *concept challenge*. Intermediate impossible starts from a totally outrageous idea that nonetheless helps to see the current situation in a new light and hence break a conceptual block. Random juxtaposition is related to the stimulus obtained by new experiences and to the use of random words, which can be used to generate new perspectives through the association of ideas. Select a word or a number of words from a book or dictionary and let your mind use their meanings as a new perspective on the issue with which you are concerned. Concept challenge requires both analytical and creative thought to challenge the assumptions behind accepted attitudes. It is not too dissimilar from the idea of reversal, which is based on turning round the initial concern to look at it from the opposite perspective; seeing a problem as an opportunity, for example.

Van Gundy (1988) divided group techniques into two main categories, those that rely on the verbal expression of the ideas, *brainstorming*, and those that are based around the silent generation of written ideas, *brainwriting*.

5.3.1. Brainstorming

According to Van Gundy (1988), classic brainstorming is based on two principles and four basic rules. The first principle is *deferred* or *postponed judgement*. Osborn, the originator of the technique, argued that the human mind is both creative and judgemental, but that training and experience tend to lead to a dominance of the judgemental over the creative. In order to encourage the creative, judgement is suspended until a later stage of the brainstorming process. The second principle holds that in order to achieve quality *quantity* is also required. Not all ideas are good ones, just as not all the photographs taken on a holiday are masterpieces. The chances of getting a good idea or a good photograph are enhanced the more that are generated or taken. The rules follow from the principles.

1. Criticism and evaluation during the generation of ideas is ruled out. It is

only in these circumstances, it is claimed, that members of the group will be prepared to relax sufficiently to express their ideas without reservation. In a normal group situation, individuals are unlikely to articulate ideas that they believe will be laughed at or criticised by other members of the group, but these may be the insights that offer a new perspective on the issue and lead to the eventual solution. Suspending judgement in any form, not only verbal but through actions and expressions, is held to be an important encouragement to the generation of such innovative, non-standard ideas.

2. Freewheeling is encouraged. The relaxed atmosphere of the brainstorm is intended to encourage ideas that might at first seem wild or wacky and for them to be expressed as they come to mind rather than assessed before they are articulated. Only a non-judgemental environment encourages this.

3. Quantity is sought. In an effective session the recorder should find it hard to keep up with the flow of ideas as group members rapidly produce them. A fifteen-minute session might easily produce over fifty ideas.

4. Piggy-backing on the ideas of others in the group is encouraged, to build on and improve them.

Most writers favour groups of around ten for effective brainstorming, six and twelve being the limits. Too few and it becomes difficult to sustain the flow of ideas, which is important to the success of the process; too many and some members of the group will be unable to participate fully. However, Rickards (1990) did recommend mini-brainstorming, with only two or three people, in certain situations, noting that creative methods should themselves be used creatively.

At the outset of a brainstorming session it is important for everyone to be clear about the issue to be considered. It is useful, therefore, to make sure that everyone can see the subject written down. It may also be useful to have a loosening-up exercise before embarking on the real thing, in order to break down reservations within the group. A session run by Doris Shallcross (1994) asked participants to brainstorm uses for odd socks left at a launderette, which certainly broke the ice.

The group facilitator can act as recorder of the ideas or appoint someone else to do it. The most important aspect of the recording is to ensure that the members of the group can see the ideas as they are recorded, to use them as a resource for development and improvement. Chalkboards, flip-charts and overhead projectors are useful ways of achieving this. The facilitator may either act as a member of the group, adding in ideas of their own, perhaps to encourage new trains of thought, or remain outside the process. Some practitioners consider it good for the facilitator to fill in gaps in the generation of ideas by adding in their own prompts, while others believe the silences are themselves valuable and avoid the danger of the facilitator dominating the generation of ideas. It may depend on whether the facilitator is a member of the group or an outside consultant brought in to manage the process.

There is no absolute rule for the length of time a session should last, but half an hour is usually quite long enough. Some suggest that the group should set itself a target number of ideas and then go beyond that target, because the extra relaxation that comes from achieving the target will release more innovative suggestions. Mini-brainstorming generates fewer ideas in a shorter time, but can still provide some useful insights (Rickards 1990).

Brainstorming, like Delphi, has attracted a lot of attention and has become a commonly used and criticised technique. Van Gundy (1988) saw its main advantages as the generation of a large number of ideas in a short time, in an environment that some of the participants find stimulating and satisfying. The inclusion of evaluation is also important to avoid the criticism that all brainstorming does is produce a lot of silly, unworkable ideas. The disadvantages and weaknesses that emerge from the research are more numerous. They include the difficulties of controlling the group and avoiding domination by a few people while others remain inhibited; the danger of adopting the technique because it is superficially attractive; wasting time producing large numbers of useless solutions to relatively simple problems; and the lack of individual recognition for ideas generated. Van Gundy made a number of suggestions for overcoming some of these problems, such as training in the procedures, careful group-selection and taking ideas in sequence from the group rather than randomly to avoid domination by particular individuals.

5.3.2. Brainwriting

Brainwriting techniques are generally similar to brainstorming, except that they are based on written rather than spoken ideas. Rickards (1990) termed such situations *nominal group*, since the members are part of a group but are working alone for some of the time. Delphi is sometimes considered to be a form of nominal group activity. Basic brainwriting uses groups of five to eight people sitting around a table. Each member writes down four ideas on the issue under consideration. These sheets of paper are then placed in the centre of the table and the ideas listed by each member are used as a stimulus for other members to develop more ideas. The process continues for twenty to thirty minutes. Variations on this are the *Card-writing, 6–3–5* and *Gallery* techniques. Card-writing requires group members to write each idea on a separate card which is then passed round the table to the next participant, who uses it as a stimulus to generate more ideas of their own. At the end the cards can be pinned up to assist in grouping ideas for evaluation. The 6–3–5 technique is similar, except that each member of a group of six participants writes one idea on each of three separate cards; these cards are then passed round the table for each participant to add one further idea to the growing list on each card. By the time they return to their originators each card will have five more ideas listed. In the gallery technique the participants move between flip charts or sheets of paper pinned to the wall adding their ideas on the selected topics and using the ideas generated by the group as a stimulus.

5.3.3. Group Support Systems

Developments in technology are leading to computer-based systems that have the capacity for brainstorming/brainwriting. Linked computer networks with the appropriate software allow groups to work together on issues while maintaining confidentiality. All members of the group are equal, because only the computer 'knows' who has contributed a particular idea. The systems record all the contributions made and reproduce them on a display and on-screen so that all members of the group can see the developing ideas and contribute to them in real time. 'Participants can all speak at once, electronically. This aids the generation of ideas and the retention of ideas that might otherwise get lost in the shuffle' (University of Houston, Clear Lake 1994). Both electronic and printed records of the session are generated for later use. As such systems develop, it is possible to foresee the development of creative networks that are not restricted to the 'same place, same time' format of manual brainstorming and brainwriting, but enable 'different place, same time' and 'different place, different time' formats. Such systems could provide useful 'jolting' mechanisms to stimulate new perspectives, or ideas banks.

5.3.4. Futures Workshops

One of the criticisms of Futures and of many of the methods discussed so far is that they are exclusive. Futures concepts and theories can be very complicated, requiring considerable study to understand them. Likewise, Futures methods often appear complex and may require a level of technical ability beyond the average individual. On the other hand, we all have a vested interest in the future, because that is where we are going to spend the rest of our lives. The danger is that the development of an academic discipline, a profession or advanced techniques in Futures will capture the future for those who have particular abilities or powers and exclude the equally concerned majority. Futures is not alone in this. There has long been an opinion that powerful groups in society not only dominate the present but also control both history and the future. They control history, it is argued, by selecting those events and perspectives on history that they consider important and that reinforce their view of the world. The continuing debates in the UK during the 1980s and 1990s about the content of the History curriculum for schools, particularly how much of it should concern British as opposed to world history, illustrate the point. It is necessary to be selective, but who makes the selection and what they select is crucial, because that determines the past that future generations will learn about.

Similar arguments are presented about the future. Dominant groups in the present are in a position to ensure that the decisions that are made reflect their interests and work towards a future favourable to them. This is nothing new, the powerful have always done so, but it is often noted that many of the techniques of Futures were developed to assist the already powerful to maintain or increase their influence. Much early activity was centred around the needs of the military. The first Delphi study concerned developments in armaments. Cost–benefit analysis was developed to assess major government proposals such as new roads and, it is suggested, to see them in a favourable light by including certain factors rather than others. Scenarios have been used by commercial interests concerned, quite naturally, to maintain or enhance their competitive position. Although the process is often justified as being in the 'public interest', the public themselves have seldom been able to play a central role. As a result, Futures has been accused of being a tool of the powerful and of helping to perpetuate, or even exacerbate current inequalities. The idea that there should be a group of professionals specifically concerned with the future and the development of educational programmes to support this has been regarded with suspicion. Bernard Shaw summed this up succinctly: 'All professions are conspiracies against the laity.'

Although the developments within government and commerce cannot be denied there is another facet to Futures that has been concerned to democratise the future and increase the opportunity for everyone to be able to influence the future in directions they would prefer. This is a strong theme of the movement for the inclusion of Futures in education. A clear indication of this was given by Hooker (1989). In setting out the main arguments for introducing futures into the curriculum he contended that it encourages 'students to understand the ways in which they can help to shape their own futures by offering them the skills to participate in that shaping'. Sisk and Whalley (1987), in common with other writers, stressed *empowerment* as an important feature of the study of alternative futures.

Outside the educational context, one of the foremost ways in which people have been involved is in the development of *anticipatory democracy* through such tools as the Futures workshop. Developed by Robert Jungk, Futures workshops are intended to allow anybody to become involved in creating their own preferred future rather than being simply subject to the decisions of experts. The idea grew out of the dissatisfaction expressed by people who were presented, in a range of different circumstances, with a *fait accompli*, and the conviction that some involvement in the making of decisions would result in more acceptable results. Jungk and Mullert (1987) give a number of examples of workshops in which people have been enabled to express their preferences for the future and be involved in bringing them into effect.

Futures workshops are group activities. Jungk and Mullert suggest that between fifteen and twenty-five is the maximum practical number for everyone to be allowed to contribute. Larger numbers can be divided into groups to run in parallel. The first sessions of the 'Imagine Houston' exercise, which I was fortunate to observe in Houston in 1994, began with about forty groups of ten people each. Each group should have a facilitator, whose role is to help the group through the process, and resources, such as paper, pens and access to photocopying. Where groups are coming together for the first time or where there are formal relationships between the members it is important to establish a relaxed atmosphere by informal introductions. Jungk and Mullert suggest that involving the group in some of the preparatory arrangements, like setting out the room or obtaining materials, can be a useful way of breaking down reservations.

The next stage is for the facilitator to outline the purpose of the workshop and the processes involved. For those unfamiliar with such activities, it is important to stress the participatory nature of the workshop and that it is concerned with helping the participants to create their own futures rather than be forced to go along with what others have decided for them. In some circumstances, particularly if they are not used to being consulted, this may be difficult for people to accept.

The first phase of the process is to involve the participants in a critique of the current situation, in order to identify issues that need attention. These can be problems or unrealised potentials that are perceived by the group. In the 'Imagine Houston' exercise, the terms 'Sads' and 'Glads' were used to encourage participants to think about those things they felt strongly about, both positively and negatively, in their city. Dator (1993a) supported the idea of noting the good things as well as the bad, particularly in circumstances where those involved feel pride in their past accomplishments. These issues should be noted as they arise. In a single group exercise this can involve writing them up on large sheets of paper on the wall; where there are a number of groups it may be necessary to have a reporting session in which the groups can share their ideas so that the most significant concerns emerge. During the identification of the issues it is important to avoid discussing them or the group will get side-tracked. Thirty to forty-five minutes is probably long enough for this phase of the process. A successful critique will generate a large number of issues that need to be prioritised for further consideration. This is usually achieved by a voting or scoring procedure, each participant having an agreed number of votes. These votes may be given a physical form by using stickers that each group member allocates to those issues they consider most important. The votes can be spread across several issues or concentrated on one, and the procedure can be open or secret.

Having identified the issues about which people feel most concerned, the workshop moves into the search for ideas to deal with them. At this stage Dator (1993a) argued that it is important to challenge participants 'to examine their own various ideas about the future [and] to express, clarify and modify their own . . . images of the future'. A productive way of doing this is to present them with different alternative futures and ask them to consider how their lives would change if these futures were to occur. Dator concluded from his experience that this is a valuable preparation for what Jungk and Mullert (1987) called the fantasy phase, in which participants are asked to imagine futures they wish to see. To be successful they argue the participants must be in a position to:

- think the otherwise unthinkable
- be enterprising and inquisitive
- be nonconformist and flexible
- open their minds to the irrational and 'off beat'
- take a chance on being wrong or failing
- shun cynical, know-all and perfectionist attitudes, and
- stand up for 'cranky' ideas

In order to achieve this it may be useful to engage in some loosening-up exercises to help people relax. A useful starting point can be to reformulate the criticisms in more positive terms in order to identify what it is that is missing to cause the concern. This may help in the development of ways to achieve the aims. The fantasy phase centres around a brainstorming exercise. Although it is important, the generation stage of brainstorming is not the end of the process. The ideas then need to be evaluated and, if anything is to change, acted upon.

5.3.5. Incasting, Visioning, Backcasting, the Relevance Tree and Envisioning

Schultz (1992) indicated that Futures workshops held by the Hawaii Research Center for Futures Studies had incorporated three other techniques of *Structured Daydreaming*: *incasting*, *visioning* and *backcasting*. 'Incasting takes people on a comparative journey across several possible futures' '(Schultz 1992). Participants are presented with different future scenarios derived from logical extensions of emerging issues and are asked to consider how these different futures would impact on particular matters of concern. This might be an institution, the experience of a particular demographic group or how well-known artefacts would change given innovative technologies. Groups of about twelve work best, larger numbers can be divided into several groups, all working on the same scenarios or each concentrating on a different one.

Visioning, a kind of three-stage brainstorming, begins with the participants being asked to set out the characteristics of their preferred future as a kind of wish-list. Schultz noted that this can be difficult, because 'Many people find it difficult to let go of the problem-identifying problem-solving perspectives that work ingrains in all of us.' She suggested that as people are generally clearer about what they do not like, problem-listing can be a useful bridge to the ideal. The negative nature of the problems is used as a basis for restating them in a positive-opportunity form. The list is then used to examine how society would function given these characteristics, using a series of questions about specific aspects such as government, social structures, education and so on. The third phase asks individuals to describe a typical day in their preferred future.

Backcasting, as its name suggests, is a kind of reverse forecasting or future history. It is also known as 'Apollo Forecasting' and is closely related to the relevance-tree technique. The starting point is a desired future state, such as President Kennedy's goal of placing a human being on the Moon (hence the name 'Apollo Forecasting', after the Apollo Programme). The technique then aims to establish ways in which this goal could be achieved. Schultz recommends the development of an 'effect-and-cause' chain, reversed because the participants are working backwards from effect to cause, to trace the path back to the present. The relevance tree is a diagrammatic presentation of the steps involved, beginning with the ultimate aim at the tip and spreading out to more detailed or earlier necessary measures lower down. A more detailed description of backcasting was given by J. B. Robinson (1990), following its use in studies in Canada within the Human Dimensions of Global Change Program. He saw backcasting as a policy tool that helps us examine the extent to which we can influence or choose our future. 'It is . . . explicitly normative, involving working backwards from a particular desired future end-point to the present in order to determine the . . . feasibility of that future and what policy measures would be required to reach that point.' He described it as a six-stage process involving some of the methods already discussed.

1. Determine objectives or the desired future
2. Specify particular goals, constraints and targets
3. Describe the present situation
4. Specify the important factors which will affect the future
5. Develop scenarios
6. Undertake an impact analysis to compare the anticipated results of the scenarios with the desirable future

The same emphasis that 'The future is not the domain of knowledge but of action' is expressed in the *envisioning* process described by Ziegler (1991). Based on experience in a wide range of different situations, Ziegler wrote of envisioning as a process 'Concerned neither with the probable or the possible but with the desirable, the imagined, the intended, the compelling, indeed, the mythic'. By moving us 'Beyond the expected and accepted', its 'Purpose is to change action and behaviour in the present by virtue of the intentioning of the participants to do just that'. The process involves moving from a deep analysis of concerns, through the creation of images, to strategies for action.

5.4. INNOVATION

5.4.1. Creative Imagery

The appreciation of the role of the subconscious in creativity has led to the development of techniques to encourage the relaxation of conscious attention and free up the imaging capacity of the brain. 'In the development of these creative skills, the major tools are increasingly sophisticated concentration and meditation techniques. Without the refinement of inner concentration and meditation, the subtle unconscious levels of the mind are never brought to conscious awareness' (Nuernberger 1984). Markley (1988) noted that the skills needed to make use of these procedures are not commonly encouraged. They are, as in brainstorming, the suspension of judgement and *passive volition*, 'essentially, letting go and allowing the desired phenomena to happen'. It is necessary, therefore, either to have an experienced guide to help you or to practice them until you become proficient enough to follow the steps on your own. One way of doing this might be to tape record the instructions and play them back with appropriate pauses in between.

The starting point for methods of this kind is mental and physical relaxation. Settle yourself comfortably—lying down if that feels better. Close your eyes, breathe deeply and let a sense of relaxed well-being spread through your body. 'Take five or ten minutes to reach a state of relaxed attention—but don't fall asleep!' (Parnes 1992). Having reached a relaxed state you are ready to start.

Parnes's 'Imaging the Future' exercise begins by imaging yourself in some favourite place, where you are happy and comfortable. (For me it would be somewhere like Simon's Seat, a peak in the Yorkshire Dales with a view across Wharfedale, on a warm summer day.) Then follow through these stages in a relaxed way:

- Imagine you are in a time machine.
- Just by your hand are a series of buttons which will allow you to select a year in the future you wish to visit and to return to the present when ready.
- Select a year.
- On the instruction of your guide press the button labelled 'Future' and image yourself in that year. Experience it with all your senses, see, hear, smell, touch for about five minutes.
- Try to remember the images you experience.
- Parnes suggests some other steps before pressing the 'Return to Present' button and slowly returning to normal consciousness.
- Spend some time noting, either in writing or drawing, the images you 'saw'.
- Examine the future you 'saw'. What would it be like? What implications would it have?
- If you are working with others share experiences and discuss your conclusions.

The 'Imagine Houston' exercise used a similar approach, asking participants to imagine themselves at a going away party prior to leaving the city. Ten years later they were to image themselves returning and to note the changes that had occurred in the city in their absence.

Markley (1988) described four methods of intuitive problem-solving and innovation that, he claimed, are useful in a wide variety of decision-making situations involving uncertainty and risk. Each method has a different aim: to clarify a problem, re-vision a problem as an opportunity, assess alternative strategies, and provide a procedure for transcendental creativity and exploration. As an example, the third method for assessing alternative strategies is reproduced as Box 7.

MANAGING, PLANNING AND CREATING THE FUTURE

> **Box 7. Assessing alternative strategies**
>
> 1. Chose several alternative policy options or strategies by which to accomplish some objective of significant concern.
> 2. Pick one strategy for initial exploration.
> 3. Relax physically, emotionally and mentally— accepting the suggestion to avoid thinking in rational, verbal and/or evaluative terms— to a suitable frame of mind for focused imagistic thinking. Imagine that the strategy is actually being implemented at the present moment, and that you are going to explore what it leads to in the future.
> 4. Using passive volition, allow yourself to be carried into the future as the strategy is implemented across time, simply watching and feeling things as they occur.
> 5. After scanning to—or beyond—the desired time frame, record the impressions that seem most relevant.
> 6. Do steps 3–5 for each strategy or option deemed of interest, including strategies that you may not support or think would work, but which other persons or interest groups are known to advocate.
> 7. Decide how next to proceed. Typical 'next steps' include one or more of the following:
>   1) Select the option or strategy that seems preferable (often it turns out to be a synthesis of several) on the basis of what you saw and felt.
>   2) Select particular questions or issues that have emerged and may require further study; use either 'visionary/intuitive' or 'rational/analytic' modes of thinking, or a combination of both.
>   3) Use what you have learned from the exercise in imagistic thinking to inform whatever decision making process is to be used.
>
> *Source*: Markley (1988).

Van Gundy (1988) concluded that such visualisation methods can be useful in generating ideas and are usually an interesting experience and fun. They are not suited to everybody, but with some training are accessible to most.

5.4.2. Making Decisions and Acting on Them

Given that alternative ways of proceeding have been identified we have to choose which to use. Unless the situation is one in which only a yes or no answer is possible, for example, to build or not build a particular facility, it may not be necessary, and indeed may be unwise, to decide upon only one course of action. A package may be more advisable. In making choices we require some method of estimating the likely results of different policies and comparing them with our aims. Techniques like impact-assessment, voting procedures and cost–benefit analysis can be useful. The *Planning Balance Sheet* and the *Goals Achievement Matrix* were developed by Lichfield as extensions of cost–benefit analysis to overcome some of its limitations. They incorporate non-monetary and non-quantifiable factors into the evaluation of alternatives, and examine the impact of proposals on the various interests involved as well as attempting to produce an overall assessment. Whether it is important to seek a 'best' solution (the one with the fewest disadvantages or the least opposition) or the one which gains most support while achieving a 'satisfactory' result will often be a matter of debate. If the best is unlikely to occur but a satisfactory policy has a good chance of being adopted, it could well be the better alternative.

Making decisions is one thing but putting them into practice is another, and one without which the planning and decision—making process is all but irrelevant. A common criticism of planners is that they may be good at devising plans but not at implementing them. Stacey (1992) contended that in dynamic, unpredictable situations plans are unlikely to be carried out because unanticipated changes render them obsolete before they can be implemented. The latter situation is neatly summed up by the planner's dilemma: 'the greater the degree of change, the greater the need for planning, otherwise precedents of the past could guide the future', but the greater the degree of change, the greater the uncertainty and 'the greater the likelihood that plans right today will be wrong tomorrow' (after Trist 1972). Stacey's advice was not to plan, except in the short term, where the future is reasonably predictable, but to adopt an open-ended learning approach to the unknowable future. In contrast, Kenney (1988) argued that these unanticipated consequences of planning reinforce the need for planning, because 'Planning in this sense becomes self-perpetuating as the unintended undesirable consequences of planning generate more planning to overcome them.' Opponents of planning might immediately conclude that doing away with planning would avoid these unintended consequences and therefore the need for planning, but we adopt planning because we believe that to achieve our desires we need to intervene. Consequences, unintended or otherwise, also follow from not planning. That we do not always get all we wanted and may get things we did not want or had not thought of—good as well as bad—does not undermine our original reasons for planning. It does suggest that planning can never be wholly rational and should be regarded as a process of learning.

The means to carry out policies and the development of the necessary support for them is an important part of the planning and decision-making process. Though it is usually depicted as coming near the end, it is more likely to lead to success if built up from the start. The acceptance of plans by those who will implement them or provide the required resources, or whose co-operation is necessary to make them effective, is often the most important factor in their successful implementation. An apparently perfect plan without the necessary support and co-operation is of little use, as is the availability of resources and support without a direction in which to apply them.

Actions do not always produce the results expected, either because other factors intervene to affect what happens or because our anticipation of the consequences was not accurate. It is important therefore to continue to monitor the changing situation in an attempt both to assess the impact of any actions and to continue learning about the way things change. Though scanning is a valuable tool in this task, it is not always easy to differentiate the results of particular decisions from other changes that are occurring. A government may take steps to reduce unemployment through training schemes and employment support, but if the general economic situation improves it will be difficult to attribute the extra jobs generated to any one cause, even though the government will claim that its policies were successful. The conclusions drawn normally owe as much or more to the starting perspective of the observer as to the changes themselves.

The temptation in planning is to assume that because we have prepared a plan and put it into effect our task is complete; we can move on to the next issue. To some extent that may be necessary to make effective use of our resources, but it assumes that our efforts will always be successful and turn out as expected. This is not always the case. Some plans completely fail to achieve their objectives, others are partially successful and some achieve almost all they set out to. Assessing the results and the changing situation will itself form part of the continuing process of issue-identification, decision-making and planning. Success for some might be the incentive for their opponents to begin a campaign to reverse the situation to one that they deem preferable. Contentious issues like capital punishment or abortion are seldom finished with as committed groups on one side of the debate or other will exert pressure to change the status quo, whatever it is and however recently it was reached.

5.4.3. Politics

Politics is not often considered to be a Futures method, but consideration of what politicians do and what politics is concerned with offers a useful perspective. Miller (1965) argued that 'Politics is about policy; and policy is a matter of either the desire for change or the desire to protect something against change.' It is, therefore, future-oriented. Just like planning, decision-making and problem-solving, it is concerned to change the current situation and bring about a better future. Political conflict centres around the kinds of debate discussed in the last section: what are the causes of the current situation, what should we be aiming for and how can we best achieve those aims?

If it is true that uncertainty is inherent, particularly in respect of the future, it is to be expected that differences of opinion will emerge about what course of action should be adopted. If we cannot know for certain that a specific policy will lead to particular results, which of a set of policy alternatives will lead to the best situation or even what the best circumstances would be, there is ample room for disagreement about what course of action to adopt. If we add in uncertainty and debate about the nature of the present situation and the past events that have led up to it, the room for honestly held differences of opinion increases.

In the absence of certainty, wide debate about what we want the future to be like and how we can best achieve it is not only inevitable but desirable. There is no guarantee that the 'best' policy will emerge from the process, but we increase our chances by widening the range of the alternatives we consider. The process of debate about the future and the actions we take that affect it is an opportunity for learning and developing ideas. One concern is the feeling that many of our political systems and attitudes, which originated in another age and which are based around an adversarial approach of arguing from fixed positions, may not be appropriate to the world we live in now. Politics with a Futures perspective would be an open learning process. It would have clear aims but be prepared to adapt to change and new information and accept the multiplicity of interests and opinions impinging on the issue. That may sound like a political system unlike any that we know, but it may be one that we need to develop if we are to avoid some of the worse predictions of doom.

5.5. CONCLUSIONS

There is a wide range of methods available for thinking about and planning for the future. Some are relatively unknown and underused, some even a little scary on first acquaintance. Others we accept without thinking, using them regularly without realising they are in fact Futures methods. None can guarantee that we get it right, but the realisation that there are so many and careful use of them can make the future less daunting, and encourage us to create a better future rather than just attempt to predict it.

PART THREE

CHALLENGES AND OPPORTUNITIES FOR THE 21ST CENTURY

CHAPTER SIX
THE FUTURE AS PARADOX

The concept of paradox is not new. The word is found in both Latin and Greek, where it originally meant 'a statement contrary to accepted opinion'. Today it is defined as 'a seemingly absurd or contradictory statement, even if actually well founded' (Tulloch 1993). Both the origins of the word and the current definition suggest the difficulties we have with paradoxical situations. They do not fit the accepted wisdom and may often seem ridiculous and inconsistent. In consequence, they are often disturbing, raising questions about our established ideas and ways of doing things, and doing so in a way that, because they appear contradictory or even laughable, may be dismissed as not worthy of serious consideration. The contention of this final chapter is that as we deal with the future we would be well advised to take the paradoxes of our situation more seriously, because working with them may well help us to deal more successfully with our present and future.

It should already be apparent that dealing with paradoxes has relevance to thinking about and dealing with the future. Thinking effectively about the future is difficult, if not, in the sense of obtaining accurate and reliable foreknowledge, impossible. But it is also easy, unavoidable and vitally important if we are to move towards a future we prefer rather than one that is thrust upon us. This paradox of our relationship with the future formed the foundation of the discussion in the first three chapters. Although we often do not realise it, we have considerable experience of dealing with the future, even if gaining that experience has sometimes been painful and prone to error. Some of the ways that we have developed to deal with the future were examined in Part 2.

One of the most disturbing—and increasingly apparent—paradoxes is that we need to consider the longer-term future if we are to deal responsibly with decisions that need to be made now when we lack the necessary information to be sure we make them correctly. We need to decide rather than leave the outcome to chance, because the potential implications of the issues are so large.

The decisions must be made now for a number of reasons, including advances in scientific knowledge presenting us with new questions that, left unresolved, may take us in directions we subsequently regret; long lead times, which require decisions now for effects to occur many years hence; and the long-term consequences that will follow, whatever the decisions or non-decisions we make now. We do not have the information we need because much of it pertains to uncertain future developments, either resulting from these decisions or relevant to them.

We have always made such decisions, usually without being aware that they would have long-term consequences. Since we live with the consequences of past decisions and have begun to gain some understanding of the processes by which those consequences have come about, our age is different because we now know that the actions we take will have implications in the future, some for very long periods. We also know that we cannot predict with certainty what those implications will be, although they will be contingent upon our actions. It is an uncomfortable situation.

The temptation in these circumstances is to give up any attempt to consider the future; to make what seems to be the best of the present and let the future look after itself. This is a very understandable reaction but one that is likely to lead to unanticipated consequences that future generations, or even ourselves in a few years time, will consider could, and should, have been avoided if we had given the future sufficient attention now. Whether those consequences could have been avoided or not will remain a matter of debate, but with the added benefit of hindsight we will always be open to that criticism. Complaining that hindsight is always easier than foresight will be treated as an unacceptable excuse, particularly where it is held that our short-sighted failure to look ahead is largely responsible for the consequent problems. Although we cannot guarantee accuracy by making an attempt to anticipate the consequences of our actions and proceeding cautiously in our areas of ignorance, at least our chances of avoiding regret and of obtaining a favourable future are increased. Not attempting to do so almost certainly ensures that, unless we are exceptionally lucky, the future will not turn out as we would have preferred. If we wish to take a responsible approach to the future we need to consider the future consequences of our actions, even when we know we cannot do so with absolute certainty. Responsibility requires that we accept the paradox of our situation and, though we cannot resolve it, work through it rather than attempt to pretend it does not exist.

Unfortunately, accepting paradoxical situations that cannot be resolved but must be worked through does not fit with many of our established attitudes and preferred ways of proceeding. We frequently talk, for example, of problem-solving, the process by which we identify a problem and attempt to solve it to create a situation in which it no longer exists. We are happy with the idea that we can devise and implement a solution that will be effective and enable us to move on to the next, often unrelated, problem. We know from experience that our solutions may not work out as anticipated and have varied success rates—though this is not welcome knowledge. We frequently prefer to forget such limitations and believe that this time we will get it right. Although our actions may ease the original situation, they too often create reactions that in turn create or reveal other, potentially even worse problems. For example, many of the urban planning policies of the 1950s and 1960s, which at the time were considered to be solutions to the problems we then recognised, themselves played a role in the creation of the urban problems of the 1980s and 1990s. The new housing developments, which seemed to provide much better accommodation than the slums in which people then lived, are now condemned as worse than the houses they replaced. The new roads that were built to improve access to city centres have not reduced congestion, because more traffic has filled the extra space and we now face serious problems of pollution, both local and global, resulting from traffic fumes. These are complex issues without simple explanations, but they serve to illuminate the paradox. We are comfortable with certainty; we like to think that we know, and that we can make clear decisions with predictable outcomes. We favour strong leaders with clear vision who know what the future is going to be. Uncertainty, doubt and leaders who show all too clearly the difficulties of making the right decision and acknowledge their inability to make problems disappear like a conjuror are not popular. Paradoxically they are probably more closely attuned to our situation than the know-alls.

The situation is not too different from the riddle 'Which would you prefer, a watch that was always five minutes slow or one that said twelve o'clock all the time?' The 'clever' answer is supposed to be the latter, because it is right twice a day, at midday and midnight, whereas the former is always wrong. That may be so, but for all except twenty minutes of the day, the five minutes either side of midday and midnight, the first watch is more accurate than the second, despite the fact that it is always wrong. From this perspective it would seem better to be a bit wrong all the time than right occasionally and wildly wrong most of the time. Recognising this as the nature of our relationship with the future—that we are not in a position to know with certainty that we are right about it and must accept that we are always likely to be a bit wrong—may be a wiser, if not an immediately attractive, approach. It may be a more mature approach, which our increasing understanding of the complexities of our world requires as humanity moves from the adolescent enthusiasm of industrialism to the chaos of postmodernism.

A further paradox of our relationship to the future is that, although we spend much of our time looking forward to it and making arrangements concerning it, we can never experience it, because, like tomorrow, the future never comes. The future always advances ahead of us, stretching tantalisingly out in front of us as we journey on in the changing present. At least this is how we appear to experience it. If it is so unattainable why should we bother with it? The reason, of course, is that today is yesterday's tomorrow. Although tomorrow never comes, tomorrow becomes today, just as today becomes yesterday. The future is always ahead of us, but the present was the future in the past, just as the past was once the present, and further back in time than that, the future. It remains a paradox, but one we have become used to living with. The central argument for Futures revolves around the growing conviction that because what we are doing today has much greater implications for tomorrow than ever before, we need to pay much more attention to the effect we are having on the future than past generations ever did.

Our inability to know or experience the future may go some way towards explaining another paradox of our time. At the very moment that we are beginning to realise the scale of the potential future consequences of our actions, society, particularly in the West, is becoming more present-oriented. We seem to live in a 'now' society where only the moment is important: instant news from anywhere, the soundbite, the limited attention span, the satisfaction of wants now rather than later, short-term gain rather than long term investment. McArthur (1994) reported that Reuters, the worldwide news service, defines historic data as 'anything over a minute old'. At one level, this concentration on the immediate present is quite understandable. It is all we have; the past has gone, we can do little about it, and the future has yet to come. We do not know what the future holds; it may be better, it may be worse. For a variety of reasons the late twentieth century has been a prone to pessimism about the future, and if we are convinced it is going to get worse whatever we do, there is some logic in enjoying the moment while we can. If all we are able to be certain of is our current existence, it is sensible to make the best we can of it before one of the many threats we perceive transpires. As long as our luck holds we can continue to enjoy the present; we will bother about the problems if and when they arise. A particularly strident example of the mood is provided in the song 'I want it all' by the group Queen. It includes the lyric 'I want it all, I want it all, I want it all, and I want it now'. So much for posterity or the consequences of our actions.

We do live in the present and it is quite reasonable to wish to make that present as pleasant as possible, because that is all we have. Past generations were, perhaps, too prepared, particularly in social and economic affairs, to defer the satisfaction of their wants. A little impatience can be a good thing, but it does leave us with a paradox: can we live for now and for the future without compromising the latter? Unlikely if all we consider is now and let the future take care of itself. The need to go beyond 'Nowism' in the interests of future generations was argued by Yazaki (1994).

Several writers have already suggested that the concept of paradox is useful in understanding the world of the late twentieth century. Makridakis (1990) put forward a number of paradoxes arising from his experience of forecasting, planning, strategy and creativity. For example, he suggests, 'Organisations must often take risks to succeed, yet risk taking, by its very nature, can lead to failure. On the other hand not taking risks can also lead to failure.' Elsewhere, both Naisbitt (1994) and Handy (1994) made paradox a central theme of their work.

Naisbitt (1994) centred his argument around one major *Global Paradox*, that 'The larger the system, the smaller and more powerful and important the parts'. This is reflected, he argued, in the apparently contradictory developments of a global economy, which suggests a concentration of power in the hands of major transnational companies, and both a breaking-up of these giants into smaller parts and a growing cultural and political tribalism, which distributes power more locally. We may be moving towards a global economy, but culturally and politically there are trends in the opposite direction, as past mega-states like the Soviet Union break up into their constituent parts. This causes him to rework the 'Think Globally, Act Locally' mantra of the ecologists into a 'Think Locally, Act Globally' guide for business.

The global paradox has other facets. In our global life, given the right equipment, we can know and see what is happening anywhere in the world from anywhere in the world. We can consume goods produced on the other side of the planet and travel round the world in less time than it took to travel from London to Paris (just over 200 miles) fewer than 200 years ago. Despite the combination of this shrinking world and an estimated 100 million international migrants, major refugee movements and rapid growth in international tourism, only about 2 per cent of the world's population live outside the country of their birth (Mather and Bond 1993). The vast majority of people, in other words, remain close to their origins; it is only a small minority who are global citizens with a global perspective.

One relatively recent development that is changing the way we experience the world is global communications, and particularly television. Traditionally, governments have jealously guarded their control over the media within their jurisdiction, and television has been no exception. Now, with satellite communications, that control is breached. No longer is it possible for governments to restrict their citizens to approved sources of information. Some fear that such global broadcasting will lead to cultural imperialism, as Western values are beamed into non-Western lives. There is that danger, but other results are possible as the world's poor are made more aware of their relative poverty by greater exposure to Western affluence. Why should they be prepared to accept the imbalance any longer? The West may find that lifting the veil of ignorance unleashes increased pressures for a fairer world. It has been argued, for example, that access to West German television was a significant factor in creating the circumstances that led to the collapse of East Germany in 1989.

We may be one world but exposure, either on television or by direct experience, to the lives of those who live very differently from ourselves may just as easily lead to reaction and hostility as understanding and tolerance. In some countries, notably in the Muslim world, there is a sharp reaction against the subjugation of indigenous culture to dominant Western values. We are all inclined to favour our own habits and frequently react against different ways of doing things, particularly if we feel that they are being imposed on us. To witness the attraction of the familiar it is only necessary to observe the British queuing for bacon and eggs and a cup of tea on the Cross Channel ferry from France. No doubt French visitors to Britain cannot wait to get home to decent coffee and good food. Perhaps they do not even come, because they believe such things, like good weather, are unavailable in the UK. Whatever the cause, it is clear that the French, like the British, Americans, Japanese and probably all other national and cultural groups believe that their ways are best and are just as likely to fight to protect their individuality as accept homogenisation.

Minor examples maybe, but there is a serious issue behind them. National and cultural differences have historically been a major cause of conflict. Just because the privileged few—businessmen, academics and tourists—are global in their outlook does not mean that the local hostilities have gone away. Indeed, several commentators have suggested that the post-Cold War era is just as dangerous, perhaps even more so, in local and regional terms, than the superpower face-off ever was. It is only necessary to consider the conflicts in the former Yugoslavia, the former Soviet Union, Africa and elsewhere to realise that we are far from one global happy family. Despite some significant successes in the Middle East and South Africa in the 1990s, a major concern of the twenty-first century will be dealing with conflict in one form or another between competing interests and groups. Some of these conflicts have their roots centuries and even millennia ago, and both sides have claims that may be mutually exclusive but equally legitimate if viewed from differing perspectives. Paradoxically, the global world we now live in can give these local disputes a wider relevance. When we knew nothing of them because information never reached us, we could not feel any concern for the conflicts or responsibility towards the groups involved. Now, when they are headline news, the global community is drawn in. The growing involvement of the UN and the USA, with some help from its allies, in an increasing number of local conflicts indicates this trend, as does the tendency for action groups to extend their campaigns beyond their immediate locality into the global forum, using the capacities of modern communications to increase the impact of their cause.

6.1. NINE PARADOXES OF MATURE ECONOMIES

Concentrating on developments in the developed countries, Handy (1994) presented nine paradoxes of mature economies, which, he suggested, explain 'what is going on in our societies and why some confusion is inevitable'. He supported the view that we are in an era of change when many of our past ideas no longer hold and our good intentions have a habit of producing unpleasant surprises. He regarded paradox as inevitable. It is not comfortable, but recognising it and dealing with it is, he contended, the only way to proceed. He outlines paradoxes of *intelligence, work, productivity, time, riches, organisations, ageing, the individual* and *justice*.

6.1.1. The Paradox of Intelligence

The paradox of intelligence revolves around the emergence of intelligence or information as a central factor in continued economic success. Intelligence is a new form of property, but it is not controllable like the forms of property we are used to. It is sticky, leaky and tricky but, as Naisbitt (1994) suggested, 'should make for a more open society'. If it does it will challenge many of the assumptions of our existing society, most notably its power structures as the *nouveau information riche* compete with the owners of capital, just as they competed with the landowners in the past. It is sticky because, as Stonier (1983) argued, information can be passed on to others without the original 'owner' losing possession. Theoretically, we could all possess it at once; but because control of information bestows power, only the information that the controllers want to pass on is likely to be so widely disseminated. It is leaky because information and intelligence cannot be so closely controlled as land or capital. Intelligence, in particular, is an personal attribute that people carry with them. If they decide to take it elsewhere it is difficult to stop them, unless we indulge in draconian restrictions. The very nature of information and the means by which it can be spread does make control more difficult. It is tricky because intelligence is difficult to measure with conventional accounting tools. Traditional approaches have considered people a cost of production and have attempted to reduce labour as a means of cost-reduction. Regarding people as an asset—because they possess intelligence, the vital factor of production for the twenty-first century—throws these concepts into turmoil. As a result, established notions of property are inapplicable.

6.1.2. The Paradox of Work

The paradox of work arises because employment serves several purposes in industrial society. It gives individuals status, self-esteem and income, and provides the economy with labour. Increasingly these purposes are creating tensions between the individual's needs and those of society. Competitive pressures for efficiency and the replacement of labour by capital are leading to reductions in employment, which in turn lead to a more divided society. Those in work increasingly have too much work and reasonable amounts of money, but too little time to enjoy the fruits of their labours, while those without employment have all the time but no money. Loss of income from employment, for what appear to be sound commercial reasons for a company, destroys individual status and self-esteem and undermines established social systems and assumptions. It also reduces the ability of individuals, as consumers, to purchase the goods and services available, thus enhancing the competitive pressures for price cuts through further reductions in wage costs and a downward economic spiral. Only the creation of new jobs with comparable incomes, or some other method of providing income, can counter the trend. At the same time, as Wedell (1983) noted, we have the absurdity of much useful work that could be done—particularly in improving the environment and the social conditions of the sick, old, handicapped and poor—and millions of unemployed. This is the paradox of having much that needs doing but no way of employing the people without jobs to do it, because to do so would cost more than we are prepared to pay. If we want that work done and want to avoid the social consequences of unemployment new approaches to work and circulating income are likely to be necessary.

One of our problems is that we think work and employment are the same thing. They are not. They may overlap, but much work occurs outside employment and different employment situations involve a considerable variation in the amount of work required to fulfil their obligations. Housework, home-improvement, gardening and charitable activities all involve work, in the sense of physical or mental effort, but when it is not paid for it is not employment and is not counted in official statistics. If it was, the numbers 'in work' would dramatically increase and the economy would 'grow' by about 50 per cent.

Women have traditionally done most of this work without pay or recognition. Paradoxically, this work within the household is at least as important to society as work outside the household in the formal economy, which men have traditionally been paid to do. Without the former the latter cannot function effectively. Western societies are beginning to see the significance of this type of work as the traditional role of women changes. As more women enter employment rather than work for nothing, the support systems provided by their unpaid work, and taken for granted by society, are breaking down, often with disturbing social consequences. Finding alternative ways to provide these vital social supports will require creative solutions; suggesting that women should return to their earlier unpaid role is unlikely to be one of them.

6.1.3. The Paradox of Productivity

Changes in employment are partly fuelled by the paradox of productivity, which concentrates paid work in the hands of fewer people. Pricing work through employment and regarding labour as a cost rather than a resource lead to pressures for greater efficiency, but they also destroy jobs because they become too expensive. Except in low-wage economies, capital-intensive production is both cheaper and increasingly capable of producing all the manufactured goods we need. Consequently, jobs are shed from manufacturing industry just as they were from agriculture in the past. A further result is what Gershuny (1987) called the 'self-service economy', which is itself a paradox, in that while service industries are growing service consumption is either declining or not growing as quickly as might be expected. This occurs to a large degree because it is cheaper to 'do it yourself' than to pay someone else to do it for you. This is seen in a wide range of situations, from painting the house rather than employing someone to do it, through self-service shops and petrol stations, to driving our own cars rather than using public transport. In order to reduce costs in the service industries, suppliers shift the work involved in providing the service on to the customer. Suppliers' costs are reduced because they no longer have to pay anyone to do the work; as customers, do it for nothing! If we costed our time spent filling the supermarket trolley or driving to work we would realise that paying someone else to do it would be much cheaper and would create employment at the same time. One driver with 70 passengers on a bus or 1,000 on a train could be paid far more than normal rates if the cost of our own driving time was available to the public transport operator. We do not cost our time, so we think we are getting a bargain, do it ourselves and limit job-creation. Ironically, the British Department of Transport uses estimates of saved driver time as part of its justification for building new roads, but not in the evaluation of public transport investment.

Thus, the scale of the shift from manufacturing to service employment is less than was once expected. The new service jobs, which were to replace those lost in manufacturing, failed to materialise. Many of the new service jobs that have been created are part-time, casual and poorly paid in comparison to the industrial jobs they have replaced, creating a further paradox, in which the creation of new jobs does not lead to the expected increase in purchasing power or feelings of economic well-being that we traditionally expect.

6.1.4. The Paradox of Time

The ability to produce more with less has led to a paradox of time. Although it takes less time to produce the same, those in employment seem to work longer, not shorter hours, while those out of work have time on their hands—a new version of the 'haves' and 'have-nots'. It is a manifestation of a Haitian proverb that says if work was such a good thing the rich would keep it all to themselves. To a larger extent than ever before they are now doing just that. Globally, this has been true since the Industrial Revolution, as employment developed in the rich industrial countries. Despite the exploitation of cheap labour in the developing countries, employment remains concentrated in the rich countries. Unemployment may be a growing problem in the West but in the rest of the world unemployment, underemployment and non-employment are a way of life.

On a global scale another paradox of employment may be emerging—the division between the highly paid managerial group mostly located in the advanced economies and the low-paid production workers in the developing economies. In between are the now-redundant manufacturing workers in the advanced economies, who lack the skills to compete for managerial jobs and demand wages too high to allow them to compete for production work. Some service industries are beginning to show a similar split, as data-preparation, for example, is being shifted to cheaper labour economies. Instant worldwide communications mean that such tasks can be carried out anywhere.

6.1.5. The Paradox of Riches

Global comparisons lead to the paradox of riches, which revolves around the observation that historically economic growth has usually been associated with growing markets based on expanding populations. This was certainly true of the UK in the nineteenth century, when the growth of industry coincided with an explosion in the population. According to Zey (1994), population growth provides the necessary incentive to continued economic growth. He contended that among the reasons for the lower growth of the more developed economies are their declining birth rates and ageing populations. If present trends continue, several of these countries will experience declining populations and static or declining markets in the twenty-first century. The potential growth markets of the future are in the less developed world, where the population is young and growing; but unless the developed world is prepared to invest in those countries to boost their economies the potential will remain unrealised. In the short term such investment is likely to reduce employment further in the developed countries, so it is often opposed, despite the potential for long-term benefit for both the developed and developing worlds.

6.1.6. The Paradox of Organisations

The paradox of organisations comes from their changing nature. Whereas they were once seen as 'a castle, a home for life for its defenders', they are becoming 'more like a condominium, an association of temporary residents gathered together for their mutual convenience' (Handy 1994). We have grown used to depending on organisations and to their having a certain stability, but to be effective in the twenty-first century they must become flexible and impermanent.

One area in which we have come to rely on organisations is in the provision of employment. Since the Industrial Revolution we have come to expect an employer to provide us with a job, a package of work for payment. Before the Industrial Revolution, and in most of the world still, that expectation did not, and does not exist. Most people work in order to maintain a subsistence existence, not for regular payment. If the nature of organisations is changing to become more flexible, their employment needs are likely to change. They are likely to want fewer permanent employees and more who are contracted only for specific tasks. Once those tasks have been completed, the 'job' will disappear. Could we be entering the post-employment age as well as the postindustrial one?

6.1.7. The Paradox of Ageing

Unfortunately, our ideas, concepts and particularly our social arrangements and expectations seldom keep up with the changes in our economy or our society because of the paradox of ageing. 'Every generation perceives itself as justifiably different from its predecessor, but plans as if its successor generation will be the same as them' (Handy 1994). It won't, but because the older generation makes the rules, the rules don't fit the emerging reality. When change was nonexistent or slow, it did not matter; one generation lived very like the one before and the one after. But the economy and technology in particular have moved on at an increasing pace from *Dombey and Son* via the 'Generation Gap' to the multiple career, interspersed with retraining or continual learning. Social, legal, cultural and political systems are lagging behind, still working to an outdated set of assumptions.

6.1.8. The Paradox of the Individual

The paradox of the individual, Handy suggested, was best captured by Jung, who argued that to be truly ourselves, as we are increasingly encouraged to be, we need others as well. Competition is necessary, as an incentive, but is not sufficient. To achieve what we desire as social animals, co-operation is also necessary. In these terms, neither the individualism of *laissez-faire* capitalism nor the collectivism of socialism are enough, on their own, to address the needs of emerging society. Socialism may have failed dramatically in the 1980s but capitalism, although apparently triumphant, is also in crisis, unable to produce the sustainable society unaided. Social, economic, environmental and political challenges multiply.

6.1.9. The Paradox of Justice

Many issues these days, as Naisbitt (1994) noted, are not 'right versus wrong' but 'right versus right', or even perhaps 'wrong versus wrong'. Many ethical issues seem to be like this; should a terminally ill patient in excruciating pain be kept alive because we can defer death, or helped to die with dignity? Should a green field be retained because it provides a habitat for a rare species, or should it be developed to provide housing for the homeless or jobs for the unemployed? Your answer will most probably depend on your perspective and whether the interests of rare species, the homeless or the unemployed are of most value to you. Handy saw this as the paradox of justice. He summed it up in a reference to capitalism, which 'depends of the fundamental principle of inequality—some may do better than others—but will only be acceptable in a democracy if most people have an equal chance to aspire to that inequality'. Inequality and the chance of individual advancement may provide incentive but too much inequality and a perceived lack of opportunity are likely to lead to resignation or revolution.

6.2. SOME FURTHER CONTEMPORARY PARADOXES

The paradoxes put forward by Naisbitt and Handy may appear to provide enough challenges as we enter the twenty-first century, but it is relatively easy to extend the list. Here are some more that have become apparent during the preparation of this book. You may also wish to add more of your own.

6.2.1. The Paradox of Technology

There is increasing concern that the technology that has underpinned our Western lifestyles since the Industrial Revolution is causing damage to the natural processes of our planet. The Greenhouse Effect, the hole in the ozone layer, acid rain, nitrate pollution, over-fishing, diseases like asthma attributed to air pollution and cancer to other environmental causes, are blamed on technological developments that have taken place in the last 200 years. As these developments accelerate, the potential problems multiply but paradoxically it is that same technology and the scientific knowledge on which it is based that have given us the ability to begin to understand the natural processes on which we depend. It was technology, for example, that gave us the truly amazing view of 'Spaceship Earth' that so clearly encapsulates our situation. Without our technology we would not be in a position to realise what we are doing, but nor, of course, could we have done it. Having opened Pandora's box we are going to need that technology, and more, to clean up the mess we have made in the past and to find ways of creating a sustainable future that is acceptable to the human population. It is unlikely that we have all the necessary knowledge to undo our past mistakes without further research and just stopping technology and returning to a preindustrial lifestyle, even if it was possible, would not help us with our inherited problems. Although it is important to take a more cautious attitude to technological innovation, doing all we can to assess the likely impacts of developments before we adopt them, the unexpected can be favourable as well as damaging. Stopping now would mean foregoing the benefits as well as the costs. Attempting to maximise the former while minimising the latter through careful impact-assessments seems the most promising approach to take, despite the uncertainties involved.

In the light of our experience it would appear wise to take a more considered approach to the development of technology in the future, but it is not possible to prove beyond reasonable doubt that technological advance should be halted. On what grounds should we stop now, rather than at some other time in the past or the future? When did, or will, the balance shift between benefit and cost? Some might argue that the shift occurred at the beginning of the industrial period, or even the Neolithic, while others insist there is no reason to believe we are anywhere near the limits yet. It is an issue worth debating but it is very difficult to reach a definitive conclusion.

Technology itself will also remain a paradox. It enables us to produce lifestyles beyond our wildest dreams or threats darker than our darkest nightmares. The changes during the twentieth century, both for good and ill, would leave our great-grandparents astonished, were they able to return to see them. Without further advances in technology we are likely to be left with the problems of the past without the hope of dealing with them in the future. Although we would then avoid new problems arising from new technologies, we would also forgo the undoubted benefits to be obtained. Turning our back on technology is unlikely to help, because it is not in essence a technological problem, but a human one. It is our use of the technology and the choices we have made about which technologies to develop and how to develop them that have caused the problems.

The greater the understanding that we obtain about the nature of human technology and its advantages and disadvantages, the greater the moral and ethical dilemmas we face. Nuclear power and many existing technologies have already raised wide-ranging debates, but developing technologies are going to raise even more. Genetic engineering has the potential to enable us to eliminate many hereditary diseases, but it also provides the possibility to influence other characteristics, such as intelligence, appearance, physical ability and the like. Where should the line be drawn? Is it better to stop research and avoid the issues but condemn further generations to suffering from potentially curable diseases, or run the risk of misuse? Nanotechnology or molecular manufacturing, according to Drexler, Peterson and Pergamit (1992), has the potential to 'help us get what we want: high quality products at low cost with little environmental impact', but can we avoid the equally large potential for misuse? Drexler *et al.* concluded that it looks a tough problem. Paradoxically the real issue for the twenty-first century may not be the technology but the uses we make of it, the ethical dilemmas that raises and the political means at our disposal to resolve them. If the twentieth century has taught us anything about ourselves and our technology, it is that these are the questions we need to face.

6.2.2. The Paradox of Information

One of the requirements of creating a sustainable future is more information about both natural and social processes. We need to know more about how the planet functions and how we humans interact with it, and about the other lifeforms we share a home with. But how can we cope with all the information we need? We are already suffering from 'infoglut', but sources of information, whether academic journals, television channels or the infant information superhighway are proliferating. It may be that much of the content of any media is junk, but apart from the issue of who decides what is and what is not junk and what is and what is not important, how do we make the important information more attractive than the junk?

In the UK and probably most other Western countries, the most popular newspapers and television programmes are the tabloids and the soap operas. They seldom deal with the kind of issues that futurists believe important and generally adopt a relatively straightforward, even simple approach, without reference to the complexities and paradoxes discussed here. It may be tempting to take an elitist stance and condemn both the media and their audiences, but if, as has been argued before, it is likely to be necessary to obtain the support of the majority for decisions with important implications for the future, it is an inadequate response. If a sustainable future can only be attained by a democratic approach, the majority must inform themselves, rather than be informed, about the issues. This can only be achieved if the issues are raised in a popular way in a popular format. Staying aloof or imposing apparent solutions is unlikely to work, because they will be undermined.

6.2.3. The Paradox of Education

To enable people and societies to cope with the modern world, it is generally agreed that we need better and more highly educated individuals. At the same time, education is criticised for failing to provide the necessary skills and attainment levels are deplored. Furthermore, the employment prospects for both educated and unskilled people are relatively poor. Graduate unemployment is relatively high and a major concern among final-year students is their ability to get a job when they complete their studies. The prospect for those who have little education and few skills is even worse. Partly in consequence, many young people see little point in education. If there are no jobs, why bother? And if getting a degree is no longer a route to well-paid employment, why spend years in higher education acquiring a useless degree and debts it will be difficult to pay off? Better to enjoy the present while we can.

This links to Handy's paradox of ageing. The education system is controlled by adults, quite often middle-aged adults. In government, curriculum and examination boards, education committees, school boards and the classroom they decide what is to be taught. Too often it reflects the world they have lived in rather than the one in which their children will live. An illustration of the domination of education by outdated concepts might be the experience of my younger son, who spends a considerable amount of his time reading, but who found the books specified for his English Literature course by the British National Curriculum unutterably boring. By choice he read books by authors like Isaac Asimov, David Eddings and Terry Pratchett, who was recently described as 'This country's greatest living novelist . . . the Dickens of the 20th century'. Such books relate to his interests and the late-twentieth-century world in which he lives. For English Literature he had to read Thomas Hardy, Wordsworth and Shakespeare—all important authors in English culture, but from periods of the past quite foreign to a sixteen-year-old. The lifestyles they described and the language they used have little to connect them with the life of a teenager into computers, role-playing games and rock music. Reading them is no doubt considered by the curriculum designers to be 'good for him', but that must be doubtful if he is turned off the classics for life as a result. Might it not be better to encourage his interest in reading by relating to his world and attempting to link his experience to the development of the rich heritage of literature? After all, the authors we now consider classics, like Dickens and Shakespeare, wrote for their own age about issues of their time, not to persecute the young of generations a century or more in the future. They might be very surprised, if they were able to return, to find that we valued their writings so highly. It is also interesting to note that David Lodge, who wrote the screenplay for a television production of *Martin Chuzzlewit*, contended that if Dickens were alive in the late twentieth century he would write for television.

An understanding of history is an important part of any education, because so many current issues have their roots in the past and cannot be understood without that context. On the other hand, their resolution usually requires new thinking and an openness to experimentation and novel approaches, rather than a repetition of the old.

6.2.4. The Paradox of Change

As a natural process, change is inevitable, unless time stands still. Both the world we live in and our own bodies are continually changing. The processes of growth and decay are more natural than stability. They are usually gradual, but change can also be rapid, like volcanic eruptions and hurricanes. Change in human affairs can be both exciting and frightening. Without change life can be boring, the same routine day in, day out. Change—meeting new people, having new experiences, discovering new things—can add spice to life and stimulate personal development. It can also be stressful. Psychologists have developed scales of stress associated with events in our lives, like moving house or the death of a near relative. Too much change can make us ill.

To deal with change we need to accept its inevitability and respond creatively rather than defensively, realising that we create change as well as experience it. Despite the apparent pace and amount of change we are experiencing, we can neither change everything at once nor cope with the stress total change would induce. We need a certain level of stability in order to operate. The limitation on our ability to change what we have is made more significant by our growing numbers and the physical stock we have created. Our physical capital, such as our cities, has been built up over decades, centuries and even millennia. To change it all would take so much effort and cost so much as to make it impossible, except over an extended period. Some estimates suggest that the rate of renewal of the urban fabric in the UK is only about 1 per cent per annum. This is broadly in line with the rate of change in the housing stock, which can be estimated from information on the total number of houses and the current rate of building. Twenty-one million household spaces were counted in the 1991 Census in England and Wales. In 1993, 155,438 new dwellings were built. At that rate it would take 136 years to replace the existing housing stock if the demand remained the same. Given that it is likely to continue to increase, as it has been doing in recent years in response to changes in the structure of the population, it is likely to be much longer—up to 800 years according to Burns (1986) or 4,000 years if Malpass (1995) is correct.

The greater the capital stock the more resources have to be devoted to its maintenance, particularly if it is likely to be needed for a longer period of time. Successful companies make allowances for depreciation, new investment to replace old and maintenance. Those that do not usually go out of business as competitors using up-to-date methods produce better products more efficiently. Societies, and particularly governments, seem more reluctant to maintain their infrastructure. It is always more attractive to cut taxes or keep prices low than to spend the money maintaining roads, schools, hospitals, sewers or houses. It will not matter for another year; things will not get much worse.

Building new things can be glamorous; good publicity can be obtained opening new facilities, but spending on maintenance is dull, with little publicity value. It has no sex appeal. As a consequence, maintenance budgets are squeezed and facilities run down. Spending on maintenance or replacements for outworn facilities can always be put off just a little longer; the difference a short delay will make is not going to be serious. These incremental delays are insignificant in themselves but as they accumulate our infrastructure becomes gradually worse. All of a sudden, it seems, we are faced with major problems, as Victorian sewers collapse, inadequately maintained railways suffer increasing breakdowns and hundred-year-old schools and hospitals are condemned as inadequate for modern standards. The potential costs of the failure to maintain are suddenly horrifying. For example, in 1994 it was estimated that bringing unfit housing in the UK up to current standards would cost £12.6 billion, nearly twice the government's total annual spend on housing (Simmons 1994).

It seems likely that nomadic hunter–gatherer societies were in certain respects more flexible than modern societies. Within a very short time they could move from one place to another, because, unlike us, they were unencumbered by the large fixed capital we have accumulated. They were probably more able to move because, being fewer in number, there was also less likelihood of their colliding with other groups who would defend their 'territory'. When natural or manmade disasters strike in the modern world, there is much less flexibility. Modern nation states with fixed territories, which they jealously guard against outsiders, are not prepared to make room for the victims of misfortune from elsewhere. Neither are their peoples, who see their position threatened by an influx of outsiders.

These observations suggest another underlying paradox. At a time when change is said to be occurring at an ever-increasing speed, we are likely to run up against an increasing number of barriers to change—economic, social, cultural, ecological and political. In Britain, for example, where the legacy of history is long and space and resources limited, it is already clear that any proposal for change will run into opposition, often from entrenched interests with reasons to protect the status quo. Almost any proposal for development will inspire opposition—housing, a road, the rail link between London and the Channel Tunnel, forestry, reducing the number of cars in a city centre, or a high-tech business park on a green-field site. Individuals and communities with legitimate interests and rights will campaign long and hard to protect those interests. Almost any policy proposal or action will invoke an equal and opposite reaction. In any society that claims to be a democracy, those interests must be heard. This takes time. As a result of the extent of entrenched interests and the scale of our fixed capital investment, our society takes longer and longer to change direction; it is like an ever-larger supertanker, when the sea conditions seem to demand a much more manoeuvrable craft.

6.2.5. The Paradox of Cities

The fact that cities are a scene of contrasting fortunes and lifestyles is not new. One of their abiding attractions has been their variety, which has often been contrasted to the more restricted opportunities of the countryside. They have always been centres of wealth and culture, high-points of civilisation, and pits of deprivation, but as the population becomes more urban, particularly in Latin America, Africa and Asia, the contrasts become starker. People are attracted to cities by the promise of a better life, but when they get there, if the promise proves elusive, it is much more difficult to maintain subsistence than in a rural community.

An urban population is more dependent on a wide range of impersonal linkages for its survival than a rural population. Before the Industrial Revolution in Europe, and in most of the world until recently, most people lived a subsistence lifestyle, growing their own food and making their own clothes. It may have been a hard life and one we would find unattractive, but it was not dependent on a host of unknown others, as Western lifestyles have become. Our food, our clothes, all our consumer goods, and the power to heat our homes and operate all the gadgets all depend on a network of unknown and far-flung systems and people. When we turn on a light switch we give no thought to the source of the electricity, the environmental effects of its production, the way it has reached us or the people involved in making it possible. Only when something breaks down or someone in the chain decides not to perform their part of the task do we pay any attention to the complex network involved; most likely to curse or complain. The more complex the network and the more links involved, the more prone to disruption the system becomes. It is rather like Naisbitt's Global Paradox in the sense that the larger and more complex the system becomes, the more power to disrupt it the individual links have.

Cities are changing in response to the wider forces of our society. The traditional city was a tight-knit, densely populated, built-up area where inhabitants lived and worked in close proximity. Since the middle of the twentieth century, first in North America and subsequently in Western Europe, this pattern has changed. The mobility made possible by trains and buses and then by the car has encouraged people to move to the edge of the city, separating their homes from their place of employment. As those who could afford to do so moved further out, many of the traditional city-centre services followed. First shops, then entertainment and some offices moved from the city centre to the suburbs or out of town. Loss of traditional industries left large areas derelict, while the location of employment shifted to new locations. Left behind in this transition were the poor, who were unable to move out and who lost the services previously provided by the town centre. This has exacerbated the ghettoisation of the city, with the poor trapped in the inner city and the better-off behind their security devices in the suburbs or beyond. The new telecommunications technologies have the potential to increase this divide, both socially and spatially. As a consequence, some observers have declared the age of the city to be past. However, although they may no longer live within the boundaries of the city, the better-off are just as much a part of the city as ever. Connections to the wider community, whether physical or by telecommunications, are a vital part of life beyond the traditional boundaries of the city. The city as we knew it in the past may be dead, but the city in the Western world is alive and evolving into a new, possibly global or virtual form. In the Third World the rapidly growing cities are also producing a new form, in terms of urban areas larger than we have ever experienced before.

6.2.6. The Paradox of Success

As Kahn (1978) noted, several of the problems we now face are the result of success in solving past problems or in developing the lifestyle of the advanced economies, which we usually consider to constitute progress over earlier generations. The environmental challenges we now face are a prime example. Our very success in creating the consumer society has created a series of consequences that we now regard as problems, some of considerable concern.

The invention of the internal-combustion engine and the explosion of road traffic have had an important influence on the pattern of life in the West in the twentieth century. Cities have spread as car owners have been able to move to suburban locations. Shops and places of employment and entertainment have followed, particularly in North America but increasingly in Western Europe, too. The car is now a symbol of freedom and status, 'one of the last enclaves where we have almost complete dominance and self-determination. We can go where we want, when we want and take however long we want' (Graham 1994). Access to a car is almost an entrance requirement to enjoyment of the late-twentieth-century lifestyle, and convenient road transport is considered a necessity for successful economic development, both nationally and locally.

It has been suggested that if we had known what the effects of the car would be when the internal-combustion engine was invented, we would probably not have proceeded with its development. Apart from the problems of congestion and consumption of land, road vehicles make a major contribution to air pollution. Carley (1992) quotes Dutch estimates that suggest that the world vehicle fleet is the largest single source of global air pollution, producing 17 per cent of the main greenhouse gas, carbon dioxide. Road transport is also claimed to be responsible for 20 per cent of climatic change, 20 per cent of acidification, 70 per cent of smog, 50–85 per cent of the airborne lead, 60 per cent of nuisance and 5 per cent of waste—this at a time of continued growth in vehicle numbers. On the basis of recent trends, traffic in the UK is forecast to increase by 142 per cent by 2025 and the world vehicle fleet from 500 million in the 1990s to 1,000 million in 2010 and 1,500 million by 2030. If these forecasts are correct, the impact will inevitably increase, even with improvements to fuel efficiency and pollution-control. This raises questions about the capacity of the Earth to cope. If the motor industry had not been so successful and the car not so attractive to consumers, the problem would be nowhere near as great.

6.2.7. The Future as Paradox

Assuming we accept that in making decisions about such issues we have a responsibility to consider the future, how can we know what the consequences will be and how we can achieve the future we prefer? We know that it is almost inevitable that the effects of our actions will affect the future, just as the decisions of our ancestors have affected our present. But we also know that predicting the impacts of our decisions and the nature of the future is, at best, an imprecise art. To make the correct decisions we would need to plan in the certainty of knowing what the future will be; but that certainty is unattainable. Should we decide not to decide? Possibly, but a decision not to decide is as much a decision, from which consequences flow just the same. Our responsibility to the future is something we cannot avoid but, paradoxically, something we cannot discharge in the knowledge that we are doing the right thing.

Many of the paradoxes discussed here raise issues with which humanity has wrestled for centuries. Most religions and philosophers throughout history have struggled to resolve such problems. What grounds are there, then, for suggesting that an understanding of the inevitability of paradox is useful to us as we face the future, and for taking our responsibility more seriously than before?

The basic human condition—that current generations influence the life chances of their descendants—has not changed. Ever since early humanity learned to plant seeds and harvest the results, if not before, our future has been contingent on our present actions. The effect was greatly increased by the Industrial Revolution, as we know to both our benefit and our cost. The difference is that we are the first generation to *realise* the impact that we have made and are making.

Human choice and action are increasingly influencing not only our effect on our environment, which affects our own life-chances (the day this was written air-pollution warnings were being issued for much of the UK), but also our effect on other lifeforms and on each other. It is the realisation of this responsibility for the future that is the difference. It is a realisation born of our increasing knowledge and the knowledge that human influence, due mainly to our numbers and the advance of our technology, has become more significant. Paradoxically, our individual short-term interests may not coincide with the longer-term interests of humanity and the Earth. Our struggle to obtain or maintain a comfortable style of life could be jeopardising our future.

It is an awesome, even scary responsibility, but also an exciting prospect. It is scary because we are always moving towards a future in which uncertainty is inherent. We cannot know all we would like or need to know in order to make decisions we can be sure will be correct. It is also scary because we appear to be in a period of major changes that make the future less predictable than we believe it used to be. Many of our established ideas and traditional structures appear to be breaking down, and without them the future looks threatening. Perhaps it would be better to ignore it and hope it goes away.

It is also exciting. Perhaps we are engaged in a transformation that historians will eventually consider as significant as the Industrial Revolution. The use of the term postindustrial society suggests as much. As a description it is not very positive, because it indicates where we have come from rather than what we have become. But it also suggests that we are still in the process of creating the new society, with all the opportunities that offers. In large measure it is open to us as never before to create the future, to establish the new structures and ideas that will shape the twenty-first century. It is an exciting prospect. If we wish to take up the challenge, the Future is Ours.

*The future is not out there, waiting to be discovered;
future*s *are in here, ready to be created.*

REFERENCES

Alexander, J. (1992), *The Astrological Manager: A New Approach to Business, Success and Destiny*, Anness, New York.
Amara, R. (1981), 'The Futures Field: Searching for Definitions and Boundaries', *The Futurist*, February, pp. 25–9.
Ariansen, P. (1994), 'Sustainability, Morality and Future Generations', paper to the First Global Future Generations Forum, Kyoto, Japan, 24–26 November.
Armstrong, J. S. (1978), *Long Range Forecasting: From Crystal Ball to Computer*, Wiley, New York.
—— (1987), 'Forecasting Methods for Conflict Situations', in G. Wright and P. Ayton (eds.), *Judgemental Forecasting*, Wiley, Chichester, pp. 157–76.
Ash, T. G. (1991), 'Future Indefinite', *Independent*, 3 January, p. 23.
Asimov, I. (1960), *Foundation*, Panther, St Albans.
Barney, G. O. (1980), *Global 2000 Report to the President of the US*, Pergamon, New York.
Beach, L. R., Christensen-Szalanski, J. and Barnes, V. (1987), 'Assessing Human Judgement: Has it been Done, Can it be Done, Should it be Done?', in G. Wright and P. Ayton (eds.), *Judgemental Forecasting*, Wiley, Chichester, pp. 49–62.
Beckman, R. (1988), *Into the Upwave: How to Prosper from Slump to Boom*, Milestone Publications, Portsmouth.
Bell, D. (1976), *The Coming of Post Industrial Society*, Penguin, Harmondsworth.
Bell, W. (1993), 'Why Should We Care About Future Generations', in H. F. Didsbury (ed.), *The Years Ahead: Perils, Problems and Promises*, World Future Society, Bethesda, pp. 25–41.
—— et al. (1971), *The Sociology of the Future*, Russell Sage, New York.
Benford, E. (1982), *Timescape*, Sphere Books, London.
Benveniste, G. (1973), *The Politics of Expertise*, Croom Helm, London.
Berlin, I. (1969), *Four Essays in Liberty*, Oxford University Press, Oxford.
Bohler, E. (1973), 'Psychological Prerequisites of Forecasting and Planning', *Technological Forecasting and Social Change*, 4, pp. 317–22.
Bolch, B. and Lyons, H. (1993), 'Apocalypse Not: Science, Economics and Environmentalism', Cato Institute, quoted in *Future Survey*, 15(7), p. 15.
Boniecki, G. (1980), 'What are the Limits to Man's Time and Space Perspectives', *Technological Forecasting and Social Change*, 17, pp. 161–174.
Boulding, E. (1976), 'Futuristics and the Imaging Capacity of the West', in M.

Maruyama and A. Hawkins (eds.), *The Culture of the Future*, Mouton, Atlantic Highlands, NJ, pp. 7–31.

Boulding, E. (1978), 'The Dynamics of Imaging Futures', *World Future Society Bulletin*, 12(5), pp. 1–8.

Bowonder, B., and Miyake, T. (1993), 'Technology Forecasting in Japan', *Futures*, 25(7), pp. 757–77.

Branch, M. (1990), *Planning: Universal Process*, Praeger, New York.

Bratt, E. C. (1958), *Business Forecasting*, McGraw Hill, New York.

Bronowski, J. (1973), *The Ascent of Man*, BBC Publications, London.

Bryson, B. (1989), *The Lost Continent*, Secker & Warburg, London.

Budd, A., Dicks, G., and Robinson, B. (1982), 'A Small Step Ahead—Unless We Slip on Oil', *The Sunday Times*, 14 March.

Burns, P. (1986), 'The World We Live in', lecture to the School of the Environment, Leeds Polytechnic, by the Chief Executive of Crown Paints, 14 January.

Camill, K. (1982), 'National Strategy is Boosting Japan into Fifth Generation', *Computer Weekly*, 25 February.

Carley, M. J. (1992), 'Settlement Trends and the Crisis of Automobility', *Futures*, 24(3), pp. 206–18.

—— and Derow, E. O. (1983), *Social Impact Assessment: A Cross Disciplinary Guide to the Literature*, Westview Press, Boulder, CO.

Central Statistical Office (1981), *Social Trends 12: 1982*, HMSO, London.

—— (1992), *Social Trends 22: 1992*, HMSO, London.

Chadwick, G. (1971), *A Systems View of Planning*, Pergamon, Oxford.

Chapman, G. (1976), 'Economic Forecasting in Britain 1961–1965: A Critique of Assumptions', *Futures*, 8(3), pp. 254–260.

Chapman, P. F. (1978), 'Forecasting Energy Futures: Paradoxes and Their Resolution', *Built Environment*, 4(4), pp. 275–80.

Chisholm, R. K., and Whitaker, G. R. (1971), *Forecasting Methods*, Irwin, Homewood, IL.

Choucri, N. (1991), 'Global Environment and Multinational Corporations', *Technology Review*, 94(3), pp. 52–9.

Clark, B. D., Bisset, R., and Wathern, P. (1980), *Environmental Impact Assessment: A Bibiolography with Abstracts*, Mansell Publishing, London.

Clarke, A. C. (1962), *Profiles of the Future*, Pan, London.

Clarke, I. F. (1979), *The Pattern of Expectation 1644–2001*, Jonathan Cape, London. Reissued 1996, Adamantine Press, London

Cleveland, H. (1989), 'The Future of Futurists: What Matters and What Works', *Futures*, 21(4), pp. 390–6.

Coates, J. F. (1974), 'Some Methods and Techniques for Comprehensive Impact Assessment', *Technology Forecasting and Social Change*, 6, pp. 341–57.

—— (1978), 'Technology Assessment', in J. B. Fowles (ed.) *Handbook of Futures Research*, Greenwood, Westport, pp. 397–421.

—— et al. (1986), *Issues Management: How You Can Plan, Organize and Manage for the Future*, Lomond, Mt Airy.

Cook, L. (1986), 'The State Scanning Network: An Issue Identification System for State Policy Managers', *Futures Research Quarterly*, 2(1), pp. 65–77.

Cooper, D. F., and Chapman, C. B. (1987), *Risk Analysis for Large Projects: Models, Methods and Cases*, Wiley, New York.

Copeland, R. M., Dascher, P. E., and Davison, D. (1980), *Financial Accounting*, Wiley, New York.

Coveney, P., and Highfield, R. (1990), *The Arrow of Time: A Voyage Through Science to Solve Time's Greatest Mystery*, W.H. Allen, London.

Cross, N. (1982), *Control of Technology. Unit 8: Methods Guide*, Open University Press, Milton Keynes.

Dator, J. (1993a), 'From Future Workshops to Envisioning Alternative Futures', *Futures Research Quarterly*, 9(3), pp. 108–12.

—— (1993b), 'American State Courts, Five Tsunamis and Four Alternative Futures', *Futures Research Quarterly*, 9(4), pp. 9–30.

Davis, C. H., and Fitzsimmons, J. A. (1991), 'The Future of Nuclear Power in the United States', *Technological Forecasting and Social Change*, 40, pp. 151–64.

de Bono, E. (1970), *Lateral Thinking: Creativity Step by Step*, Harper & Row, New York.

Delbecq, A. L., Van De Vem, A. H., and Gustafson, D. H. (1975), *Group Techniques for Program Planning: A Guide to Nominal Group and Delphi Processes*, Scott, Foremand and Co., Glenview, IL.

Della Vecchia, R. M. (1986), 'Futuristics Education: An Avenue of Hope for Today's Student', *Futures Research Quarterly*, 2(4), pp. 31–40.

Department of the Environment (1990), *Our Common Inheritance: Britain's Environmental Strategy*, HMSO, London.

Dickson, G. C. A. (1991), *Risk Analysis*, Witherby, London.

Done, K. (1982), 'Japanese Export Onslaught', *Technology Week*, 13 February.

Drexler, K. E., Peterson, C., and Pergamit, G. (1992), *Unbounding the Future: The Nanotechnology Revolution*, Simon & Schuster, London.

Duke, R. D. (1978), 'Simulation Gaming', in J. B. Fowles (ed.), *Handbook of Futures Research*, Greenwood, Westport, pp. 353–67.

Duncan, O. D. (1969), 'Social Forecasting: The State of the Art', *The Public Interest*, 17, pp. 88–118. Reprinted in F. Tugwell (ed.) (1973) *Search for Alternatives: Public Policy and the Study of the Future*, Winthrop, Cambridge, MA, pp. 23–49.

Eger, A. F., and Smith, G. (1987), 'Construction Forecasting: The Delphi Approach. A Survey of Canadian Office Construction for 1986', *Land Development Studies*, 4, pp. 3–16.

Ellis, K. (1973), *Prediction and Prophecy*, Wayland, London.

Encel, S., Marstrand, P. K., and Page, W. (1975), *The Art of Anticipation: Values and Methods in Forecasting*, Martin Robertson, London.

Enzer, S., and Wurzburger, R. (1982) 'LA 200 + 20: Some Alternative Futures for Los Angeles 2001', executive summary, Center for Futures Research, University of Southern California, Los Angeles, CA.

Evans, J. St B. T. (1987), 'Beliefs and Expectations as Causes of Judgemental Bias',

in G. Wright and P. Ayton (eds.) *Judgemental Forecasting*, Wiley, Chichester, pp. 31–48.
Ferguson, M. (1980), *The Aquarian Conspiracy: Personal and Social Transformation in the 1980s*, J.P. Tarcher, Los Angeles, CA.
Ferkiss, V. C. (1977) 'Futurology, Promise, Performance, Prospects', *The Washington Papers*, 5(50), Sage, Beverly Hills, CA.
Field, B., and MacGregor, B. (1987), *Forecasting Techniques for Urban and Regional Planning*, Hutchinson, London.
Firth, M. (1977), *Forecasting Methods in Business and Management*, Edward Arnold, London.
Foley, G., with Nassim, C. (1981), *The Energy Questions*, Pelican, Harmondsworth.
Fowles, J. B. (1978), 'The Problem of Values in Futures Research', in *Handbook of Futures Research*, Greenwood, Westport, pp. 125–40.
Frankenfield, P. J. (1993), 'Simple Gifts: Complex Environmental Hazards and the Responsibility to Leave a Controllable World', *Futures*, 25(1), pp. 32–52.
Friend, J. K., and Jessop, W. N. (1969), *Local Government and Strategic Choice: An Operational Research Approach to the Process of Public Planning*, Tavistock, London.
Galbraith, J. K. (1969), *The New Industrial State*, Penguin, Harmondsworth.
Galtung, J. (1976), 'The Future: A Forgotten Dimension', in H. Ornauer, H. Wiberg, A. Sicinsky, and J. Galtung (eds.), *Images of the World in the Year 2000: A Comparative Ten Nation Study*, Mouton, Atlantic Highlands, NJ, pp. 45–120.
Gattey, C. N. (1989), *Prophecy and Prediction in the 20th Century*, Aquarian Press, London.
Gershuny, J. I. (1987), 'The Future of Service Employment', in O. Giarini (ed.) *The Emerging Service Economy*, Pergamon, Oxford, pp. 105–124.
Gibson, L., and Gibson, W. (1974), *Complete Illustrated Book of Divination and Prophecy*, Souvenir Press, London.
Godet, M. (1987), *Scenarios and Strategic Management*, Butterworths, London.
—— (1993), *From Anticipation to Action: A Handbook of Strategic Perspective*, Unesco, Paris.
Gordan, A., and Suzuki, D. (1991), *It's a Matter of Survival*, Harper Collins, London.
Graham, A. (1994), 'No U-Turn for the Car Culture', *Yorkshire Post*, 27 October, p. 10.
Graham, A. K., and Senge, P. M. (1980), 'A Long Wave Hypothesis of Innovation', *Technological Forecasting and Social Change*, 17, pp. 283–311.
Hage, J. (1981), lecture at Bradford University Management Centre, December.
Hall, P. (1980), *Great Planning Disasters*, Penguin, Harmondsworth.
Hamel, G., and Prahalad, C. K. (1994), *Competing for the Future*, Harvard Business School Press, Boston, MA.
Handy, C. (1994), *The Empty Raincoat: Making Sense of the Future*, Hutchinson, London.
Harman, W. W. (1976), *An Incomplete Guide to the Future*, Stanford Alumni Association, Stanford, CA.

—— (1983), 'Integrated Impact Assessment: The Impossible Dream', in F. A. Rossini and A. L. Porter (eds.), *Integrated Impact Assessment*, Westview Press, Boulder, CO.
Harvey, D. (1989), *The Condition of Post-Modernity*, Basil Blackwell, Oxford.
Henshel, R. L. (1978), 'Self-Altering Predictions', in J. B. Fowles (ed.) *Handbook of Futures Research*, Greenwood, Westport, pp. 99–123.
Hewitt, V. J., and Lorie, P. (1991), *Nostradamus: The End of the Millennium. Prophecies 1992–2001*, Bloomsbury, London.
Hirschorn, L. (1980), 'Scenario Writing: A Developmental Approach', *Journal of the American Planners Association*, 46(2), pp. 172–183.
Hooker, C. (1989), 'Future Studies: Its Role in Education', in R. A. Slaughter (ed.), *Studying the Future: An Introductory Reader*, Commission for the Future and The Australian Bicentennial Authority, Victoria, pp. 47–50.
Hoos, I. R. (1978), 'Methodological Shortcomings in Futures Research', in J. B. Fowles (ed.), *Handbook of Futures Research*, Greenwood, Westport, pp. 53–66.
Huss, W. R., and Honton, E. J. (1987), 'Scenario Planning: What Style Should You Use?', *Long Range Planning*, 20(4), pp. 21–9.
Ignatieff, M. (1993), 'Poverty of Desire is our National Failing', *Observer*, 24 January, p. 19.
Inayatullah, S. (1990), 'Deconstructing and Reconstructing the Future: Predictive Cultural and Critical Epistemologies', *Futures*, 22(2), pp. 115–41.
Ingelstam, L. E. (ed.) (1974), *To Choose a Future*, Swedish Ministry of Foreign Affairs, Secretariat for Future Studies, Stockholm.
Jenkins, J. (1993), 'Apocalypse Tomorrow', *New Statesman and Society*, 29 January, pp. 24–5.
Johnston, D. F. (1978), 'Social Indicators and Social Forecasting', in J. B. Fowles (ed.), *Handbook of Futures Research*, Greenwood, Westport, pp. 424–48.
Jones, B. (1990), *Sleeper's Awake: Technology and the Future of Work*, Oxford University Press, Oxford.
Jones, H., and Twiss, B. C. (1978). *Forecasting Technology for Planning Decisions*, Macmillan, London.
Jouvenel, B. de (1967), *The Art of Conjecture*, Weidenfeld & Nicolson, London.
Judge, A. (1993), 'Metaphors and the Language of Futures', *Futures*, 25(3), pp. 275–88.
Jungk, R., and Mullert, N. (1987), *Future Workshops: How to Create Desirable Futures*, Institute for Social Inventions, London.
Kahn, H. (1978), *The Next 200 Years*, Abacus, London.
—— and Wiener, A. J. (1967), *The Year 2000: A Framework for Speculation on the Next Thirty-three Years*, Macmillan, London.
Kaufman, D. (1976), *Teaching the Future: A Guide to Future Oriented Education*, ETC Publications, Palm Springs, CA.
Kay, A. (1994), 'The Best Way to Predict the Future is to Invent it', occasional lecture to the Programme on Information and Communication Technologies, London, 26 May.

Kenney, M. L. (1988), 'Planning th Future: A Voyage of Discovery', *Futures Research Quarterly*, 4(4), pp. 49–74.

Kettle, M. (1993), 'If Only We had Known About Hindsight', *Guardian*, 16 January, p. 25.

Kliever, G. (1992), 'The 10,000-Year Warning: Alerting Future Civilizations About Our Nuclear Waste', *The Futurist*, 26(5), pp. 17–19.

Klosterman, R. E. (1994), 'Large-Scale Urban Models: Retrospect and Prospect', *American Planning Association Journal*, 60(1), pp. 3–6.

Kondratiev, N. (1935), 'The Long Waves in Economic Life', *Review of Economic Statistics*, 17, pp. 105–15.

Kuhn, T. (1970), *The Structure of Scientific Revolutions*, University of Chicago Press, Chicago, IL.

Lal, D. (1992), 'Green Imperialists', in D. Fishburn (ed.), *The World in 1993*, Economist Publications, London, p. 16.

Land, G., and Jarman, B. (1992), *Breakpoint and Beyond: Mastering the Future Today*, Harper Business, New York.

Lewis, C. D. (1982), *Industrial and Business Forecasting*, Butterworths, London.

Lichfield, N., Kettle, P., and Whitebread, M. (1975), *Evaluation in the Planning Process*, Pergamon, Oxford.

Linstone, H. A. (1973), 'On Discounting the Future', *Technological Forecasting and Social Change*, 4, pp. 335–8.

—— (1978), 'The Delphi Technique', in J. B. Fowles (ed.), *Handbook of Futures Research*, Greenwood, Westport, pp. 273–300.

—— and Simmonds, W. H. C. (eds.) (1977), *Futures Research: New Directions*, Addison-Wesley, Reading, MA.

Loveridge, D. (1977), 'Values and Futures', in H. A. Linstone and W. H. C. Simmonds (eds.), *Futures Research: New Directions*, Addison-Wesley, Reading, MA, pp. 53–64.

McArthur, R. (1994), 'European Printing and Publishing in the Multi-media/Communications Economy', paper delivered at 'The New Communications Age' Conference, Leeds Metropolitan University, 28 October.

Mack, R. P. (1971), *Planning and Uncertainty: Decision Making in Business and Government Administration*, Wiley, New York.

McKie, D. (1973), *A Sadly Mismanaged Affair*, Croom Helm, London.

McNulty, C. (1992), contribution to an informal seminar on Futures at Leeds Metropolitan University, March.

Makridakis, S. (1990), *Forecasting, Planning and Strategy for the 21st Century*, Free Press, New York.

——and Wheelwright, S. C. (1989) *Forecasting Methods for Managers*, 5th edn., Wiley, New York.

Malpass, P. (1995), 'What Future for Social Housing in Britain', *Housing Review*, 44(1), pp. 4–7.

Marien, M. (1977), 'The Two Visions of Post-Industrial Society', *Futures*, 9(5), pp. 415–31.

—— (1991) 'Scanning an Imperfect Activity in an Era of Fragmentation and Uncertainty', *Futures Research Quarterly*, 7(3), pp. 82–90.
Markley, O. W. (1988), 'Using Depth Intuition in Creative Problem-Solving and Strategic Innovation', *Journal of Creative Behaviour*, 22(2). Reprinted in S. J. Parnes (ed.) (1992), *Source Book for Creative Problem Solving*, Creative Education Foundation Press, Buffalo, NY, pp. 330–40.
Martin, B. (1989), 'Infamous Last Words', *Guardian*, 16 May, p. 5.
Martino, J. P. (1993), *Technological Forecasting for Decision Making*, 3rd edn., McGraw Hill, New York.
Masini, E. B. (1993), *Why Futures Studies*, Grey Seal, London.
Maslow, A. (1952), *Management and Motivation*, Prentice Hall, Englewood Cliffs, NJ.
Masser, I., and Foley, P. (1987), 'Delphi Revisited: Expert Opinion in Urban Analysis', *Urban Studies*, 24, pp. 217–225.
Masser, I., Svidén, O., and Wegener, M. (1992), *The Geography of Europe's Futures*, Bellhaven, London.
Mather, I., and Bond, M. (1993), 'Migrants Can't be Stopped', *European*, 8–11 July, p. 1.
May, G. H., and Green, D. H. (1981), 'Employment Forecasts Neglected by Local Authorities', *Futures*, 13(2), pp. 93–106.
Mead, S. (1974), *How to Get to the Future Before it Gets to You*, Michael Joseph, London.
Meadows, D. H., Meadows, D. L., Randers, J., and Behrens, W. W. III (1972), *The Limits to Growth*, Earth Island, London.
—— —— —— (1992) *Beyond the Limits*, Earthscan, London.
—— Richardson, G., and Bruckmann, G. (1982), *Groping in the Dark: The First Decade of Global Modelling*, Wiley, New York.
Mendell, J. S. (1978), 'The Practice of Intuition', in J. B. Fowles (ed.) *Handbook of Futures Research*, Greenwood, Westport, pp. 149–61.
Mensch, G. (1979), *Stalemate in Technology*, Ballinger, Cambridge, MA.
Miles, I. (1978), 'The Ideologies of Futurists', in J. B. Fowles (ed.) *Handbook of Futures Research*, Greenwood, Westport, pp. 67–97.
—— (1993), 'Stranger than Fiction: How Important is Science Fiction for Future Studies', *Futures*, 25(3), pp. 315–21.
Miller, J. D. B. (1965), *The Nature of Politics*, Penguin, Harmondsworth.
Millett, S. M. (1988), 'How Scenarios Trigger Strategic Thinking', *Long Range Planning*, 21(5), pp. 61–8.
Milne, T. E. (1975), *Business Forecasting: A Managerial Approach*, Longman, London.
Naisbitt, J. (1984), *Megatrends*, Futura, London.
—— (1994), *Global Paradox*, Morrow, New York.
—— and Aburdene, P. (1990), *Megatrends 2000*, Pan, London.
Nanus, B. (1982), 'QUEST: Quick Environmental Scanning Technique', *Long Range Planning*, 15(2), pp. 39–45.

Neufeld, W. P. (1985), 'Environmental Scanning: Its Use in Forecasting Emerging Trends and Issues in Organisations', *Futures Research Quarterly*, 1(3), pp. 39–52.
Nisbet, R. (1971), 'Has Futurology a Future?', *Encounter*, November, pp. 19–28.
Nore, P., and Osmundsen, T. (1988), 'Norway: The Privileged Corner of Europe. Three Scenarios for Norway Towards the Year 2000', *Futures*, 20(5), pp. 565–77.
Northcott, J. (1991), *Britain in 2010*, Policy Studies Institute, London.
Nuernberger, P. (1984), 'Mastering the Creative Process', *The Futurist*, 18(4), pp. 33–6.
Nystrom, H. (1979), *Creativity and Innovation*, Wiley, Chichester.
OECD (1965), *Techniques of Economic Forecasting*, OECD, Paris.
—— (1979), *Interfutures: Facing the Future*, OECD, Paris.
OPCS (1989), *Population Projections 1987–2027*, HMSO, London.
Orheim, O. (1992), 'The Norwegian Glacier Centre', publicity pamphlet.
Ornstein, R. (1972), *The Psychology of Consciousness*, Freeman, San Francisco, CA. Quoted in D. Loye (1978) *The Knowable Future: A Psychology of Forecasting and Prophecy*, Wiley, New York, p. 38.
—— and Ehrlich, P. (1989), *New World: New Mind*, Methuen, London.
Osborn, A. F. (1963), *Applied Imagination*, 3rd edn., Scribner, New York.
Parente, F. J., and Anderson-Parente, J. K. (1987), 'Delphi Inquiry Systems', in G. Wright and P. Ayton (eds.), *Judgemental Forecasting*, Wiley, Chichester, pp. 129–56.
Parnes, S. J. (1992), *Visionizing: State-of-the-Art Processes for Encouraging Innovative Excellence*, Creative Education Foundation Press, Buffalo, NY.
Pearce, C. (1971), 'Prediction Techniques for Marketing Planners', Associated Business Programmes.
Pearce, D., Markandaya, A., and Barbier, E. B. (1989), *Blueprint for a Green Economy*, Earthscan, London.
Pecci, A. (1981), *One Hundred Pages for the Future*, Pergamon, Oxford.
Pedler, K. (1981), *Mind Over Matter: A Scientist's View of the Paranormal*, Thames Methuen, London.
Pflaum, A. M., and Delmont, T. (1987), 'External Scanning: A Tool for Planners', *Journal of the American Planners Association*, 53(1), pp. 58–68.
Phillips, M. (1994), 'Power to the People in the War on Crime', *Observer*, 24 April.
Pohl, F. (1993), 'The Uses of the Future', *The Futurist*, 27(2), pp. 9–12.
Polak, F. (1973), *The Image of the Future*, Elsevier, Oxford.
Popcorn, F. (1992), *The Popcorn Report: Revolutionary Trend Predictions for Marketing in the 90s*, Century Business, London.
Popper, K. (1988), 'The Allure of the Open Future', *Guardian*, 29 August, p. 8.
Porter, A. L., Roper, A. T., Mason, T. W., Rossini, F. A., Banks, J., and Wiederholt, B. J. (1991), *Forecasting and Management of Technology*, Wiley, New York.
Radford, T. (1994*a*), 'Star Trek Showing the Way', *Guardian*, 22 February, p. 10.
—— (1994*b*), 'September's Children Born with Football Boots on', *Guardian*, 14 April, p. 24.

Renfro, W. L. (1987), 'Issues Management: The Evolving Corporate Role', *Futures*, 19(5), pp. 545–54.
—— (1993), *Issues Management in Strategic Planning*, Quorum, Westport.
—— and Morrison, J. L. (1982), 'Merging two Concepts: Issues Management and Analysis', *The Futurist*, 16(5), pp. 54–6.
Richards, P. G. (1970), *The New Local Government System*, Unwin, London.
Rickards, T. (1990), *Creativity and Problem Solving at Work*, Gower, Aldershot.
Robertson, J. (1985) *Future Work*, Temple Smith/Gower, Aldershot.
Robinson, J. B. (1990). 'Futures Under Glass: A Recipe for People Who Hate to Predict', *Futures*, 22(8), pp. 820–42.
Robinson, M. (1992), *The Greening of British Party Politics*, Manchester University Press, Manchester.
Rossini, F. A., and Porter, A. L. (1983), *Integrated Impact Assessment*, Westview Press, Boulder, CO.
Rowe, G., Wright, G., and Bolger, F. (1991), 'Delphi: A Revaluation of Research and Theory', *Technological Forecasting and Social Change*, 39, pp. 235–51.
Sackman, H. (1974), 'Delphi Assessment: Expert Opinion, Forecasting and Group Process', R-1283PR, RAND Corporation, Santa Monica, CA.
SACTRA (Standing Advisory Committee on Trunk Road Assessment) (1992), 'Assessing the Environmental Impact of Road Schemes', Department of Transport, HMSO, London.
Sadler, P. (1992), 'Biotechnology and the Challenge of Choice', in S. Moorcroft (ed.), *Visions for the Twenty-First Century*, Adamantine, London.
Sardar, Z. (1993), 'Colonising the Future: The Other Dimension of Futures Studies', *Futures*, 25(2), pp. 179–87.
Saunders, P. (1980), *Urban Politics*, Penguin, Harmondsworth, citing D. Philips (1973), *Abandoning Method*, Josey Bass, San Francisco, CA.
Schell, J. (1982), *The Fate of the Earth*, Jonathan Cape, London.
Schnaars, S. P. (1987), 'How to Develop and Use Scenarios', *Long Range Planning*, 20(1), pp. 105–14.
Schultz, W. (1992), 'Words, Dreams and Actions: Sharing the Futures Experience', in B. Van Steenbergen, R. Nakarada, F. Marti, and J. Dator (eds.) *Advancing Democracy and Participation: Challenges for the Future*, selections from the Twelfth World Conference of the World Futures Studies Federation, Barcelona 17–21 September 1991, pp. 201–6, Centre Catala de Prospectiva and Centre UNESCO de Catalunya, Barcelona.
Schwartz, P. (1992), The Art of the Long View: Scenario Planning—Protecting Your Company Against an Uncertain World, Century Business, London.
Shallcross, D. (1994) at the 'Creative Problem Solving for Organisations' Conference, Centre for Innovation and Creativity, Leeds Metropolitan University, 18 March.
Sicinski, A. (1976), 'Optimism versus Pessimism', in H. Ornauer *et al.* (eds.) *Images of the World in the Year 2000*, Mouton, Atlantic Highlands, NJ, pp. 23–42.
Simmons, M. (1994), '12.6bn repair bill for unfit housing', *Guardian*, 8 November, p. 5.

Simon, W. (1974), 'Reflections on the Relationship Between the Individual and Society', in *Human Futures*, IPC Business Press.

Sisk, D., and Whaley, C. E. (1987), *The Futures Primer for Classroom Teachers*, Trillium Press, Toronto.

Slaughter, R. A. (1984), 'Towards a Critical Futurism: Part 3. An Outline of Critical Futurism', *World Future Society Bulletin*, 18(5), pp. 17–21.

—— (ed.) (1989), *Studying the Future*, Commission for the Future and Australian Bicentennial Authority, Victoria.

—— (1990), 'Assessing the QUEST for Future Knowledge: Significance of the Quick Environmental Scanning Technique for Futures', *Futures*, 22(3), pp. 153–66.

—— (1993), 'Looking for the Real Megatrends', *Futures*, 25(8), pp. 827–49.

Smith, B. (1976), *Policy making in British Government: An Analysis of Power and Rationality*, Martin Robertson, London.

Smith, F. M. (1982), 'Innovation: The Way out of the Recession?', *Long Range Planning*, 15(1), pp. 19–29.

Smith, I. (1983), 'No Future in Prediction', *Guardian*, 15 December, p. 9.

Smith, N. I., and Ainsworth, M. (1989), *Managing for Innovation*, Mercury Business Books, London.

Southern California Edison (1988), 'Planning for Uncertainty: A Case Study', *Technological Forecasting and Social Change*, 33(2), pp. 119–48.

Springett, P. (1994), 'Lloyd's Reveals a Further £2bn Loss', *Guardian*, 18 May, p. 1.

Stacey, R. (1992), *Managing Chaos: Dynamic Business Strategies in an Unpredictable World*, Kogan Page, London.

Steerman, J. D. (1985), 'An Integrated Theory of the Economic Long Wave', *Futures*, 17(2), pp. 104–31.

Stewart, H. B. (1989), *Recollecting the Futuure: A View of Business Technology and Innovation in the Next 30 Years*, Dow Jones/Irwin, Homewood, IL.

—— (1991), 'Recollecting the Future', *Futures Research Quarterly*, 7(1), pp. 6–16.

Stonier, T. (1983), *The Wealth of Information*, Thames Methuen, London.

Stretton, H. (1976), *Capitalism, Socialism and the Environment*, Cambridge University Press, Cambridge.

Stover, J. G., and Gordon, T. J. (1978), 'Cross Impact Analysis' in J. B. Fowles *Handbook of Futures Research*, Greenwood, Westport, pp. 301–28.

Suzuki, D. (1992) *Inventing the Future: Reflections on Science, Technology and Nature*, Adamantine, London.

Svidén, O. (1988), 'Future Information Systems for Road Transport: A Delphi Panel-derived Scenario', *Technological Forecasting and Social Change*, 33, pp. 159–78.

Toffler, A. (1970), *Future Shock*, Bodley Head, London.

—— (1980), *The Third Wave*, Collins, London.

—— (1990), *Powershift: Knowledge, Wealth and Violence at the Edge of the 21st Century*, Bantam Books, New York.

Tonn, B. E. (1988), 'Philosophical Aspects of 500-Year Planning', *Environment and Planning A*, 20, pp. 1507–22.

—— (1991), 'The Court of Generations: A Proposed Amendment to the US Constitution', *Futures*, 23(5), pp. 1041–50.
Tough, A. (1992), *Crucial Questions about the Future*, University Press of America, Lanham. Revised edition (1994) Adamantine, London.
—— (1993), 'What Future Generations Need from Us', *Futures*, 25(10), pp. 1041–50
—— (1994), 'What Future Generations Need from Us', in Institute for the Integrated Study of Future Generations, *Why Future Generations Now*, published for the Future Generations Alliance Foundation, Kyoto, pp. 78–95.
Trist, E. L. (1972), 'The Structural Presence of the Post-Industrial Society'. Reprinted in N. Cross, D. Elliott, and R. Roy (eds.) (1974) *Man-Made Futures: Readings in Society, Technology and Design*, Hutchinson Educational/Open University Press, London, pp. 107–17.
Tulloch, S. (ed.) (1993), *Complete Wordfinder*, Reader's Digest, London.
Twiss, B. C. (1981), lecture to a course in forecasting at Bradford University Management Centre.
University of Houston, Clear Lake (1994), *Research Institute for Computing and Information Systems Review*, 6(1).
Van Gundy, A. B. Jr. (1988), *Techniques of Structured Problem Solving*, 2nd edn., Van Nostrand Reinhold, New York.
Vlek, C., and Otten, W. (1987), 'Judgemental Handling of Energy Scenarios: A Psychological Analysis and Experiment', in G. Wright and P. Ayton (eds.), *Judgemental Forecasting*, Wiley, Chichester, pp. 267–89.
Wack, P. (1985), 'Scenarios: Uncharted Waters Ahead' and 'Scenarios: Shooting the Rapids', *Harvard Business Review*, 5, pp. 71–89, and 6, pp. 139–50.
Wagar, W. W. (1992), *The Next Three Futures: Paradigms of Things to Come*, Adamantine, London.
Webler, T., Levine, D., Rakel, H., and Renn, O. (1991), 'A Novel Approach to Reducing Uncertainty: The Group Delphi', *Technological Forecasting and Social Change*, 20, pp. 253–63.
Wedell, E. G. (1983), 'The Time Has Come to Lift Adam's Economic Curse', *Guardian*, 26 January, p. 15.
Wells, H. G. (1932), 'Wanted: Professors of Foresight', BBC broadcast 19 November. Reproduced in R. A. Slaughter (ed.) (1989), *Studying the Future*, Commission for the Future and Australian Bicentennial Authority, Victoria, pp. 3–4
Wenz, P. S. (1988), *Environmental Justice*, State University of New York Press.
Westcott, R. W. (1976), 'The Anthropology of the Future as an Academic Discipline', in M. Maruyama and A. M. Hawkins (eds.), *Cultures of the Future*, Mouton, Atlantic Highlands, NJ.
Westman, W. E. (1985), *Ecology, Impact Assessment and Environmental Planning*, Wiley, New York.
White, L. Jr. (1974), 'Technology Assessment from the Stance of a Medieval Historian', *Technology Forecasting and Social Change*, 6, pp. 359–69.
Williams, R. (1976), *Keywords: A Vocabulary for Culture and Society*, Fontana, Glasgow.

Williams, T. (1981), lecture to the Forecasting for Strategic Planning Seminar, Bradford University Management Centre, November.

Wise, G. (1976), 'The Accuracy of Technological Forecasts 1890–1940', *Futures*, 8(5), pp. 411–19.

World Commission on Environment and Development (1987), *Our Common Future*, Oxford University Press, Oxford.

Woudenberg, F. (1991), 'An Evaluation of Delphi', *Technological Forecasting and Social Change*, 40, pp. 131–50.

Yazaki, K. (1994), 'Going Beyond Boundaries for Our Future Generations', in Institute for the Integrated Study of Future Generations, *Why Future Generations Now*, published for the Future Generations Alliance Foundation, Kyoto, pp. 12–19.

Yeomans, K. A. (1968), *Introducing Statistics*, Penguin, Harmondsworth.

Zentner, R. D. (1975), 'Scenarios in Forecasting', *Chemical and Engineering News*, 6 October, pp. 22–34.

Zey, M. G. (1994), *Seizing the Future: How the Coming Revolution in Science, Technology and Industry will Expand the Frontiers of Human Potential and Reshape the Planet*, Simon & Schuster, New York.

Ziegler, W. (1991), 'Envisioning the Future', *Futures*, 23(5), pp. 516–27.

Zohar, D. (1983), *Through the Time Barrier: A Study of Precognition and Modern Physics*, Paladin, London.

INDEX

Aberfan Disaster 115, 117
Aburdene, P. 43, 129
Access credit card 10
accidents 96–7, 177
   at airports 95
   environmental 177
   nuclear 78–9, 88, 178
Africa 212
   famine 79
ageing population 93, 221
   paradox 217–18
agenda, future 91–4
aims 24–5
Ainsworth, M. 190
airports 81, 96
   London: growth 54–6, 59, 71; location 176
air quality, internal-combustion engine and 79, 226
air traffic 50, 71, 187
   airports 53–6
Alexander, J. 117
alternative futures 100
alternative strategies 201
ambitions 24–5
American West 77
analytical forecasting 139–45
Anderson-Parente, J. K. 153
anticipations 23, 100
appointments 23–4
Apollo forecasting 198
Apollo Programme 198
   moon landing 89, 110
Ariansen, P. 84
Armstrong, J. S. 148–50, 163, 179
Ash, T. G. 53
Asimov, I. 158, 222

assumptions 61–5, 142–3
astrology 115
astronomy 114–17
atom bomb, destruction 79
Aviation, Ministry of 71

backcasting 196–7
'Back to the Future' 146
'bad old days' 43
Band Aid 83
Bangladesh, floods in 79
Barbier, E. B. 85
Barnes, V. 149
Beach, L. R. 149
Beckman, R. 137–8, 147
Bell, D. 16, 18
Bell, W. 16, 18, 86
'Bellwether' states, USA 134
Benford, E. 67
Benveniste, G. 102
Berlin, I. 17
Beyond the Limits 15, 57–8
Bhopal Disaster 97
biotechnology 77
births, UK 120, 123, 125
'black-box' approach 118
Bohler, E. 19
Bolch, B. 42
Bolger, F. 152
Bond, M. 211
Boniecki, G. 5, 7–8, 18–19
Bosnia 161
Boulding, E. 4, 19, 44
boundary examination 188
Bowonder, B. 31
brain, two hemispheres of 19–20, 186
brainstorming 191–3, 197

brainwriting 193–4
Branch, M. 181
Bratt, E. C. 28
breakthroughs 171
Britain in 2010 162
British Airports Authority 56, 58–9, 95
British Foreign Office 97
Bronowski, J. 66, 69, 101
Bruckmann, G. 140, 146
Brundtland Report 15, 83–4
Bryson, B. 85
Budd, A. 63
buildings:
    projects and costs 78
    Western 89–90
Burns, P. 78, 223
Bush, Dr V. 50
Bush, George 116
business 28
    Western failure 29
    women in 171

Camil, K. 31
Canada, Global Change Program 198
Capitalism 45, 89, 181
    laissez-faire 218
card-writing 193–4
Carley, M. J. 79, 172, 266
Carrington, Lord 97
causal models 139–45
Central Statistical Office 34
census information 32, 67, 223
CFCs 48, 79, 101
Chadwick, G. 31
Chancellor of the Exchequer, UK 39
change 18–19, 92–3
    coping with 18
    desire for 92–3
    information 18
    paradox 222–4
    social 18–29
Channel Tunnel Rail Link 224
Chaos Theory 160–1
Chapman, C. B. 177
Chapman, G. 51, 53, 56–8
Chapman, P. F. 72
checklist 178, 190
Chernobyl 178

Chisholm, R. K. 29
Choucri, N. 169
Christensen-Szalanski, J. 149
choice–determinism continuum 47
Church of England, women priests in 116
Churchill, Winston 103–4
cities:
    paradox of 224–6
    urban planning 35
civilisation, future 85
Clark, B. P. 172
Clarke, A. C. 50, 51, 53, 57
Clarke, I. F. 27, 78
Club of Rome 5, 57, 70
Coates, J. F. 129, 134
colonisation 77
commerce 28, 90
commitments 25–6
communications 60
    telecommunications 153, 225
Communism 45–6
compact discs 134
Complete Wordfinder 4
computer:
    games 145, 180
    models 139–40
    simulation 180
    technology 153
concept challenge 191
Condorcet, A. 50
cone of the future 48
conjectural forecasting 163
Conservative Party 33
content analysis 129
continental drift 60
Cook, L. 171
Cooper, D. F. 177
Copeland, R. M. 11
coping with change 19
cosmos 117
cost–benefit analysis 176, 195
Coveney, P. 114
creative imagery 199–201
creativity 186–91
crime 14
crisis-management 97
Cross, N. 166
cross-impact forecasting 153–4

Crossman, R. 35
crystal balls 149
culture, Western 21
Cyberpunk 147
cycles 135–8
 cyclical 136
 economic 137
 long waves 137–8
 random 136

Darwin, C. 66
Dascher, P. E. 11
data collection 119–20
Dator, J. 108, 196–7
Davidson, D. 11
Davis, C. H. 152
daydreaming, structured 198
De Bono, E. 191
decisions 32, 103, 201–3
 lag 32–3
Declaration of Independence, US 77
Delbecq, A. L. 152
Della Vecchia, R. M. 78
Delmont, T. 170
Delphi forecasting 115, 149–53
democracy 102–4
 anticipatory 196
democratic thinking 102–4
Derow, E. O. 172
Dicks, G. 63
Dickson, G. C. 177
directed scanning 170
direction, need for 86–91
disasters, natural and manmade 11
 Exxon Valdez 97
 Bhopal 97
distribution problems 29
Done, K. 31
dreams 117
Drexler, K. E. 77, 147
Duke, R. D. 179
Duncan, O. D. 52–3

Earth, ownership of 82
earthquakes, prediction of 116
Eastern Europe 9
Eating Habits 21–2
economic cycles 137

economic forecasts 148
economic growth 87
 UK 51
economy, self-service 215
Eddings, D. 222
education 221–2
 National Curriculum 222
 paradox 221–2
Eger, A. F. 152
Ehrlich, P. 20, 96
Einstein, A. 108, 114, 117
electronic publishing 171
elitism 73
Elizabeth I 116
Ellis, K. 115–17
Embryology Authority 95
employment 72, 195, 216
Encel, S. 58, 70
energy 71, 144
 conservation 154
 consumption 71
 forecasts 71
 Gap 71
 Netherlands 163
 solar 71, 154
English language 75
 the future in 75
English literature 222
envelope curves 134–5
Environment, Department of the 82
environmental scanning 170–2
 accidents 177
 damage 177
envisioning 196–7, 199
Enzer, S. 86
ethnocentrism 73
European Community 173
Evans, J. St B. T. 148
evolution 66
experts 102–3
 Future Studies 102–3
 public involvement 103
exponential smoothing 124–5
extrapolation 118–39, 148
Exxon Valdez Disaster 97

facilitating 192–3, 196
Falkland Crisis 97–8

family 4–5
famine in Africa 79
fault trees 178
'feel good' factors 15
Ferguson, M. 16
Ferkiss, V. C. 51, 53
fertilisation, human 95
feudalism 45
fiction 171
  English literature 222
Field, B. 139, 145
films 146
  '2001' 27
  'Aliens' 27
  'Back to the Future' 146
  'Jurassic Park' 146
  'The Terminator' 27
financial forecasts, Treasury 34
financial management 29
financial markets 14
Firth, M. 119, 123, 127, 142
Fitzsimmons, J. A. 152
flight 50
  airports 53–6, 59, 71
  Wright brothers 39, 50, 81, 187
floods, Bangladesh 79
Foley, G. 71, 144, 152
forecasting 28–9, 36, 39, 53, 56–8, 60,
    70–1, 99, 100–1, 109, 114, 142
  analytical 139–45
  Apollo 198
  conjectural 163
  Dephi 115, 149–53, 193, 195
  economic 148
  herringbone 40
  judgemental 147–9
  models 140
  social 51
  technical 31, 50
Foresight, Professors of 75, 102
Fowles, J. B. 73
Frankenfield, P. J. 82
free will 46
Friend, J. K. 65
future:
  agenda 91–4
  attitudes of youth towards 78
  blueprints 100

civilization 85
cone of the 48
definition 4
  in the English language 75
European Parliament 85
everyday life 21
generations 80–6; opportunities 81;
  responsibility 80–6
government 32–6
House of Lords 85
images 100–1
impact-assessment 86
lack of 11
learning process 99–102
life on Earth 80, 90
long-term effect 80
managing 159–61
metaphors 6
next life 78
paradox of 227–8
positive images 19
responsibility 81
scenarios 161–8
threats to 11
US Congress 85
vision 89
Future Studies 102–3
  experts 102–3
  public involvement 103
  Sweden 34–5
Futures methods 111–12
Futures-thinking 37–42, 45, 48, 69–73, 99,
    104, 107–12, 227–8
  alternatives 100
  democratic 102–4
  impossible 38
  possible 38
  preferred 40
Futures Workshops 194–7

Galbraith, J. K. 30
gallery techniques 193–4
Galtung, J. 3, 5, 9
games, computer 145
gaming 178–80
Gattey, C. N. 115
genetic engineering 220
Gershuny, J. I. 215

Gibson, L. 116
Gibson, W. 116
global climate 79
global equilibrium 57
global models 144
global paradox 211, 225
global warming 93, 144
GNP 144
Goals Achievement Matrix 202
  orientation 188
Godet, M. 162–3
golden age 43
Gordon, A. 43
Gordon, T. J. 155
government:
  future 32–6
  local 33
Graham, A. 138
Grandparents 83
Greater London Council 33
Greenhouse Effect 79, 158, 169, 219
Greenhouse gases 79
'grey literature' 171
Gross National Product 144
group support systems 194
groupthink 149
Gulf War 98
Gustafson, D. H. 152

Hage, J. 31
Hall, P. 71
Hamal, G. 31
Handy, C. 147, 211, 213, 217–18, 221
Harman, W. W. 16, 176
Harvey, D. 16
Hawaii Research Center 198
Hazards 82–3
Henshel, R. L. 58–9
Hewlitt, V. J. 115–16
Highfield, R. 114
Himalayas, destruction of trees 79
hindsight 77, 97
historicism 73
history 76–80
Hitler, A. 115
Hooker, C. 195
Hoos, I. R.. 53, 67
horoscopes 27, 116

household surveys 132–3
housing 35, 223
Houston, University at Clear Lake 194
human civilization, future of 85
Human Dimensions of Global Change
  Program, Canada 198
human mind 191
human perspectives 7
hunter–gatherers 224

I Ching 116
ideas, evolution of 102
Ignatieff, M. 86
'Imagine Houston' exercise 196, 200
imaging, future 100–1, 200
imaging capacity, decline of 19
impact-assessment 94, 172–6
  future 86
Inayatullah, S. 36
incasting 196–7
Industrial Revolution 18, 72, 77–9, 217–18, 227
industry 28
  oil 162
information 18–19
  future 38
  lag 32–3
  paradox of 220–1
  speed of dissemination 18
information technology 31, 77
Ingelstam, L. E. 74
innovations 199–204
  technical 138
insurance 26, 177
  Lloyd's of London 177
intellectual capacity, lack of 19
Interfutures 16
intergenerational equity 85
intermediate impossible 191
internal-combustion engine
  and air quality 79
inventions 138, 185
inventory controls 29
issues
  Life Cycles 169
  Management 169

Janis, I. L. 149

Japan:
    planning 31, 181
    technical forecasting 51
Jarman, B. 186
Jenkins, J. 97
Jessop, W. N. 65
jet engine 81
Johnston, D. F. 113
Jones, B. 77
Jones, H. 29, 134
Jouvenel, B. de 50, 61, 69
Judge, A. 108
judgemental forecasting 147–9
Jungk, R. 196–7
'Jurassic Park' 146
just-in-time production 30
justice, paradox of 218

Kahn, H. 70, 129, 147, 162
Kaufman, D. 6
Kay, A. 157
Kennedy, President 89, 110, 185, 198
Kenney, M. L. 181, 202
Kettle, M. 95
Kliever, G. 34
Klosterman, R. E. 145
knowledge 60–9
    lack of 19
Kondratiev, N. 137
Kuhn, T. 67–70

Labour government 33
laissez faire 218
Lal, D. 70
Land, G. 186
landmark events 171
Laslett, P. 86
lateral thinking 190–1
learning process, future 99–102
legislation 33
Lewis, C. D. 127
Lichfield, N. 202
life cycles, issues 169
life on Earth, future of 80
lifestyles, Western 84
Limits to Growth 5, 8, 13, 15, 49, 57, 59, 70, 146
Lincoln, Abraham, assassination of 117

linear regression 126–7
Linstone, H. A. 13, 150, 152
Lloyd's of London 177
local government 33
    UK 51, 65
London airports:
    growth 54–6, 59, 71
    location 176
London Business School, forecasts 62–3
lone signals 171
long waves 137–9
Lorie, P. 115–16
lotteries 26–7
Loverage, D. 20
Lyons, H. 42

McArthur, R. 210
MacGregor, B. 139, 145
Mack, R. P. 64–5
McKie, D. 71
McMahon 32
McNulty, C. 164
Makridakis, S. 29, 118, 123–4, 127–8, 137, 143, 148–9, 191, 211
Malpass, P. 223
management 28
    crisis 97
    future 159–61
    issues 169
managers, forward-thinking 29
manpower requirements 29
Marien, M. 16, 171
Markandaya, A. 85
Markley, O. W. 199–200
Marstrand, P. K. 58, 70
Martin, B. 55
Martino, J. P. 127, 145
Marxism 45–6
Masini, E. B. 113
Maslow, A. 8
Masser, L. 147, 152, 163–4
Mather, I. 211
matrices 145
Mead, S. 49
Meadows, D. H. 5, 7, 15, 42, 57, 70, 79, 130, 140, 144–5, 147, 166
media analysis 129
medical knowledge 67, 92

medieval society 78, 89
Megatrends 129
Mendell, J. S. 187
Mensch, G. 138
Middle Ages 78, 89
Middle East 212
Miles, I. 73, 146
Miller, J. D. B. 203
Millett, S. M. 163
Milne, T. E. 28
mind 191
  mind-sets 189
  new mind 20
Miyake, T. 31
models:
  causal 139–45
  computer 139–40
  development 143
  forecasting 140
  global 144
  matrices 145
  population 140–2
money 11, 13
Montesquieu, C. L. S. 50
moon landing 89, 110
Moore, W. E. 16
Morrison, J. L. 169
Mother Shipton 115
motoring patterns, future 11
motorways 56
Mullert, N. 196–7
multilogue 179
multiple regression 142
mystification 73

Naisbitt, J. 43, 129, 134, 211, 213, 218, 225
nanotechnology 77, 220
Nanus, B. 170
National Environmental Policy Act 1969, USA 173
National Plan, UK 51
Netherlands, energy debate 163
Neufeld, W. D. 171
newspapers, production 85
New York Times 84–5
Newcomb, S. 50
new mind 20
new products 30–1

New World 20
Nisbett, R. 53
non-fiction 171
non-quantitive trends 129–30
Nore, P. 162
Northcott, J. 162, 164
Norway 2000 162
Nostradamus 115–16
'Nowism' 9
nuclear power 57, 71, 152, 220
  accidents 79, 88; Chernobyl 178; Three Mile Island 178
nuclear programmes 34
Nurnberger, P. 199
Nystrom, H. 186

OECD, *Interfutures* 16
oil industry 162
Old Testament prophets 115
OPEC 162
opinion polls 59
optimism 42–4
organisations, paradox of 217
Organization of Petroleum Exporting Countries 162
Orheim, O. 79–80
Ornstein, R. 20, 98
Orwell, George 146
Osborn, A. F. 191
Osmundsen, T. 162
Otten, W. 163
Our Common Future 15, 83–4
ozone layer 79–80
  depletion 48

Page, W. 58, 70
Pandora's box 219
paradigms 189
  shifts 16
paradoxes 207–28
  ageing 217–18
  change 222–4
  cities 224–6
  education 221–2
  future 227–8
  individual 218
  intelligence 213–14
  justice 218

paradoxes (*cont.*)
  organisations 217
  productivity 215–16
  riches 216–17
  success 226–7
  technology 219–20
  time 216
  work 214–15
Parente, E. J. 153
Parnes, S. J. 186–7
passive volition 199
past, understanding 4
pattern-recognition 121–8
Pearce, C. 29, 65
Pearce, D. 85
Pecci, A. 80
Pedler, K. 117
Pegamit, G. 77
pessimism 19, 42–4, 147
  of the young 78
Peterson, C. 77
Pfleum, A. M. 170
Phillips, M. 148
planet, future of 90
planning 28–9, 31, 34–5, 181–4
  Balance Sheet 202
  Japan 31
  planned economy 181
  policy-making 183
  Sweden 34–5
  urban 35
Pohl, F. 58
Polak, F. 19, 44–5, 88, 157
policy 32
  effect lag 32
  making 181–4
  politics 203–4
  UK 32
pollution 79
  internal-combustion engines 79, 226
Popcorn, F. 129
Pope John Paul I 116
Popper, K. 44, 88
population:
  ageing 93
  change 140
  models 140–2
population growth 15–17, 79, 217

births, UK 120, 123, 125
census 32, 67
projections 34; UK 120, 123, 125; USA 120, 123, 125
Porter, A. L. 154, 172
post-Fordism 16
post-industrial society 9
postmodernism 16
Prahalad, C. K. 31
Pratchett, T. 222
precautions 26
precognition 117–18
precursor analysis 134
predications 41, 53, 58, 99, 113–15
  self-altering 58
  self-defeating 58
  self-fulfilling 58
  sport 113–15
present, coping with 8
price and discount policies 29
Prince Charles 116
proactive approach 98
probabilistic methods 145
probability trees 178
problems:
  anticipation 96
  dimension analysis 189
  identification 184–6
  solving 88–9
production 29
  flexible 30
  just-in-time 30
  new developments 30
  South-east Asia 29
  Western 29
productivity, paradox 215
products, new 30–1
prophecy 115–16
prophets, Old Testament 115
prospective approach 162
Protestants 50
public transport 22
pyschohistory 158

qualitative trends 130
quantitive trends 130
Quick Environmental Scanning Technique (QUEST) 170

INDEX

Rabaut, J. P. 50
Radford, T. 116
radiation 79
radio 18
radioactive products 33–4
RAND Corporation 149, 152, 162
random juxtaposition 191
Reagan, President 117
regression, multiple 142
Relativity, Theory of 108
relevance trees 195–8
Renaissance 19, 68, 78
renewable resources 81
  wood 81
Renfro, W. L. 98–102
Reuters 210
reversal thinking 190
Richardson, G. 140, 145
Rickards, P. G. 20, 33, 189–93
Rifkind, M. 161
risk-assessment 94, 177–8
road building 78
  motorways 56
Robertson, J. 73, 92, 147
Robinson, B. 63
Robinson, J. B. 198
Robinson, M. 98
role-playing 178–80
Rossini, F. A. 172
Rowe, G. 152
Royal Commission 33
Royal Dutch Shell 162, 166

S-curves 131–4, 169
Sackman, H. 150, 153
Sadler, P. 77
satellites 83
Saunders, P. 69
scanning 170–2
  directed 170
  environmental 170
scenarios 161–8
  likely 167–8
  preparing 165
Schwartz, P. 161–4
science 78, 171
  human 114
  natural 114

science fiction 27, 60, 146–7
scientism 73
Second World War 10, 115
self-service economy 215
Senge, P. M. 138
Shallcross, D. 192
Shaw, B. 185, 195
Shell, Royal Dutch 162, 166
Sicinski, A. 42
signals, lone 171
Simon, W. 9
Simmonds, M. 13
simulation 178–80
  Nutrition Systems Game, UN 119
Sisk, D. 195
Slaughter, R. A. 4, 129, 145
Smith, B. 181
Smith, F. M. 137
Smith, G. 152.
Smith, I. 53
Smith, N. I. 190
smog 79
Social Trends, Central Statistical Office 34
socialism 45
societies 8
  change 15
  post-industrial 9
  Western 6, 9, 18, 20–1, 88, 92
solar power 71, 154
South California Edison 162, 164
Soviet Union 116, 211–12
space travel 81
Spaceship Earth 219
speculation 145–7
sport, predictions 113–15
Springett, P. 177
Stacey, R. 160, 182, 202
Stalin, J. 115
Steerman, J. D. 138
Stewart, H. B. 134, 137–8
Stover, J. G. 155
strategies, alternative 201
Stretton, H. 70
success, paradox of 266–7
Suzuki, D. 17, 43
Svidén, D. 163–4
Sweden, social policy 134
systems failure 177

INDEX

Tarot cards 116
Tech-Fix 73
technical determinism 73
technical developments 31
technical forecasting 31, 50
  Japan 51
technology 78–9, 171–2, 229
  complex 30–1
  innovations 138
  nanotechnology 77, 220
  paradox of 219–20
  S-curves 134
telecommunications 153, 225
television 18, 83
Thatcher, M. 98, 189
thinking 190–1
  lateral 190–1
  reversal 190
Three Mile Island 178
time-series forecasts 116–29
  cyclical 119
  fluctuating 119
  horizontal 118
  random 119
  seasonal 119
  trend 119
Tofler, A. 16, 18, 100, 147
Tonn, B. E. 84–5
Tough, A. 85
traffic forecasts:
  airports 53–6
  Dutch 226–7
  UK 34, 144, 226–7
transport 22, 215
  air 50, 71, 187
  motoring 11, 56
  public 22
  road building 78
Treasury, forecasts 34
trends, projection 128–9
  Megatrends 129
  non-linear 130–4
  non-quantitative 129–30
  qualitative 130
  quantitive 130
Trist, E. L. 31, 202
Tulloch, S. 4, 113, 117, 128, 147, 161, 181, 207

Twiss, B. C. 29, 128, 132, 134, 151–2, 155

uncertainty 94, 99–100, 102
unemployment 14
United Nations 15, 212
urban planning 35
  cities, paradox of 224–5
USA 212
  'Bellwether' states 134
  Declaration of Independence 77
  long-term problems 34
  National Environmental Policy Act 173
Utopianism 146

Van De Vem, A. H. 152
Van Gundy, A. B. 181, 186, 188–91, 193, 201
Victorian period 78
Viking period 77
visioning 196–7
Vlek, C. 163

Wack, P. 162
Warfield, J. N. 162
wave power 71
weather forecasting 114
Webber, M. M. 181
Webler, T. 152
Wedel, E. G. 214
Wegener, M. 163–4
  continental drift 60
Wells, H. G. 75, 102
Wenz, P. S. 81
Westcott, R. W. 20
Western culture 21
  marketing 130
Western Europe 10, 17
Western lifestyles 84
Western societies 8–9, 18, 20–1, 88, 93
  change 18
  work patterns 18
Westman, W. E. 172
Whaley, C. E. 195
Wheelwright, S. C. 29, 118, 123–4, 127–8, 143, 148–9
Whitaker, G. R. 29
Wiener, A, J. 162
Williams, R. 45
Williams, T. 17

Wilson, Harold 32
Wise, G. 50, 53, 56
women:
  in business 171
  work 214–15
women priests, Church of England 116
wood 81
work:
  patterns 8
  paradox of 214–15
  women 214–15
World 3 Model 144, 166
World Commission on Environment 15, 83–4

worldviews 189
workshops, futures 194–7
Woundenberg, F. 152
Wright Brothers 39, 50, 81, 187
Wright, G. 152
Wurzburger, R. 86

Yazaki, K. 211
Yeomans, K. A. 128

Zentner, R. D. 164, 166
Zey, M. G. 70, 216
Ziegler, W. 199
Zohar, D. 177

About the Author

GRAHAM H. MAY is Principal Lecturer, Faculty of Design and Built Environment, at Leeds Metropolitan University, UK. He is a professional member of the World Future Society and a member of the World Futures Studies Federation. He referees articles for the journal *Futures* and is prime mover of the newly founded UK Futures Group.